W9-AJT-214

SIX PRESIDENTS,
TOO MANY
WARS

SIX PRESIDENTS, TOO MANY WARS

‹ ★ ★ ★ ★ ★ ›

BILL LAWRENCE

Saturday Review Press

NEW YORK

Published simultaneously in Canada by
Doubleday Canada Ltd., Toronto.

Library of Congress Catalog Card Number: 71–182475

ISBN 0–8415–0143–2

Saturday Review Press
230 Park Avenue, New York, New York 10017

Printed in the United States of America

Design by Tere Lo Prete

For Jacque

ACKNOWLEDGMENT

Over four decades, at home and abroad, many people gave of their time and their expertise to shape my career as a reporter, and in the writing of this book. It would be impossible to acknowledge all of them, but special thanks are due to a few: James E. Lawrence, Larry Becker, Boyd Lewis, Lyle C. Wilson, Arthur Krock, Arthur Hays Sulzberger, Edwin L. James, James C. Hagerty, Elmer Lower, Bill Sheehan, David Buksbaum, David W. Jayne, III, Alex Dreier, Larry Newman, and Milbrey Rennie. I am most grateful to A. M. Rosenthal, managing editor of *The New York Times*, and his secretary, Nancy Curran, for making available my old by-line files from the *Times*.

No person other than I can be blamed for the shape of the editorial judgments rendered herein.

B. L.

SIX PRESIDENTS,
TOO MANY
WARS

CHAPTER

I

By 1972, I had been a reporter for forty years, spent eleven terms at the White House with six Presidents, and, in between, reported on entirely too many wars.

It has been an exciting, exhilarating experience for a boy from Nebraska, roaming the world in peace and war and, somehow, getting involved personally in the news.

I've had a grandstand seat on history, and while some of it has been grim, especially in wartime, it has for the most part been a lot of fun.

Now is a time for taking stock, and for telling many of the untold tales about the stories I've covered all over the world.

I've been in Washington more than thirty years, covering all or parts of every Presidential term since Franklin D. Roosevelt's second. There were two with Harry Truman, two with Dwight Eisenhower, one, unhappily brief, with John F. Kennedy, two with Lyndon B. Johnson, and now Richard Nixon's first. I came to know all these men well, well enough so each of them called me "Bill." But to me, respectful of their high office, even at this late date, they were always "Mr. President," even though I had known some of them well enough before they entered the White House to address them as Jack, or Lyndon, or Dick. Protocol says that your closest, most intimate friend becomes "Mr. President" on the instant he is elected and you do not drop this form of salutation even at the request of the President.

I've golfed, fished, and sailed with some of our Presidents, more with John F. Kennedy than the others, and I found with Kennedy that a round of golf could be much more fruitful in news terms than many formal Presidential news conferences. John Kennedy thoroughly enjoyed "leaking" a news story, and I was lucky enough to be the recipient of so many breaks on big stories.

Any White House correspondent enjoys a unique vantage point from which to watch the Presidents, with and without their makeup. You get to know them on and off camera, with their guard up and down, under the most formal and informal circumstances.

A few examples:

President Roosevelt paused in his busy schedule one day during World War II to send me a handwritten chit about a former White House correspondent, Frank Kluckhohn, whom the President did not like. Kluckhohn was under brief detainment in quarters by order of British Field Marshal Montgomery and FDR's suggestion was that I try to get "a habeas corpus." When I delayed, Roosevelt chided me and I explained I could not care less when Kluckhohn was released.

"Ah, that's just the point," said Roosevelt, chuckling with glee over his own joke. "You see, under French law the prisoner cannot be released once a proceeding like that is started until the judge reaches a decision. And those courts in North Africa are so jammed it would take years before Kluckhohn's case could be heard."

The President threw back his head and laughed uproariously. For a few minutes, anyway, the cares of war were forgotten.

Or Harry Truman in the White House oval office early in 1952, telling me alone all the many reasons why he would not run again, and suggesting only a few remote possibilities that might get him into the Presidential race again. Then, becoming angry with a visiting Congressman who followed me into the office, Truman refused permission to print the authorized interview. I kept the confidence, and he never forgot it.

Dwight D. Eisenhower, in the closing weeks of his Presidency, invited me to dine with a group of other correspondents at the White House, a kind of farewell dinner. When I asked this ardent golfer and fisherman how he could possibly withstand the terrible heat in summer and bitter cold in winter of his planned home in retirement at Gettysburg, Pennsylvania, Eisenhower responded wistfully, "There are some decisions a man must allow the wife to make."

One of my biggest stories was John F. Kennedy's intention to appoint his brother Robert Attorney General. Kennedy's "leak" was made in an airliner high over the Southwest between a visit to the Vice President-elect, Lyndon Johnson, and the President-elect's vacation retreat at Palm Beach, Florida.

The President-elect and I were surrounded by other reporters, perhaps fifty of them, as we talked that night, but he kept the story for me to break alone in the *Times* two mornings later.

President Johnson, fresh from hospitalization and anxious to get to Texas, was hung up in Washington because of the need to swear in a new Postmaster General, Lawrence F. O'Brien. Johnson happily accepted my recommendation he swear in the new postal official in front of the President's own fourth-class post office in a gingerbread red general store at Hye, Texas. It rained cats and dogs that day, but a colored lithograph autographed in appreciation by both the President and O'Brien hangs proudly on the wall of my den.

I have never been close to Richard Nixon, though I've known him a long, long time. Nevertheless, on a trip to the National Governors' Conference at Colorado Springs, Colorado, in 1969, he cautioned me to "take care of yourself, remember you got pretty sick the last time you were in Colorado." His reference was to fourteen years earlier when President Eisenhower suffered his first heart attack in Denver and I was hospitalized in the same city a few days later. Because Mr. Nixon and I were not close personal friends, I could scarcely believe that he would remember fourteen years after the event that I had been ill in Denver the same time Ike had been.

It was in these and many other ways that I came to know the Presidents, the powerful men and women in the House and Senate, and the chieftains of both major political parties during my long career in Washington.

I suppose many of my friends, and most of my enemies, would classify me as a liberal, probably as a Democrat. But the truth is that I am a political independent and fiercely protect my lack of allegiance to any political party or man. I have tried to be objective, and there are Democrats as well as Republicans who can testify that my writing and reporting has often cut both ways.

True, I have had political romances, a few of them. Some involved Republicans, like my first Presidential candidate, the moderate Wendell L. Willkie; or the deeply conservative Senator from Arizona, Barry Goldwater, who carried the Republican banner to defeat in 1964; or Senator Taft's 1952 campaign manager, Tom Coleman, the party boss of Wisconsin, whom I loved deeply as a friend. On the Democratic side, I never knew any President as well as I knew Jack Kennedy, who was a close friend in and out of the White House, and, of course, there was that first association with the politically glamorous Franklin D. Roosevelt in 1938 when I was barely twenty-two.

Guy Gabrielson, who was chairman of the Republican National Committee at the time, proposed in 1951 that I become the Republican party publicity director, and nearly fifteen years later Bill Moyers suggested that I succeed him as White House press secretary to Lyndon Johnson. Make what you will of these job offers; I declined them both because I considered myself too independent for them.

This is a personal account of my professional career, not my autobiography or an account of my personal life. Gay Talese, in his book, *The Kingdom and the Power*, an account of the life and politics of *The New York Times*, has described me as a "womanizer," a reporter who was often seen with lovely women while covering the news. I have known a lot of beautiful women, and some of them have enriched my life. But these women are not in this book. The women I've known learned long ago that I don't kiss and tell, except on politicians. And even politicians know that I can keep a secret.

My journalistic career began on the Lincoln, Nebraska, *Star* back in 1932, and I hit the big time during the General Motors strike of 1936–37. On this first big front-page assignment, I found myself involved deeply and personally in the efforts to settle the GM strike in early 1937. Because of a question I asked, the UAW suddenly canceled its agreement to leave the Fisher body plants in Flint, Michigan, plants it held in violation of state court injunctions and in spite of the presence of the Michigan National Guard.

Everybody was waiting for the strikers to march out at the

quit-the-plant order, when suddenly Wyndham Mortimer, then a vice president of the UAW, came rushing down the stairs of Fisher body No. 1 to charge that General Motors had double-crossed the strikers and they were not to leave.

Mortimer was not yet halfway down the stairs when I ran to his side demanding why. "You should know," Mortimer replied. "You gave us the information." I didn't understand, and I told him so. Mortimer explained that the information on which the union was now acting to cancel an agreement patiently mediated between GM and the UAW by Michigan's Governor Frank Murphy was based on a question I had asked barely an hour earlier before I came into the struck plant with Paul Gallico, a general assignment reporter for the *New York Daily News*.

Mortimer's decision, ratified later that night by the UAW executive board and backed up by CIO boss John L. Lewis, meant that the strike and illegal occupation of GM's Flint plants would continue another twenty-five days despite the great economic and political power of GM, the presence in Flint of the Michigan National Guard, the powers of the Michigan government under Governor Murphy, a couple of court injunctions, massive newspaper editorial pressure, and the growing impatience of President Franklin D. Roosevelt and his Secretary of Labor Frances Perkins alternately aimed at GM and the UAW—sometimes at both at the same time.

When it was over, the UAW and CIO had won their first great victory and modern organized labor was on the march for the first time.

How did this come about, and how did I, who was only twenty and working for the United Press Association out of Chicago, come to be involved so deeply and so personally in this great labor dispute, the first story of any national consequence to which I had been assigned?

When the Flint local with only a handful of members began its unauthorized sit-down strike against the two Fisher body plants on December 30, I had been working for UP in its Chicago office for less than a month. Before the UP, my newspaper experience had included work for the Lincoln, Nebraska, *Star*, where I broke in at sixteen, and later with the Associated Press and *The Omaha World Herald*. But the minute GM was struck, the Detroit bureau of the UP, undermanned as UP bureaus always are, sent out a call for help.

UP's New York headquarters sent out its hard-driving chief editor, Merton T. Akers, and its finest reporter-writer, Harry Ferguson, and for some reason never known to me, the Chicago Midwestern editor chose his rawest recruit—me—to join the Detroit team. I was assigned to Flint where the strike was centered and the potential for trouble seemed greatest. Ferguson stayed in Detroit writing the main stories, including the reportorial product of those who were assigned to the corporation or union headquarters in Detroit, the governor's office in Lansing, or the struck plants in Flint.

What follows is not a definitive history of the GM strike, but simply my part in it.

Although President Roosevelt had been reelected to a second term by an overwhelming majority, he was still fighting to make his New Deal a reality. He faced the unrelenting opposition of what he called "the nine old men" on the United States Supreme Court who had systematically declared unconstitutional the principal cornerstones of his domestic policy. The Court had many highly respected allies: for example, a long list of conservative corporation lawyers recruited by John W. Davis and the Liberty League. The League did not even wait for the Supreme Court to act; it sometimes issued advisory opinions in advance that key federal laws were unconstitutional and therefore need not be obeyed.

Though these lawyers were by the very fact of their profession "officers of the court" charged with enforcing and promoting respect for the law, the Liberty League committee simply decided that none of the social-welfare laws of the Roosevelt administration were constitutional and therefore did not need to be obeyed. Like so many earlier and later champions of "law and order," these lawyers were deciding which laws they would choose to obey and which to disobey.

One of the laws thus declared "unconstitutional" by an unofficial advisory opinion was the National Labor Relations Act, usually called the Wagner Act, which guaranteed the right of workingmen to form legitimate unions and to bargain collectively with their employers. Where a union could establish, by an election conducted by the National Labor Relations Board, that it represented a majority of the workers in any plant, the company was required to grant exclusive bargaining rights to that union.

The law, fiercely resisted by employers, was declared constitutional by the U.S. Supreme Court in February, 1937, in a series of fiercely divided 5-to-4 decisions.

As incredible as it may seem now, the Liberty League's "lawyers committee" held the Wagner Act to be unconstitutional, saying among other things:

> Production is not commerce. The processes and incidents of production, such as labor, are not commerce, even though the products of such activities subsequently find themselves in interstate movement. Although production may have some impact on interstate commerce, the effects on commerce of the labor expended in production is remote and indirect. . . .

Industries which since have known the crippling effects of nationwide strikes affecting just one giant corporation to say nothing of an entire industry, like the railroads, can testify now to the faulty judgment of these lawyers on whom they were dependent in 1935, 1936, and 1937.

And the lawyers' committee concluded its advisory opinion with these words:

> Considering the [National Labor Relations] act in the light of our history, the established form of government, and the decisions of our highest court, we have no hesitancy in concluding that it is unconstitutional and that it constitutes a complete departure from our constitutional and traditional theories of government.

When the unauthorized General Motors sit-down strike began in late December, 1936, few companies had been complying with labor's federal charter.

And in Flint, the UAW didn't simply strike. It imported from Europe the weapon of the sit-down strike, in which workers stayed at their factory posts but refused to work. It was the first sit-down strike against any U.S. corporation. This was why nationwide cries of outrage greeted the strike.

GM, through its president, William S. Knudsen, and a friendly press, denounced the strikers who had illegally seized corporate property. GM swiftly obtained a court injunction declaring the strike illegal and requiring the strikers to end immediately their occupation of the two Fisher plants.

In Flint, a dreary "company town," the police moved to dislodge the strikers from the plants. On January 11, a police cordon was placed around the Fisher No. 2 plant, the one most lightly held by the union. In the midst of a bitter cold wave, police turned off the heat in the building and attempted to halt the supply of food to strikers occupying the plant.

While I looked on, police joined battle with the union pickets outside the plant. The resistance was directed on a loudspeaker by Victor Reuther, brother of the famous redhead, Walter, who later was to head the UAW for so many years. Union combatants outnumbered the police, and in the frigid cold they grabbed fire-hoses which they sprayed upon the police who turned and ran.

One of the reporters, recalling the great Battle of Bull Run during the Civil War, promptly named this encounter the "Battle of the Running Bulls," a name that was to stick forever.

This first outbreak of violence caused Michigan's new governor, Frank Murphy, to send the Michigan National Guard into Flint to preserve law and order, but never, as it turned out, to enforce the court orders requiring the union to give up its possession of the two GM plants.

Indeed, it soon became apparent that the first court order was unenforceable, unworthy of public respect. The union discovered and made known the fact that the Genessee County Court judge who issued the order, Judge Edward Black, was himself the owner of $219,000 worth of GM stock.

GM's lawyers and public relations men pleaded ignorance of Judge Black's large stock holdings and conflict of interest. I never was satisfied myself whether the corporation had intentionally initiated its lawsuit before a judge who was a corporate stockholder. In fact, there had been no need to transgress the conflict-of-interest prohibition because any Genessee County judge, stockholder or not, certainly would have sided against the union and for the company in the highly charged atmosphere in Flint.

It was against this backdrop that the union continued its illegal possession of GM property and the company maintained its unwillingness to obey the federal law requiring collective bargaining with legitimate unions. It was the tough and at times seemingly impossible job of Governor Murphy, himself in office only a few days, to try to find common ground for compromise between these two lawbreakers. Murphy was the first Democratic governor of Michigan in a long time, and labor expected much of him. The CIO, led by the legendary John L. Lewis, had dug deep into its union treasury to help elect Democrats, including Roosevelt to a second term. Lewis angrily demanded that Roosevelt reward his labor friends and punish his corporate enemies.

On January 15, Governor Murphy persuaded negotiators for the company and the union to agree to a truce. If the union would evacuate the struck plants, GM would begin on January 18 to bargain and would continue to bargain for at least fifteen days on the proposals put before it by the union, including the important union demand that it be granted exclusive bargaining rights for all the employees of General Motors.

While the company and union were fighting with no apparent hope of agreement, a back-to-work propaganda campaign had been started in Flint by a group that called itself the Flint Alliance, headed by a former paymaster for Buick, George Boysen. The Alliance's chief impact was in the propaganda field—releases issued from the Durant Hotel by a New York publicity man, Larry Williamson.

Most reporters regarded the Flint Alliance as a "company union," which could be depended upon to disappear whenever GM wanted it to. Certainly no one of us dreamed that it might be a barrier to the GM-UAW truce so patiently and painfully constructed by Governor Murphy in mid-January.

On the big day set for evacuation·of the Flint plants, Sunday, January 17, I awakened early in my room at the Durant Hotel and began to plan my day of work that should have marked the end of the General Motors strike. On my way to breakfast with Paul Gallico, I decided to stop off at the Flint Alliance and see what Larry Williamson might have to say.

When I knocked on Williamson's door, it opened, but he was not there. I looked in his room and saw on the desk where publicity handouts customarily were kept a large pile of releases, one of which began with the information that bargaining talks between the Flint Alliance and GM would begin a couple of days later, as agreed upon in a telephone conversation between George Boysen and William Knudsen.

As I moved back toward the elevator, continuing on my way to breakfast, I ran into Williamson and told him I had just seen the publicity releases in his room. I asked about the telephone call be-

tween Boysen and Knudsen, and Williamson told me it had occurred in the last few hours, since the GM-UAW truce had been
arranged by Governor Murphy.

At breakfast, Gallico and I were planning the day's campaign on
what we believed would be the last day of the strike in Flint. It
was a somewhat improbable alliance—Gallico, nearing forty,
already enjoying a famous name in American journalism, and I,
just under twenty-one, the raw recruit. But Gallico, a tall, powerfully built man, also was a kind of "rookie" as far as news reporting
was concerned. He had come out of Columbia University to be
the movie critic for the *Daily News* in the early twenties, and for
the last twelve years he had been the sports editor, writing a brilliant
column that made him known to literally millions of Americans.
He had tired of sports and had persuaded Captain Joseph M. Pat-
terson, who ran the *Daily News*, to let him try his hand at general
reporting. The GM strike was his first attempt.

My life in Flint usually consisted of a fast tour by taxis of the
struck plants at an early hour, even before breakfast, to learn if
there had been any nighttime developments, then the conference
with Gallico back at the hotel. I had developed excellent contacts
with the union leaders and Gallico's name made it easy for him to
get to some of GM's top brass who had never heard of Bill Lawrence but certainly were impressed with the star from the *Daily
News*.

Gallico, as a star, was highly paid, and I was making about $30
a week at the United Press, but it was an easy, natural partnership.
I had strong legs in those days, but Gallico carried his share of the
load. I learned a lot from him, and his is a friendship I still cherish.

Gallico and I agreed that the best way to cover the evacuation
and the parade was to go first to the union headquarters and there
make arrangements with the local strike leader, Bob Travis, to be
transported on the union sound truck that would lead the evacuation
parade from Fisher No. 1 to Fisher No. 2. It was a sunny, though
cold, January afternoon, nobody expected any trouble, and the
assignment ahead looked simply like a colorful account of a parade
that the union would call a victory demonstration even though some
of the top leaders, including Travis and Mortimer, were not certain
the union had achieved very much in the Murphy-arranged truce.

As Gallico, Travis, and I talked in the union leader's dusty, grimy
office on the second floor of Pengelly Hall, the local union headquarters, I inquired quite casually and innocently of Travis what

his reaction was to the information I had just received: that bargaining talks soon would begin between GM and the Flint Alliance.

"Pay no attention to Poison Boysen," Travis responded breezily. "You guys better get out to Fisher No. 1 if you want to have lunch, and then ride on the sound truck. I'll O.K. it."

I attached little significance to the question I had asked Travis. I was insufficiently experienced in labor relations and negotiations to understand that any agreement for bargaining between GM and the Flint Alliance was by itself and in effect a refusal to bargain exclusively with the UAW. Of course, General Motors had said all along it would not bargain exclusively with the UAW and nobody seriously expected it to do so; but nevertheless, the UAW demand for exclusive bargaining rights was a prime issue on which the company had agreed to bargain for at least fifteen days as provided in the truce arranged by Governor Murphy.

So neither Gallico nor I had any idea that the whole strike picture was very much up in the air as we hailed a taxi and rode out to Fisher No. 1, climbed through a window, and made our way to the basement for lunch and conversation with strikers and one distinguished outside observer, Professor Robert Morse Lovett of the University of Chicago. Lovett, Gallico, and I were eating a dish of ice cream when Mortimer came down the stairs with his announcement that the evacuation was off.

Gallico and I raced across the street to a pay telephone, where I asked him to listen in as I first telephoned to the Flint Alliance's Williamson so he could repeat—with Gallico on hand as confirmation—just what he had told me earlier about the agreement between Boysen and Knudsen to negotiate.

This confirmed, I then telephoned to UP Detroit with the news that the Flint plants would not be evacuated despite the agreement with Governor Murphy, that the union was charging a double cross by the corporation. It would be some hours before the other newsmen, and the competing Associated Press, could learn the information UP now was moving on its wires.

Gallico and I then hailed a taxicab and hurried back to the Durant Hotel and the headquarters for General Motors, then manned by an old friend, Felix Bruner.

With Gallico nodding confirmation, I told Bruner what had happened between Williamson and me, between Travis and me, and the announcement by Mortimer to the strikers inside the Fisher No. 1 plant.

Bruner, for GM, protested instantly that the story given out by Williamson was false, that there were no arrangements to bargain between GM and the Flint Alliance.

I asked Bruner if he could get me a first-hand denial from Knudsen. Bruner went into another room to telephone GM's president.

In a few minutes, Bruner was back and said that Knudsen not only had denied any arrangement for bargaining with the Flint Alliance, but had added, "I never have talked to Mr. Boysen in my life, by telephone or otherwise."

I told Bruner that I would now carry Knudsen's personally authorized denial back to the UAW and see what might be done to get the truce back on the track and the union's agreement once more to evacuate the two Fisher plants in Flint.

Back at union headquarters, I talked again with Bob Travis, and he asked me to return shortly for a meeting of the UAW's executive board. Most of the top leaders, including the UAW president, Homer Martin, had been en route from Detroit anyway to watch the "victory parade"; now they had to decide whether to continue the strike indefinitely and to notify Governor Murphy formally that they would *not* adhere to the truce agreement so recently negotiated by him.

When I returned in the early evening for the UAW board meeting, Pengelly Hall was overrun by newsmen from all over the country who were in Michigan for strike coverage. There was one notable absentee, Paul Tobenkin of the New York *Herald Tribune*, who already had left Flint after sending by telegraph to his newspaper an account of the evacuation of the Flint plants as he had assumed would occur.

When Travis learned that I was milling around with the other reporters outside the union offices, he sent for me. I was ushered inside the closed doors to where the union leaders were meeting. They asked me about my part in the day's developments, and I told them just what I have written here, and what I previously had told both Bob Travis and Felix Bruner.

Just about the time I reached that point in my narrative where I reported the Bruner-produced Knudsen denial that he had ever talked with Boysen by telephone, there was a knock on the door, a request to talk to me by Gallico. Gallico handed me a publicity release from GM, a telegram from Knudsen to Boysen agreeing to a bargaining session with the Alliance later in the week.

I did not know then, nor do I know now, why Knudsen in one

breath authorized a denial that he had ever talked to Boysen about bargaining with the Flint Alliance, and then, in another breath, sent him a telegram agreeing to such a bargaining session.

Whatever the corporate reasoning, this series of events hardened the union refusal to evacuate the Flint plants until a much more meaningful agreement had been extracted from GM.

If the union had quit the plants as scheduled on that Sunday afternoon, and GM subsequently had entered into bargaining negotations with the Flint Alliance as well as the UAW, the union would have wound up losing what its members had been striking for, because they could not have hoped to have achieved exclusive bargaining rights this way.

Since there were so few UAW members in Flint, and GM's determination at that time was not to obey the Wagner Act, the union's only clout came from its illegal occupation of the company plants, and that influence would have ended the instant the plants were evacuated.

So on that Sunday evening in Flint, the mostly young leadership of the young union, backed up by some of the labor veterans supplied by the CIO, had to make a tough decision. The board members, having heard my story and then seen its confirmation in the telegram supplied by Gallico, let me sit with them as they argued back and forth. I sat inside the conference room as the telephone call was placed to Governor Murphy and he was told personally why the GM plants would not be evacuated as the union had agreed. Then, though the union headquarters outside the room was swarming with other competitive newsmen, I asked and received permission to telephone to UP in Detroit the story of that fateful decision. UP moved the story swiftly over its teletype circuits across the nation, and a few minutes later I slipped out of the union headquarters to rendezvous with Gallico and share with him this story. Perhaps another hour passed before the union gave out the news generally.

For the red-haired Governor Murphy, still in his first two weeks in office, this was a hard and unexpected setback for his peacemaking efforts, but in light of GM's behavior there was little he could do at that moment to persuade the union to quit the plants and take a chance on success at the bargaining table. The corporation remained equally unwilling to bargain with the union while its plants were occupied.

The spotlight shifted to Washington, where Mrs. Frances Perkins coupled the "please" of a woman with the power of the Roosevelt administration to seek peace, but after nearly two weeks the Secretary of Labor had little to show for her efforts except some rebuffs headlined in boxcar type. FDR, on separate occasions, berated both sides for their refusal to cooperate and got back from John L. Lewis the stinging, caustic answer that "it ill behooves one who has supped at Labor's table to denounce with equal vigor labor and its adversary when they become locked in deadly combat."

Near the end of January, GM sought a new court injunction to evict the sit-downers. There were signs as February blew in cold and gusty that the power of the Michigan National Guard and state and local police might be used to enforce the new order, which apparently was more valid than had been the Black injunction.

But John Lewis dared the governor to use the troops against the strikers and him, and, in the background, Lawrence Fisher of the Fisher body plant was cautioning the governor against shedding any workers' blood that figuratively might leave its stain on the automobiles that rolled off the assembly lines of the future.

There are reasons for believing that Bill Knudsen took the same private attitude as did Larry Fisher, but there was tougher talk from the top GM executives in New York, including board chairman Alfred P. Sloan, whose authority exceeded that of all his subordinate officials.

Cautiously, tenaciously, patiently, Frank Murphy continued to work for settlement, and finally on February 11 at an early hour in the morning, his efforts bore fruit.

The sit-downers would leave the plants and General Motors would bargain with the union for its members employed by GM.

These were not the exclusive bargaining rights sought by the union or required by the Wagner Act, but there was another clause in the GM settlement: The company would not for a six-month period bargain with any union other than the UAW without the advance approval of Governor Murphy (and he would not be likely to give such approval). For this same six-month period, the company agreed publicly that it would not remove any tools, dies, or equipment from the struck Flint plants. One of the rumors that preceded the unauthorized strike at Flint was that removal of plant equipment was in the works; and though the Flint local leaders never could confirm this rumor, they had ordered the strike anyway.

To sweeten the pot for the union, and the workers, GM agreed also to a $25,000,000 wage increase. The forty-four-day-old strike was over.

Labor was on the march after the GM strike, and I was the foot-sore reporter who followed the labor story from negotiation to negotiation, from strike to strike, from picket line to picket line, clear across the Midwest. For a young man in journalism a press association job that demanded speed and accuracy was an ideal showcase for his talents.

Many of the strikes were centered in Detroit, and I lived in hotels there for months on end. Others were in Indiana and Illinois. It was day after day of long, hard work, days merging into weeks and months that in their repetitive character all became a giant blur. Even now it is hard to straighten out the events of one strike from another, or one bit of picket-line violence from another battle-ground for labor and its foes.

When GM settled, it did not mean that all of American industry, or even all of the automobile industry, was willing to bargain with its employees organized into CIO unions.

And one at a time the CIO took on all of them. Chrysler was organized after a hard-fought strike. Surprisingly, the United States Steel Corporation settled without a strike. After some preliminary violence known as the "Battle of the Overpass," the Ford Motor Company, long considered the most anti-labor of all the big companies, suddenly and without a strike gave the UAW a "closed-shop" agreement, blanketing all its employees into the union with or without their consent.

Because Chrysler was struck after GM had settled, the Chrysler negotiations never had the impact on newspaper headlines or on the tempers of the country that the General Motors strike had.

Once again it was Governor Murphy who worked around the clock to try to bring peace between the top management of Chrysler, meaning Walter P. Chrysler himself, and the CIO, which was John Lewis.

One of the more tense negotiating periods came during the Easter holidays of 1937 when the Chrysler-UAW team was persuaded to join round-the-clock bargaining sessions in Murphy's office in Lansing.

Murphy had hoped the GM settlement would give him some relief and that it might boost his chances for the Presidency in 1940. President Roosevelt was expected to move out of the White

House rather than break that sacred American tradition against a third term, which had existed ever since George Washington voluntarily retired to Mount Vernon.

Because of Murphy's Presidential ambitions, he struck a scrupulously neutral pose and maintained that as Michigan's governor he was acting in the public interest to restore labor peace while preserving law and order.

On the Thursday before Easter Sunday, there had been a long bargaining session in Murphy's office that included Chrysler, Lewis, and assorted leaders on both sides. The discussions had continued until well after midnight. At long last reporters were summoned to Governor Murphy's office in Michigan's old capitol building, and the governor, in his low baritone, began to rumble:

"Gentlemen, in the spirit of Good Friday eve, progress has been made. Both sides have made concessions . . ." Murphy was interrupted by Texas-born J. Edward Angly, a reporter for the New York *Herald Tribune,* who asked, "Tell us, Governor, who's going to be crucified—those Chrysler guys, or those CIO guys?"

Murphy, a deeply religious Roman Catholic, could scarcely believe the words and he struggled visibly for control.

"Gentlemen," Murphy began again, "the spirit of Good Friday eve has prevailed, progress has been made. Both sides have made concessions."

This time Angly did not dare to interrupt him, and the governor went ahead to report one of the milestones on the way to settlement at Chrysler.

During that spring, as the newsmen followed company and labor negotiators from one dispute to another, we came back to Detroit one night to find our own hotel on strike. The elevators had ceased to run and the restaurants and night clubs were not dispensing food or liquor.

The town was full of important people. I decided to go to the Statler Hotel in downtown Detroit, where, panting heavily, I climbed thirteen flights of stairs to find the opera star, Lily Pons, marooned in her suite as she waited to sing at a concert in Detroit.

Miss Pons received me warmly and cooperated beautifully in filling out the interview that already had taken shape in my mind before I came to see her.

I didn't know whether Miss Pons actually had been born in France, but Lily Pons had always struck me as a French name. I asked her first about the theory that American labor had borrowed the sit-down strike technique from French workers.

"No, no, no," was Miss Póns' indignant response, punctuated by stamps of a pretty foot swirling the negligee about her shapely legs as her body moved.

She told me that at her concert on the next evening she would sit down to sing. Otherwise, she insisted, Detroit, as the city of sit-down strikes, would not be able to hear, understand, or appreciate her singing.

There was a real headline for you: Lily Pons to stage her own sit-down strike.

It was a brief light moment in a grim time, and one of the few bright stories I ever wrote from Detroit.

With contracts signed with GM and Chrysler, the union's next obvious objective was to organize the workers at Ford, where one man, Henry Ford, ruled without challenge or even question a giant company.

Old Henry, who had helped make the twentieth century move faster because of his motor cars, had never himself moved with the fashions nor accepted the prevailing ideas of this new century.

Literally standing guard beside Ford was a tough ex-boxer turned company policeman named Harry Bennett who recruited into the Ford "service department" an assortment of strong-arm men reinforced by ex-convicts paroled personally to Bennett.

Bennett's power mounted with a series of kidnappings across the country. It was known that the elder Ford feared that his children or grandchildren might be snatched by the underworld and Bennett was to protect them. Bennett's men also were most useful in seeing to it that unions did not penetrate into Ford's empire. Employees suspected of joining or even sympathizing with a union were given their dismissal notices quickly.

As a young labor reporter, it was important for me to get to know Bennett personally. I could not hope that an audience could be arranged with Ford himself.

On the first day I went to see Harry Bennett I found him in his office, an air gun of great power held between his knees, shooting off steel pellets at a target placed against the office wall. I told him I was Bill Lawrence from the UP and that we ought to get acquainted since I would be around Ford as the UAW carried on its campaign to organize Ford's workers.

Bennett grinned an acknowledgment of my self-introduction, and flipped open a manila folder on his desk and started to read off my history: Born in Lincoln, Nebraska, educated in the Lincoln school systems, briefly attended the University of Nebraska, then went to work on the Lincoln *Star*.

He stopped there. He had made his point. The Ford secret police knew all about me.

Nothing else in the interview was memorable, but the fact that Bennett and I had met, had talked amiably, that he did not find me persona non grata, all these things later were to prove important to me and my work in and near the Ford plants at River Rouge and elsewhere.

More importantly, Bennett's thugs knew that I knew their boss and, to some degree anyway, had access to him.

It was probably for this reason that I was left undisturbed, and indeed free to use company telephones, when the bloody "Battle of the Overpass" was waged in the early afternoon of May 26, 1937. The two principal victims who took a brutal battering from Ford's "service department" thugs were UAW leaders Walter Reuther and Richard T. Frankensteen, themselves union rivals for the leadership of the big and influential bloc of Ford employees who might be organized into the union.

Armed with a city permit, Reuther and Frankensteen came to the overpass over Miller Road at Gate Four to pass out handbills urging unionization of Ford workers. Their arrival had been well publicized in advance, and Bennett's men were waiting for them the instant they stepped on the elevated bridge that led to the plant gate shortly before the time for a change in shifts.

Ford's men hit swiftly, efficiently, and brutally as they moved in large numbers against Reuther and Frankensteen, pulling the jackets over the heads of the union men so they were not free to exercise their arms in retaliation for the brutal punches and kicks that then were landed. Frankensteen fought back harder than did Reuther, and took a more vicious beating for his pains. Both men were bloody when the Ford crew finished its work, and news photographers photographing the scene said Frankensteen looked like he might never rise again.

Reuther was dumped savagely in the cinders alongside the path leading to the overpass, and still was under heavy attack when Ford's men saw a group of UAW women leaving streetcars to join in distributing handbills. They too were beaten by Ford's thugs.

Ford won that battle but lost the war. As *Time* magazine was to comment in its next issue, "it looked very much as if that brutal beating might hurt Henry Ford as much as it hurt Richard Frankensteen."

Though he was to stay and fight for many another day, in the end it was Ford who surrendered in 1939 and gave the amazed leaders of the UAW more than they could have hoped for—a closed shop with union membership for all Ford's production workers.

I was in Washington, covering the headquarters of the CIO and the United Mine Workers, when the astounded leaders of the UAW came to John Lewis for advice.

Should they accept Henry Ford's offer?

Some felt that the Ford management purposely was offering the union more than it could digest, more members than the leaders could control, with some danger that a flood of pro-Ford members might make the UAW a "company union." But John L.'s advice that night was to "take it." The auto union did, and had surprisingly little trouble continuing as a completely independent union in its dealings with Ford.

But there were strikes and troubles elsewhere, and these took me away from Detroit, back to my "home" in Chicago where I had lived for a brief time before hitting the road on an endless series of labor assignments.

In retrospect, no sit-down strike was more important than the one called by the Steel Workers Organizing Committee against the Fansteel Metallurgical Corporation in North Chicago, which I covered from its start to its bloody finish. It was not a struggle between a giant like General Motors and a little union, for Fansteel itself was a small company, employing fewer than 400 workers. One hundred of them seized two company buildings inside a seven-and-a-half-acre complex ringed by a high fence made of steel wire.

Yet Fansteel was to be the landmark case because this was the first sit-down strike ended by violent eviction of the strikers and it later was to provide the vehicle for the Supreme Court's first decision that sit-down strikes were illegal and sit-down strikers lawfully could be discharged under the Wagner Act, which act the Court had sustained by the time of this ruling. I had moved to Washington by the time the Supreme Court acted, and covered the end of the legal case as well as the strike itself.

But there was nothing about the beginning of the strike on a cold afternoon of mid-February, 1937, that marked it in any way as different from the scores of others I had covered, or ignored, as the drive of labor to organize swept across the Middle West.

My first connection with Fansteel was in the pre-dawn hours of February 19, 1937, when I boarded a North Shore railroad train from Chicago and rode out to the struck plant in North Chicago. The UP office in Chicago had been tipped off that sheriff's deputies enforcing a court order would be attempting early that morning to evict the strikers.

Fansteel was a small company which extracted rare metals from ore, including tungsten, tantalum, molybdenum, and other exotic materials. Perhaps its most identifiable product was the writing point on Eversharp pens, but Fansteel sold only to other manufacturers, not to the general public. And this fact of economic life was the prime reason Fansteel's officials could press for eviction of the men who held their plant by force. They did not need to fear, as GM officials obviously had feared, that any blood that was shed would be splashed on products that members of the general public, including union members and their sympathizers, would decide to buy or not to buy in a competitive market.

There were, in fact, two efforts to throw out the sit-down strikers by force, one on the morning of February 19 led by Sheriff Lawrence Doolittle and seventy-five deputies. This one failed as the sheriff's men fell back under a barrage of railroad spikes, iron tools, and bottles of sulfuric acid hurled from the plant windows by the embattled sit-downers. Sheriff Doolittle was injured slightly, but his pride was hurt more as the strikers turned back his force of deputies while newsmen from Chicago did a blow-by-blow account of the battle. The sheriff also was scared, and told company officials he wouldn't go through that kind of an ordeal again.

Later that morning, during postmortems about the battle, some of the newsmen were talking at the Waukegan Hotel in nearby Waukegan with one of the young company lawyers, Harold Keele. For some reason, which no one recalls today, they got into a discussion of a little-used expression, "puerile sophisticate," and that set in motion a train of events which led eventually to the eviction of the strikers.

Keele, who thirty-five years later in 1971 was still practicing law in Chicago, recalled that he argued the expression "puerile sophisticate" could not be used properly because the two words were incompatible. But as he thought about the words and their derivation from the ancient Greek, his mind went back to the siege of Troy and the Trojan Horse, and suddenly he had an idea that he thought might solve the stalemate.

We would build from lumber a hollow tower approximately six feet square and twenty feet high which could be mounted on the rear of a truck and backed up against the building. The tower was to have sides which could open out and the top could be thrown open to allow the men concealed within the tower to step out on top of the building or to enter at the level of the windows on the second floor. The inside of the structure was to be furnished with cleats which would serve as a ladder so that the men could ascend to the different levels.

In order to secure secrecy the structure was built in Chicago and brought to Waukegan, lying horizontally on a truck, after midnight on Thursday, February 25. Somewhere around six o'clock on Friday morning, February 26, the truck was driven into the Fansteel enclosure, the tower raised by ropes to an upright position on the truck, and the attacking deputies entered the tower. The truck was then backed against one of the buildings occupied by the men.

It was met by efforts of the men inside to set it afire by throwing down upon it burning papers and rags, but this had been foreseen and the tower had been wetted down with water before it had been raised on the truck.

At the same time as the truck was backed against the building the sheriff's men sent a number of tear-gas shells into the buildings. Since no one present had had any experience with modern tear gas, enough tear gas was used to have evacuated twenty buildings instead of two.

Word of the expected attack had gotten out and a considerable crowd had gathered on the Northwestern Railway tracks just outside the company's premises. On the road beyond the tracks my wife and Winthrop Hiram Smith [who was then managing partner of the offices of E. A. Pierce and Company and who subsequently became operating head of Merrill Lynch, Pierce, Fenner and Smith] and his wife, who were friends of mine, were in my car for the purpose of watching the proceedings. The tear gas drifted to the east across the tracks and the road and practically immobilized all those on the rear embankment and the road.

The men within the plant began to leave the back entrance of the buildings as soon as the gas hit the buildings. We had purposely left the rear of the buildings unguarded to enable the men to get out. At the same time that the teargas attack was launched, the men inside the tower opened the "hatches," climbed onto the roof of the building, and descended into it. They were equipped with gas masks, and by the time they reached the interior of the buildings all of the employees had left. Someone in the crowd had had the forethought to bring wire cutters and a hole had been cut in the cyclone fence at the rear of the buildings. Through this the men escaped.

The company took possession of the buildings but the tear gas had settled into the basements and its was several days before the buildings could be used. The only injuries sustained by anyone were minor and they were inflicted on the deputies by objects thrown from the buildings and from the Northwestern Railway embankment. Jack Froelich, one of the deputies who was alongside me, was struck by an object which gashed his head and he was knocked out. After the wound had been sewn up he returned to the attack.

Once again, before the attack was launched, the Chicago UP office had been tipped off in advance, and, once again, I was on the scene to report the battle and the successful eviction of the strikers. In those days, our principal rival news service, the Associated Press, got most of its news from the carbon copies of stories written by reporters for AP member newspapers. None of them were in a hurry. I was, and the UP led AP by hours on this story, by now a national sensation because at long last sit-down strikers had been forcibly thrown out. This no doubt was what the silent majority of its day fervently wanted.

Wherever there was trouble in those days, I was on hand, an overworked, underpaid, but terrifically eager reporter. There was never a day off, it seemed. The one topcoat I owned was so drenched with tear gas that I could swing the coat about in a heated room and make other occupants of the room start to cry. By now, I had developed immunity to the gas.

CHAPTER
2

A meeting of the Republican National Committee in Chicago in 1937 provided the springboard for my move to the United Press bureau in Washington. Politics always had interested me more than anything else, and though I was to continue covering organized labor in Washington, I knew my chance at a big political story would come one day. And a Washington post, under the direction of UP bureau manager Lyle C. Wilson, was considered a prize plum.

The Republicans, down to an all-time low of eighty-nine seats in the 435-member House of Representatives, were in Chicago to talk about a possible mid-term convention, which wasn't very important in the long run.

What was important to me was the chance to meet some important GOP leaders, and to impress them as favorably as I could in the hope they might carry word of me back to Wilson in Washington.

In the National Committee deliberations, the key Republican Congressional strategist was Representative Joseph W. Martin, Jr., who had started his climb in the Republican hierarchy that eventually would take him to be Speaker of the House in the Eightieth Congress.

Working alongside Martin was white-haired Earl Venable, at that time executive secretary of the Republican Congressional Campaign Committee but who had come to Washington many years before as an aide to Senator William E. Borah of Idaho. I told both Martin and Venable of my wish to move to Washington for the UP, and enlisted their active support as lobbyists in my campaign to persuade Lyle Wilson I was vital to his Washington operations.

Venable was a fixture at the National Press Club bar, where Lyle Wilson usually retreated after his day of running the Washington bureau. Back in Washington, Venable told Wilson that buried out in Chicago was a young fellow named Bill Lawrence of high competence and a great desire to work out of Washington.

Not long afterwards Joe Martin gave the same message to Wilson. Since Wilson could not know this was an inspired campaign, his interest was piqued at least. After a few months I was ordered to the Washington office.

I was twenty-two, it was January, 1938, and Washington was a town filled with magic for a young reporter. FDR was midway through his second term, and though I was at first assigned in Washington to continue my work on the labor beat, opportunities to go to the White House were frequent. FDR held news conferences twice a week in the White House oval office, and even the youngest reporter in Washington was welcome to quiz the President.

FDR's ready availability made a deep impression on me. No President before or since maintained anything like his level of press-conference activity. Through his twelve years in the White House, in peace and even in World War II, Roosevelt held an average of more than eighty news conferences annually—a figure that becomes even more astounding if one notes that President Richard M. Nixon held only four news conferences in and out of Washington during the whole of 1970.

In 1938, FDR's preoccupation was domestic issues, for we neither knew nor cared much about the world outside. In a little less than two years when Europe went to war in September, 1939, this was to change, but meanwhile FDR was concerned with the still sluggish economy, continuing heavy unemployment, and the strike momentum created by the organizing efforts of the CIO and its leader, John L. Lewis.

My job was to cover all of the labor news from Washington, including the American Federation of Labor and its president, William Green. But the AFL took a back seat to Lewis in capitalizing on the Supreme Court's belated decision that the Wagner Act was constitutional and must be obeyed by the nation's employers, large and small.

For Lewis' United Mine Workers of America, there was one bit of unfinished business, one major soft coal field that had not yet been organized. That was "Bloody Harlan," the county in Kentucky so named because its soil had been drenched with the blood of many violent murders. Some of this bloodshed was connected with the union's efforts to organize the coal fields, but most of it was not. Harlan County was simply a violent place in which to live and its record of unsolved homicides matched that of any county in the nation.

In 1938, Lewis called a UMW strike against the Harlan County coal operators, determined to break their united front against his coal miners. Fearful of the almost inevitable violence, Governor A. B. (Happy) Chandler called out the Kentucky National Guard. Chandler at that time had national aspirations hinging on FDR's decision to seek a third term.

As soon as the Harlan strike began, Lyle Wilson ordered me to cover it. Though I had been exposed to physical danger in the picket-line violence of Michigan and Illinois, and luckily had escaped any injury, I now had a feeling of some fear as I left for Kentucky.

There was a kind of psychological fear created by the very name of "Bloody Harlan" and I freely admit now that I quaked a little at the prospect of traveling into an area where independent newspaper reporters—considered pro-labor if they were not totally pro-management—had on occasion been beaten badly while trying to tell the story.

As the bus crawled up the mountain road toward Harlan, my tension increased a little when I saw a sign on the edge of the road that read "Prepare to Meet Thy Maker." It had been erected by one of those snake-handling fundamentalist Protestant sects that flourished among the mountaineers, but it was not exactly the kind of message that would relax an already nervous young reporter.

I made my way to the Harlan Hotel, squarely in the center of the small company town, and had barely entered my room when the sound of gunfire erupted in the street directly in front of the hotel. On the sidewalk lay the body of a man, and standing nearby was an officer of the Kentucky National Guard. The Guard officer said the man had been shot by a deputy sheriff, "but it has nothing to do with the strike." This last bit of information apparently ended the National Guard's interest in the shooting, and mine as well. Run-of-the-mill homicides were too frequent in Harlan County to interest the outside world.

The hotel was jammed with out-of-town reporters, including Don Whitehead of the Associated Press, Bob Casey of the *Chicago Daily News*, Kenneth Campbell of *The New York Times*, and others.

With the National Guard on duty, the potential for violence was reduced greatly so far as the strike was concerned. Nevertheless, the reporters had organized a kind of "dawn patrol" in which we traveled from mine tipple to mine tipple early every morning looking for news of trouble that might have come in the night. There was remarkably little violence of any kind.

My contacts were very good with the UMW leaders, headed by George Titler, a district leader whom I had come to know through Lewis in Washington, but I had only a passing acquaintanceship with the coal operators. My chief competitor, Don Whitehead, was on the other hand an old-timer in this area, with close friends among the coal operators and with a brother, Kyle Whitehead, who was employed on the local Harlan County newspaper. Don Whitehead's wife Marie was a mountaineer herself and knew the wives of many of the coal operators.

Perhaps because the National Guard was on hand and thus the coal operators could not break the UMW strike violently, Lewis' men had succeeded this time in closing the Harlan County mines and were able to keep them closed. The federal government had sent in surplus food which undermined the old coal company weapon of hunger, usually applied against striking miners who had to get their meager food provisions from the company stores that suddenly cut off all credit when a strike was called.

For once not all the cards were stacked in favor of the companies, and to the visiting reporters it soon became apparent that this struggle would be over when the first major coal company decided to come to terms with John Lewis and grant to him the closed shop he was demanding for the UMW.

Because of my fear that Whitehead's friendships among the coal operators would result in some big break on this story for him, I had to work twice as hard as I might otherwise. I kept in closest touch with my union friends.

One night, with no advance warning, Titler telephoned me at the hotel to come to his office at once, and there he showed me a contract that had been signed only minutes before by Armstrong Matthews, president of the Black Star Coal Company.

In those days, the cracking of the Harlan County coal operators' united front was big news across the nation, and was worthy of a "flash" on the United Press wire, a flash being the priority rating given to news that transcended even a "bulletin" in importance. I picked up the telephone in Titler's office, quickly telephoned the United Press office in Washington, and dictated a flash, then a bulletin and a few more paragraphs of explanatory material.

Then I headed for the Western Union office near the hotel where I wrote hundreds of words about the union's great victory in Harlan. All the operators now would perforce follow the Black Star Coal Company's example and sign up with Lewis.

When I had finished the night leads for the morning papers, I began to work on the "overnight" story that would be transmitted in the early morning hours to the afternoon newspapers in the country.

As the minutes ticked away, there were telephone calls from Washington, asking for reassurance that my information was correct because they thought it strange that only the United Press should be carrying this information. The Associated Press wires had nothing resembling my story.

There is an old saying in the newspaper business that stories sometimes can get too exclusive for too long. After a time I also became concerned because Whitehead was not filing the same information that I had been given.

Probably another hour passed before Whitehead showed up at the telegraph office to file a routine overnight story containing none of my information about Black Star's capitulation. Quickly I told Whitehead about the big break during his absence, and inquired where he had been.

Whitehead was redheaded, and quick to anger, and as I talked the blood rushed to his face, turning it red.

"I'll be a son-of-a-bitch," Whitehead exploded. "Armie Matthews is an old friend of Marie and of me. Tonight he invited us to dinner and after dinner suggested a few rubbers of bridge. But first he said he had something to tend to downtown so he excused himself for a few minutes. When he came back, he said nothing about his business downtown. We played bridge for a couple of hours, and then I came here."

Whitehead had been sitting right on top of the story I had just beaten him on. The outcome might just as easily have been reversed, with me the uninformed victim.

Over the years Whitehead and I have become the closest of friends and companions, covering World War II and later the Korean War together. He swears he never was beaten so badly on any story in his life, and we never have failed to recall the Harlan County anecdote whenever and wherever we have met all over the world.

The mountaineer in Marie Whitehead never let her forget the incident either. Years later at a big party where the Matthews were sharing a table with the Whiteheads, Marie turned on the coal company head and told him he was "a son-of-a-bitch who let Bill Lawrence get that big scoop and nearly cost Don his job." Don's job was never in danger, but Marie never forgave her former friend from Harlan County.

CHAPTER

3

During 1938 and 1939, my professional activities remained centered upon organized labor as Europe moved toward and then into war while the United States technically kept out, though there could be little doubt that the Roosevelt administration and the American majority, in their hearts, favored the cause of Britain and France despite the restrictions of the Neutrality Act.

But in 1940, I made my first trip with a President during a year in which I also attended my first national political conventions and drew the full-time assignment of covering a Presidential nominee. For me it was a fateful year, the beginning of a professional adventure that has never failed to excite me.

My first journey with a President was a one-day round-trip by railroad between Washington and Charlottesville, Virginia, where President Roosevelt delivered a major speech before watching his son, Franklin D., Jr., receive his Bachelor of Laws degree at the University of Virginia. There was no honorary degree for the President that day because Virginia maintains a proud tradition of never awarding an honorary degree to anyone. There was an old

Virginia law professor, however, who maintained that FDR Jr.'s bachelor's degree in law was itself honorary because the young man, then married to Ethel DuPont, had not distinguished himself in the classroom.

But the main business of this trip was the President's speech, which though long scheduled was given added significance on that day—June 10—because it was the day when Italian dictator Benito Mussolini finally summoned the courage to strike a tottering France from behind. The German Army already had flanked the Maginot Line and the fate of France had been sealed even before Mussolini made his belated move. It underlined the Italian dictator's cowardice.

On the trip I was a glorified messenger boy for Tom Reynolds, then the White House correspondent for United Press.

FDR's prepared text was given out in mimeographed form on the Presidential special train after it pulled out of Washington, crossed the Potomac, and headed for Charlottesville via Culpepper. I remember that all the reporters on the train, but especially those representing the wire services, dumped literally tens of thousands of words of press copy on an unsuspecting Western Union office at Culpepper. The joke around the UP office in Washington thirty years later was that some of the material we filed that day was now beginning to arrive from Culpepper.

From Charlottesville I not only had a text to dictate, but I also had a new lead, one that would create a world sensation when the words were spoken.

The new lead I gave them by telephone was to be held on the desk until the President spoke. In its original form, FDR's text had made no mention of Italy's attack upon France. The reason probably was that his foreign policy advisors, some of them intent on aiding the Allies, and others intent on keeping the United States neutral, were not in agreement on what the President should say. As the train rolled through Virginia beyond Culpepper, Stephen T. Early, then press secretary to the President, came into the drawing room occupied by Reynolds and me and showed us the large-type reading copy of FDR's text on which the President had inserted, in ink, his now famous reference to "the hand that held the dagger has now plunged it into the back of its neighbor."

Strong talk indeed from the President of a country that was continually reasserting its unwillingness to engage in Europe's war.

My own guess is that the foreign policy advisors still hadn't resolved their differences, but the President, fretting under the restraints of neutrality, decided to go ahead anyway. So far anyway, Roosevelt was just talking; he still was a long way from the Lend-Lease formula under which the United States would arm the Western Allies and the Soviet Union.

For some reason, Early showed the "dagger in the back" interpolation only to Reynolds and me among the newsmen, and so the UP had a nice built-in advantage of a few minutes on the wires after Roosevelt actually spoke the words. We also enjoyed the virtue of being right, which George Durno of International News Service did not. Because of a free association of ideas, as Roosevelt talked about the Italians, Durno thought he heard the President say that the hand that held the "stiletto" had plunged it into the back of its neighbor, and he reported it thus. Durno was kidded about that mistake for years, and he in turn jokingly sought to persuade Sam Rosenman, editor of the Roosevelt papers, to change the official text from "dagger" to "stiletto" so that Durno would be proven right by history.

Steve Early was in a chatty mood that day on the train, and he talked freely with Reynolds and me about the big question then perplexing Washington and the nation: Would Roosevelt seek a third term?

Early told us that unless there was some drastic change in the world situation favorable to the Allies, it was his opinion Roosevelt would run. He was the first official I ever heard say it, and in a few months the Democratic convention at Chicago proved Early right, after going through the motions of a phony draft.

The speculation among Democratic politicians and the public about whether Roosevelt would try to violate the anti-third-term tradition begun by our first President continued for weeks thereafter, and, indeed, for some persisted until the Democratic convention had concluded its "draft."

Meanwhile, the Republicans sensed great victory opportunities to be gained from capitalizing on anti-third-term sentiment if Roosevelt ran again. If he did not, they welcomed the easier job of competing for the White House against a non-incumbent, who lacked the publicity and other advantages of a sitting President.

The first national political convention I ever saw or covered was the Republican conclave in Philadelphia's Convention Hall in June, 1940. There was a host of candidates, including a comparative dark horse named Wendell Willkie. But the front runner was New York

District Attorney Thomas E. Dewey, who was capitalizing on a "crime buster" record after a series of brilliant prosecutions in the nation's largest city.

Even before the Republicans could buckle down to the serious business of writing a platform and nominating a President, Roosevelt, from Washington, struck a surprising blow. As the dangers of United States involvement in war seemed to be mounting, and the Allied cause appeared less hopeful, Roosevelt added two of the most eminent Republicans to his cabinet in a bipartisan move that he said demonstrated his desire for national unity in a time of potential peril to the Republic.

In the final pre-convention week when Philadelphia was swarming with Republican leaders and would-be Presidents, Roosevelt announced the nomination for Secretary of War of Henry L. Stimson of New York, a Republican elder statesman beyond challenge who had served earlier in the cabinets of Republican Presidents. And he chose as Secretary of the Navy Frank Knox, the Chicago publisher who had been the 1936 Vice Presidential running mate of Presidential nominee Alf M. Landon of Kansas. In the weeks of secret negotiations that preceded this Roosevelt-made bombshell bursting in the midst of assembled Republicans, the President had tried and failed to get former Governor Landon to join the cabinet as well. But Landon told me later that his price was too high for Roosevelt. Landon had insisted upon an advance public renunciation by Roosevelt of a third-term nomination.

Stimson and Knox did not insist on a lot of conditions. Although Republicans, they were ardent aid-to-Britain advocates and they welcomed this opportunity to move the President closer to relaxation of the Neutrality Act then in effect.

The announcement of the Stimson-Knox appointments while the Republican faithful were assembling in Philadelphia was enough to drive orthodox Republicans nuts, as I found out that day racing around Philadelphia from hotel to hotel seeking comments from the GOP's top leaders.

By chance, I was the only press association reporter interviewing Republican chairman John D. M. Hamilton when he decided to go before the Republican National Committee already meeting that day to hear delegate contests on the roof of the Bellevue-Stratford Hotel in downtown Philadelphia.

Hamilton's face flushed with anger as he told the National Committee members of the Presidential announcement that Stimson and Knox had joined the Roosevelt cabinet.

"Since that time," Hamilton went on, "I have been in contact with both the Congressional leaders, the Senatorial leaders, and other leaders of our party who hold positions of eminence, and as a result of my talks with them, I have seen fit to issue a statement, which I trust will meet with the approval of the committee.

"This statement is issued for a twofold purpose. The first is that these gentlemen, having entered the cabinet of the President of the United States, are no longer qualified to speak as Republicans, or for the Republican party."

Republican committee members whooped and clapped their applause as Hamilton read Stimson and Knox out of the party. Hamilton was not through. He then went on to brand the Democrats as "the war party," if for no other reason than the appointments of Stimson and Knox.

"The second part of the statement," Hamilton said, "is directed to the thought that both Colonel Knox and Mr. Stimson having long desired to intervene in the affairs of Europe, that the Democratic party now, by their appointment, has become the war party of this country, and we may accept that issue at its face value."

Hamilton's motion for approval of his action brought a chorus of loud seconds and then a unanimous vote of angry Republican leaders. Seconds later, the National Committee chairman said he had been informed by the Illinois delegation that Colonel Knox, on entering the Roosevelt cabinet, already had resigned as a delegate-at-large to the convention from Illinois and this produced cries of "Good" and "Fine" from various members of the committee. Others applauded but their anger showed how deeply the Roosevelt blow at the two-party structure had been felt.

When the convention itself began the following week, there was no clear-cut favorite for the Presidential nomination. But the press was filled with speculation about the moves of dark horse Willkie, who had entered the Presidential battle after all the primary elections were over. The well-organized Willkie partisans outside Convention Hall brought terrific pressure upon the delegates in a snowstorm of telegrams and letters that conveyed a simple message: "We want Willkie."

At fifty, Willkie was a handsome extrovert who could be described in today's terms as a man with tremendous charisma who had undoubted political sex appeal. Republican women swooned over him, and men as well found him extremely attractive because of his earthy qualities. He was clearly looking for a fight with Roosevelt, and was ready to carry the battle to the White House.

He was not without experience in this jousting with FDR because as a lawyer-turned-utilities-executive he had already done battle with the federal government over the Tennessee Valley Authority and had extracted far more money for the southern utility properties of Commonwealth and Southern than the federal government had offered initially or the power company had had reason to expect. Financially Willkie was comfortably well-to-do, but not rich by most measuring standards. He was a well-known member of the Eastern Establishment, an interventionist in foreign affairs, and usually conservative on domestic issues, especially on economic questions.

The Republican keynoter that year was the young Minnesota governor, Harold E. Stassen, who promptly dropped his neutrality and became the floor leader for Willkie as soon as he delivered the keynote speech. Early leaders in the balloting were Thomas E. Dewey, then district attorney in New York, and Robert A. Taft, in his first term as a Senator, and there was a clutch of favorite sons. But Wendell Willkie was the favorite of the galleries packed by the Willkieites, who had charge of convention arrangements. Their chants of "We want Willkie" were loud and continuous, and finally the worn-out delegates gave the nomination to Willkie on the fifth ballot.

If John Hamilton and the Republican National Committee thought they had put the "war party" stamp on FDR and the Democrats, they had not reckoned with the Presidential candidate their own party chose. Mr. Willkie believed as ardently in aiding the Western Allies as did Roosevelt, Knox, and Stimson, and it was not at all hard to gain Willkie's approval of Roosevelt's deal after the Dunkirk disaster to provide the British with fifty over-age American Navy destroyers in return for U.S. bases on British possessions in the western hemisphere. Without Willkie's advance word that he would approve the deal, Roosevelt might not have had the political courage to go ahead with this essential aid to Britain in the middle of a political campaign.

Later in the campaign, Willkie was to charge that Roosevelt was taking us into war secretly and to forecast that soon after the election American boys would be on transports headed for a foreign war if FDR was reelected. Roosevelt countered with his Boston speech in which he promised "again, and again, and again" that he would not send American boys to fight in a foreign conflict. A few months after the campaign, when Roosevelt and Willkie again were allies on foreign policy issues, Willkie was to be closely questioned by the Senate Foreign Relations Committee about his charges. Willkie characterized them as "just campaign oratory," which was true, but which also was damaging to Willkie's credibility and prestige.

A few weeks later, the Democrats met in the Chicago Stadium and Roosevelt played out his role of reluctance in the face of a third-term "draft." First there was a letter from the President releasing all Democratic delegates pledged to him to vote their own convictions and asserting his own wish for retirement, but from loudspeakers everywhere there boomed the call for Roosevelt's renomination. Inquiring reporters found a microphone manned by Chicago's superintendent of sewers—a product of the Chicago Democratic machine—deep in the bowels of the stadium and it was he who led the pro-Roosevelt chants.

Harry L. Hopkins had a direct telephone line from his Blackstone Hotel suite to the White House. He called the signals for the convention, paying little heed to the sensibilities of Democratic National Chairman James A. Farley, who dreamed of securing the nomination for himself if FDR would keep the promises he had made to Farley and decline another term. But it was not to be.

Nor was there any sunshine for other would-be Democratic Presidential aspirants including Indiana's Paul V. McNutt, "tall, tan, and terrific," as the Washington society writers had called this handsome Indiana politician when he returned from an assignment in the Philippines to run for President. Millionaire Jesse Jones of Texas had ambitions too, but they were shattered on the rocks of Roosevelt's continuing desires.

It was all over in one ballot. Roosevelt had the nomination again, though the sentiment was far from unanimous.

Vice President Garner, as sticky and sharp as a Texas cactus, was another Democrat who opposed a third term for Roosevelt, and now he had to be dealt out of second place on the ticket. Roosevelt's Vice Presidential choice was his Secretary of Agriculture, Henry A. Wallace, of Iowa, with whom politicians felt uncomfortable.

Now the delegates were astounded, boiling mad, and ready to reject Roosevelt's selection if a quick vote had been permitted.

Roosevelt's managers had to stall for time, and to defer a ballot for Vice President, even calling Mrs. Roosevelt to the platform for a speech that was clearly out of order once the Vice Presidential nominating process had begun.

Paul McNutt had set his sights on the Vice Presidency when he found the doors to the Presidential nomination blocked by FDR, but now he was trying to withdraw his name from consideration. But the howling delegates on the floor wouldn't let him make his speech of abdication.

All across the floors, aides of Hopkins were telling the angry delegates that if they wouldn't give Roosevelt Wallace as Vice President, then the President would take the unprecedented action of refusing the Presidential nomination that only minutes before had been voted him.

At the White House in Washington, listening by radio to the actual convention proceedings and by telephone to the reports of Hopkins, Roosevelt told his speech writer, Sam Rosenman, to prepare a speech declining the nomination.

James F. Byrnes of South Carolina, then a Senator, and later to be a Supreme Court Justice, an assistant to the President, Secretary of State (under Truman), and finally the governor of South Carolina, had wanted the Vice Presidency for himself. But Roosevelt had told Byrnes that the Catholics, through Cardinal Mundelein of Chicago, had vetoed Byrnes because the South Carolinian who had been a Catholic at birth had changed his religion to marry Maude, who was from a hardshell Southern Protestant family. Byrnes loyally helped put out the fire against Wallace and joined other convention officials in declaring Wallace's nomination official over the protests of many delegates.

At the end of the Chicago convention, Lyle Wilson told me that the UP executives in New York, at his urging, had picked me to cover the Presidential campaign of Wendell Willkie. I was twenty-four years old, and my pay was $55 a week.

I joined the Willkie campaign in a cornfield near Elwood, Indiana, his birthplace, where perhaps 100,000 persons had joined for the last of those formal notification ceremonies where a candidate for President was told belatedly by a committee of party officials that he had, in fact, been nominated and the candidate accepted the nomination.

Willkie accepted all right. He charged into the battle furiously challenging "the champ" to debate him face to face on the third-term issue. Roosevelt paid no attention to the challenge, but Secretary of Interior Harold Ickes applied the needle of ridicule to Willkie as "a barefoot lawyer from Wall Street."

After Elwood there was a month-long preparatory period in Rushville, Indiana, a small town to the south of Indianapolis where the Willkies long had maintained a home. The Republican candidate opened his office on Main Street, and this provoked the inevitable news stories that he had moved his headquarters from "Wall Street to Main Street." This was, of course, the thrust of that Willkie preparatory period in the cornfields of Indiana.

Rushville was not a hard assignment for the campaign reporters. We all lived in The Lollis House, a small but clean hotel operated by Leo and Mary Durbin who spared no effort over and above the call of duty to make their Eastern visitors happy.

Our principal problem was Wendell Willkie himself. He was simply too accessible, too willing to be quoted on any subject, entirely too available for interviews, exclusive or otherwise. If one reporter saw him alone and got a good story, another reporter would go to Willkie to complain about being left out of the first interview. Willkie would appease the second reporter by giving him a better story than he had given the first one. And a third might top the first two. Finally, in a treaty of self-preservation, most of us agreed informally to write nothing from Willkie that we did not all get at the same time. Undoubtedly, it was an agreement in restraint of trade, as the lawyers in the Justice Department Antitrust Division might have described it, but it was necessary if any of us were to survive this "campaign rest" at all.

It is one of the happy facts of American political life that the reporters assigned to a Presidential campaign usually *like* the candidate to whom they are assigned even if, politically, they might favor the opposing candidate. There have been exceptions, of course, of which I suppose Richard Nixon remains the most conspicuous. He didn't like most of the reporters, and they didn't like him. And when Nixon exerted an effort to become "the new Nixon" and curry favor, most of the reporters recognized it as an effort and did not respond to the courtship.

Anyway, in Willkie's time and in others, songs and skits were written, often sung and acted out in the candidate's presence, and he got as much fun out of them as anybody.

Thirty years later one of them is running through my mind as this is written, and what follows is based entirely on memory:

Up in the air with Willkie,
He delights to fly around,
Up in the air with Willkie,
Even when he's on the ground.
Never have been so busy,
Watching him makes us dizzy,
We never can tell just where we're at,
We dare not go away,
For all of us fear he'll go to bat
With something more to say.
Up in the air with Willkie,
Wendell Willkie, hip, hip, hooray.

Out on the stump with Willkie,
Jesus, how he covers ground,
Out on the stump with Willkie,
Making speeches by the pound.
Nothing he loves like chatter,
We pick it off the platter.
We're out to save Democracy
And preserve the American Way.
That's what Mr. Willkie says,
And, Brother, that ain't hay.
Out on the stump with Willkie,
Wendell Willkie, hip, hip, hooray.

Often there were news conferences, some of them held in the shade of an apple tree in the backyard of the Willkie residence, and there was even a song for these occasions:

In the shade of the old apple tree,
There's a handout for you and for me,
When Willkie sits down,
On the bugs and the ground,
He wants to debate Franklin D.
But Franklin is keeping quite still
And we hope that forever he will,
For we'd rather wait than cover a debate
And wait in the bar for a fill.

Perhaps some of the lyrics left something to be desired poetically, but in those days they were fun even when sung discordantly.

In that small-town atmosphere, living so close together, we got to know Willkie intimately and he came to know and like most of us. In my case, he became a friend for life, and a kind of public relations man for me, using his friendship with publishers all over the country to tell them that I was a young, underpaid, top-notch political reporter for the UP who would be a valuable addition to their staffs. Out of this Willkie propaganda came numerous job offers that I reluctantly declined from the Cowles brothers, who already had a publishing empire in Des Moines and Minneapolis and later were to add *Look* magazine and other publishing properties. Willkie's high praise was instrumental too in arousing interest from Arthur Hays Sulzberger and other executives of *The New York Times*, where I worked for the next twenty years after the Willkie campaign.

Willkie's pace was unrelenting almost to the very end. It was an old-fashioned whistle-stop campaign made mostly by train, and we spent something like fifty-two days on the train. Willkie prided himself on the pressure from the public that had produced his nomination at Philadelphia, and throughout his campaign he paid as little attention as possible to regular Republican politicians. He didn't even like to talk to the politicians by telephone. Because candidates did not in those days campaign on Sundays, we spent many weekends aboard the train parked in a railroad freight yard outside a city where politicians would find it harder to reach the candidate in person or by telephone.

Willkie's speech writers rode in the second car from the rear, a combined office and sleeping car called the "Squirrel Cage." Once a Republican state official charged aboard the train angry because the schedule for his state had been changed time after time without apparent reason. He demanded to know "Who is running this campaign anyway?"

Pierce Butler, Jr., a white-haired attorney from St. Paul and son of a Supreme Court Justice, had the answer. "Have you ever been in a whorehouse on Saturday night when the Madam was away and the girls were running it to suit themselves?" Butler asked. "That's how this campaign train is run."

Willkie was a large, powerfully built man who poured all of his strength and more than his vocal chords could endure into that uphill campaign to deny a third term to Roosevelt.

On his second day out, headed west from Chicago, Willkie astounded the press car and his campaign audiences along the tracks in Illinois by asserting that it was FDR who had been responsible for the loss of Czechoslovakia to Hitler.

"FDR telephoned Hitler and Mussolini, and urged them to sell Czechoslovakia down the river," Willkie shouted from the rear platform in a voice that already was beginning to crack from the strain.

It was the first rear-platform speech I had ever covered, and I caught his final remark in my typewriter and tossed it to Western Union to send to the UP Chicago bureau. In Chicago, a new lead was put on my story under my by-line quoting Willkie to that effect. But after many minutes went by, the UP offices in Chicago and New York established that the AP and INS were not carrying similar dispatches. UP Chicago sent a telegraphic directive to me to telephone the office, but I got that telegram just as the train was ready to leave the next stop so the call had to wait one more stop. Meanwhile the *Chicago Daily News* appeared with an altered version of Willkie's remark—one that made more sense—and the Chicago desk revised my account to make it conform to that of the *Chicago Daily News*. When I called in farther down the road, ready with an exact stenographic text of the Willkie speech that proved me right the first time, the Chicago desk again had to revise my account.

Later that same day, Willkie's voice gave out completely, and a high-priced throat specialist who treated the Hollywood motion-picture stars was flown from the West Coast to come aboard our campaign train.

That night the UP "night lead Willkie" signed by me was a curious one:

"Doctors tonight enjoined silence for Wendell Willkie a few hours after he charged incorrectly that President Roosevelt telephoned to Hitler and Mussolini and urged them to sell Czechoslovakia down the river."

The wires were filled for hours with the explanations by Willkie's press secretary, Lem Jones, of what Willkie had "meant to say."

Willkie bore no grudge against me, then or ever, for anything I reported. Once he got his voice back, he talked from dawn till midnight nearly every day except Sundays and we reported nearly every word of it. Our hours were even longer than his, because we not only had to report his first and last speeches, but also had to write additional accounts about the last after his workday of speeches had ended. Often about the time we were ready to close our typewriters and fall into bed, there would be a knock on the drawing room door, and there would stand Willkie, on the prowl for companions to join in a drink and some more conversation. We never turned him away.

Willkie allowed another press freedom in reporting his campaign. He let a reporter stand on the rear platform with the official party so the "pool" reporter could come back to the working press car and tell the other reporters what had happened on the rear platform, what was said between the candidate and some of his visitors, and other events that were not audible over the loudspeakers to the reporters who stayed aboard the train while Willkie talked along the trail.

Sometimes an overenthusiastic Democrat would let fly with an egg, fresh or otherwise, or a tomato aimed at the Republican nominee. On one such occasion, in Wisconsin, I caught a fresh egg on the arm and the yellow stain dripped down my gabardine suit coat. Nobody thought Willkie's life was endangered, or mine either, and there was no loud outcry because of such incidents. Willkie laughed at my discomfort and the fact that I had to change suits. He was happy he hadn't been hit himself. But it did not provide the basis for campaign oratory about "law and order" as did a few objects flung at President Nixon in the heat of a campaign thirty years later.

Incredible as it may seem now, in these later days of slick, highly scheduled campaigning, Wendell Willkie actually ran out of campaign appearances in the final days before the election, just before he was to make the traditional campaign-ending appearance in New York City.

The train pulled to a stop in the railroad yards of the Jersey flats, not far from the Hudson River and in full view of the New York skyline. Feverishly, Willkie and his campaign advisors discussed whether new speeches in other places should now be scheduled in the interval before the campaign ended. Finally, Willkie decided that there was a trend running in his favor among the nation's electorate and it might look panicky if he were now to arrange some unexpected speeches in faraway places in the day or two before the campaign was to end. So no more talks were scheduled, and the train sat in the Jersey flats for days. In the daylight we walked alongside the train with Willkie and he talked, and talked, and talked.

Finally in New York, he ended the campaign at Madison Square Garden, and a few hours later, the people voted. There was not and had not been a trend in Willkie's direction and he was soundly beaten by Franklin Roosevelt.

As I look back on it now, I am certain no Democrat other than FDR could have withstood the Willkie challenge that year.

CHAPTER

4

I came out of the Willkie campaign with a $20-a-week wage increase, from $55 to $75 a week, from the United Press, a spectacular raise and almost unprecedented in those days for the UP.

The Willkie campaign had been an unparalleled success for me.

My boss and friend Lyle Wilson never tired of telling about his boy "Willie" and the impression the young reporter had made on the UP's New York executives.

As Wilson told it, on the morning after the 1940 election, he was having a pre-lunch drink with Earl J. Johnson, then vice president and general manager for news of UP. Johnson was in a happy mood; the election was over, and there had been few complaints from client newspapers that the UP had been beaten or had favored one candidate over another. UP felt sensitive primarily about charges its news stories might be slanted in favor of Willkie, because most American newspaper publishers always supported FDR's opponent, including Roy W. Howard, the principal stockholder in the UP.

"Your boy did a good job," Johnson told Wilson. "No complaints about his stories at all. How old is he anyway?"

Lyle Wilson grinned, then said, "Twenty-four."

The drink that Earl Johnson was holding fell to the floor and the glass shattered.

"You son-of-a-bitch," Johnson said to Wilson. "Don't you *ever* assign a boy to do a man's work in the future!"

Now Johnson was as strongly on my side as Wilson had been all along, and between them they cooked up for me a new assignment to cover the United States Senate, a post Wilson had held many years earlier and which he thought was the best beat in Washington.

Though I worked hard and made many good friends in the Senate, I did not like the assignment. My basic uneasiness there made it easier for *The New York Times* to lure me away a few months later by offering me a job in its Washington bureau.

But first there was the story of Lend-Lease proposed by Roosevelt after his third-term victory and now the target of the nation's isolationists led by the America First groups.

When Roosevelt first briefed Congressional leaders on details of his Lend-Lease bill before it went to Congress, UP was soundly beaten on the story by the *Times* and its star Washington reporter, Turner Catledge. Frantic calls to catch up went out from the UP Washington desk and I was summoned to work very early. An habitual early riser, Senator Walter F. George, then chairman of the Senate Foreign Relations Committee, was already at work in his Washington office.

Like the other Congressional leaders, Senator George had been enjoined to silence by Roosevelt, but the old Georgia Senator took pity on me and my sad tale of my disgrace at being beaten on such a big story. Senator George not only told me all that Roosevelt had said to the Congressional leaders, but he also provided me with an interpretation of what the Lend-Lease Act would in effect authorize and permit.

Senator George asserted the Roosevelt proposal would alter fundamentally many understandings of existing international law. It had always been the practice during wars, for example, to intern a belligerent warship if it entered a neutral port by accident or design. Now, Senator George said, Roosevelt proposed to change all that, to permit an American shipyard, for example, to repair a British warship that might have been damaged by German naval gunfire or the torpedo of a German U-boat. Under the Roosevelt proposal, said Senator George, a heavily damaged British battleship might steam into New York harbor and on to a shipyard for repair, and he did not know how, except by force, the American authorities could prevent German warships or submarines from following their target into the very heart of an American city.

George's illustration furnished the lead for UP's catch-up story, and when it appeared in afternoon newspapers from coast to coast I not only had matched Catledge's *Times* story, I had a bigger story of my own. This coup was due to Senator George, who really didn't know me very well.

It was not long after this incident that Turner Catledge approached me in the Senate press gallery one day and inquired whether I might be interested in coming to work for *The New York Times*. He suggested I get in touch with Arthur Krock, the *Times'* chief Washington correspondent and the head of its Washington bureau.

Krock, a giant among Washington newsmen, was a cultured, soft-spoken, Kentucky-bred man of infinite charm who received me cordially and questioned me about my newspaper background and my interest in coming to the *Times*.

Krock had great personal power at the *Times* and was the sole authority in Washington. Unlike in later periods when the New York office was to assert its authority, then he alone had the power to hire and to fire in the capital. At the end of our conversation, he politely offered me a job, suggesting a salary of $75 a week. That happened to be exactly what I was making at UP thanks to the big raise that had come at the end of the Willkie campaign.

I told Krock that while it had always been my ambition to work on the *Times*, I was not unhappy with the UP and I would like a few days to think over the proposal he had just made to me. He assented graciously.

Then I began to wrestle with my own heart and mind. Lyle Wilson was away in Europe and I could not counsel with him. My other associates at UP in whom I confided thought I would be crazy to pass up a *Times* offer.

I picked up a telephone to call Earl Johnson at UP's New York office, and told him of my job offer from the *Times*. I reminded Johnson that I was basically a reporter, that I had little or no interest or talent for management, and I wondered whether over the long haul if $150 a week—double my present salary—did not constitute about the top salary I could ever hope to command from the UP.

Johnson agreed that was a probable top figure. I told him I believed that over the years my opportunity to earn more probably was greater with the *Times* and that therefore, regretfully, that was the choice I would make. Johnson agreed that my decision probably was the right one for me, though an unhappy one for UP.

Then I telephoned Krock, told him of the internal struggle through which I was passing, of my "leaning" toward the *Times* and simultaneously of my happiness with UP.

"Could you," I inquired of Krock, "give me just some little extra reward—say five dollars a week more—that would salve my conscience as I leave UP?"

This conversation was by telephone so I do not know what Krock's facial expression or other visible signs of reaction were. He only said gently, "Of course, Mr. Lawrence, if you will come, we will pay you eighty dollars a week."

And so it was agreed that I would make the switch, but not for another few weeks so that I could finish reporting for UP the struggle over Lend-Lease on Capitol Hill. Krock had approached me to replace a member of the *Times* bureau who was to retire, but not for some weeks, so his need for me was not an urgent one, and he recognized my unwillingness to leave UP in a lurch since I was in charge of Lend-Lease coverage in the Senate where most of the battle was centered.

During the period between my agreement to go to the *Times* and my actual starting date, there was an incident between Krock and me that I think annoyed him at first but in retrospect gave him pleasure. At least he has told the story many times since it happened.

In that spring of 1941, there was the customary dinner given by the White House Correspondents Association for the President of the United States, and the ballroom on the top floor of the Willard Hotel was jammed with correspondents, politicians, and other news sources, all attired in dinner jackets and black ties. Wendell Willkie was one of the guests, and I had spent some time with him that afternoon, learning that after the dinner he would go to the home of Krock to join other guests for an after-dinner drink.

Roosevelt was, of course, the guest of honor, and by now he and

Wendell Willkie were pretty good friends despite the bitter campaign oratory only a few months before.

When such a dinner broke up, it was customary for all other guests to remain in their places until the President was wheeled from the room in his chair. That night, just before dinner adjourned, Roosevelt had called Willkie to his side and they had chatted together at the head table. Then the final gavel was banged, Roosevelt was wheeled away, and Willkie disappeared so quickly I could not reach him through the crowd of other dinner guests.

But as a reporter I felt I had to know what Roosevelt had said to Willkie. It might be a story.

After the dinner, I waited for perhaps thirty minutes, then placed a telephone call to Krock's home.

The telephone was answered by a voice that I assumed was that of the butler, and I asked politely to speak with Mr. Willkie.

After a brief pause, the same voice returned with the message that Mr. Willkie was unavailable to speak on the telephone because he was "engaged with guests."

"Look," I responded brusquely, "this is Bill Lawrence of the United Press, and I have no doubt that Mr. Willkie is engaged with guests. But you tell him that Bill Lawrence wants to talk to him personally, and you make sure he gets that message. Then if Mr. Willkie says he is too busy with guests to talk to me, that's okay. I'll understand that. But you give him my message."

Again there was a pause and I waited on the telephone.

This time it was Willkie who came to the telephone and who told me, in response to questions, about the chitchat that he had carried on with the President. What they said was of no importance then, so I don't remember it now; in any event, it was no story. So I thanked Willkie and moved quickly to other after-dinner drinking events that were in progress around the Willard Hotel.

On the following Monday, I was at work for UP in the Senate press gallery when I was called to the telephone. It was Turner Catledge from the *Times*.

"Boy," he said excitedly, "what did you say and do to Mr. Krock?"

"Nothing," I responded. "Oh, I did call his house and some butler tried to keep me from talking to Wendell Willkie but I brushed him aside. . . ."

Catledge interrupted me. "That was no butler," he said. "That was Mr. Krock. He just called me in to ask about you, and I reminded him that he had been looking for a long time for a young reporter who wouldn't take no for an answer."

Years later Krock told the story with great relish, once to a National Press Club luncheon audience where one question had been, in effect, *why* had he ever hired Lawrence?

With a broad smile in my direction, Mr. Krock responded that his action had been motivated by "the worst example of bad manners and one of the finest examples of intensively determined reporting I had ever encountered up to that time."

Mr. Krock was not only a great newspaperman, but he was also a fine gentleman and his manners were as perfect as mine were imperfect. There was a bit of reserve between him and his staff. He usually addressed men of the Washington bureau as "Mister" so and so, and hardly anyone dared to call him anything but "Mister Krock."

I was on a mutual first-name basis with many of the nation's leading politicians including Presidential candidates (though never Presidents) long before I ever moved into the tiny circle that might refer to Mr. Krock as "Arthur," and then I cracked that barrier on a social occasion. When I came back from a European assignment in 1948, a dinner was given for me by Mrs. Gilbert Harrison, wife of our former Minister to Switzerland with whom I had become friendly during a crossing on the liner *America*. Mrs. Harrison had a big old magnificent house behind the British Embassy, was an acknowledged leader of Washington society, and had summoned to the black-tie dinner for me people like Senator Taft, Walter Lippmann, and the Krocks.

Just after he reached Mrs. Harrison's door that night, Krock took me aside and handed me a yellow envelope, commanding me to read its contents instantly. I moved out of the range of other arriving guests and hurriedly tore open the envelope which contained a note on the office memorandum form that bore the printing "Memo from A.K."

I could scarcely believe what I read. Addressed to "Mr. Lawrence," the memo's basic message was: "At an affair like this [meaning the Harrison party], please don't call me Mr. Krock. Address me as Arthur, or A.K., or if that is too rotarian for you, simply call me Krock without the mister." It was signed "A.K."

Sure enough in the first circle among the conversing guests before dinner, I moved into his group and promptly called him "Mister Krock."

"Bill, didn't you read my message?" he inquired sternly.

"Yes," I said, and there was a long pause before I could form the next word. "Yes, Arthur."

Socially it might now be "Arthur" and "Bill," but inside the office it would still be Mister Lawrence and Mister Krock.

My colleague C. P. Trussell, known as "Peck" to all his colleagues and several Presidents, was working at his desk one day when Krock said something flattering to him about a recent dispatch but addressed him as "Mister Trussell."

"How long do I have to be around here," Trussell inquired, "before you'll start calling me 'Peck' like everybody else does?"

"I'm sorry," Mr. Krock replied, "I was raised that way."

Later as a member of the Pulitzer Prize committee he was to campaign for a Pulitzer Prize for Trussell's general coverage of Congress during the year 1948.

If you were one of "Krock's boys," you could do no wrong. New York desk men had to think twice before they changed a word of copy flowing out of the Washington bureau.

Gay Talese in his fascinating account of the internal politics on the *Times* in the book *The Kingdom and the Power* has described the Washington bureau under Krock as "the last of the great fiefdoms," maintaining its independence from the seat of power in New York, where the paper was published and edited. So it was.

CHAPTER
5

My first long-term assignment for the *Times* in the spring of 1941 was the American preparations for war, first embodied in Roosevelt's goal that America would become "the arsenal for the democracies," providing the weapons and supplies that would keep first Britain and later the Soviet Union in the war against Hitler and Mussolini.

In those days, the country remained divided and there was no national will to become a mighty arsenal. Roosevelt was still on the defensive against the outcries of the America Firsters, whose leaders included Colonel Charles A. Lindbergh, a prophet of gloom about England's war-making potential and one who looked to his friends in Germany to win a quick victory because of superior air power.

FDR was unwilling to delegate great powers to mobilize American industry, and his first steps to build an armament industry on top of an expanding civilian economy were faltering and uncertain. He recruited some big names—William S. Knudsen from General Motors, Sidney Hillman from the CIO's Amalgamated Clothing

Workers, Donald Nelson of Sears, Roebuck and Company, and Sidney Weinberg from Wall Street among many, many others. To these he added a mix of tried and tested New Dealers like Bob Nathan, Leon Henderson, Paul Porter, and big Ed Pritchard.

Knudsen and Hillman were designated as joint captains, each with a veto over the other, and the whole machine suffered from lack of firm and positive direction. Roosevelt was unwilling to seek any new production authority from the Congress, which was much more lukewarm about aiding the Allies than he was. Proclamations of limited, then full, national emergencies were made by the President to invoke old laws still on the statute books from World War I.

From time to time, Roosevelt gave "fireside chats" designed both to alert the American people and to give new heart to the British in their lonely war against Hitler. But FDR was careful not to get too far out in front of public opinion which was slow to reach the conclusion that a German victory in Europe would necessarily affect the future security and prosperity of the United States. Indeed, public opinion never moved that full distance until the Japanese struck their surprise, devastating blow at Pearl Harbor on December 7, 1941.

As the business and labor leaders and their partners from the New Deal began to explore the productive requirements of Roosevelt's rearmament goals, Washington was filled with good stories, but it took a lot of leg work to bring them out.

A newspaper partnership was formed to meet this new Washington challenge. It consisted of Alfred Friendly, then a reporter on the *Washington Post*, and me. We prowled the town, working separate sides of the street, and pooled our joint information to write stories every night. Together, Friendly and I covered the never-ending feuds between the businessmen and the New Dealers and Roosevelt's constant prods to both groups to get moving.

Enormous miscalculations were made. Experts investigated the available sources for the production of steel and aluminum, just to mention a couple, and concluded there was enough steel and enough aluminum to meet foreseeable military and civilian demands even if the country moved into all-out war. The expert studies were wrong by several thousand percent.

Perhaps the hardest job was to interest the Detroit automobile industry in the war production effort. Detroit's automakers just wanted to make cars, period. And the elder Henry Ford, who had received a German decoration not long before, saw no merit at all in taking contracts to make weapons for the British. Ford said he'd make weapons for his own country, but not for the Western Allies. The big trouble was that though Roosevelt talked about 50,000 tanks and 50,000 planes, he did not have the money from Congress to place any real big orders for the American military machine.

So Detroit kept on making cars up to and even beyond Pearl Harbor. Its executives turned a deaf ear on criticism from outside, whether the critics were high in government or lowly reporters. I remember one trip to Detroit in company with a left-wing reporter, I. F. Stone, who, in a play on words, said our job was not to "retool" the auto industry but to "reghoul" it. We had no impact on Detroit either, and neither did a high-power committee of labor and management headed by Cyrus S. Ching, the six-foot-eight-inch labor mediator who had come to government from the U.S. Rubber Company headquarters.

After Pearl Harbor and the declarations of war, and faced with the huge production goals Roosevelt had outlined to Congress, Bill Knudsen finally gave the order for the automobile industry to stop entirely its production of automobiles for civilian use. But even then, the industry resisted. Charles E. Wilson, then president of General Motors and later to be President Eisenhower's Secretary of Defense (and a very poor one indeed), headed the auto industry representatives who came to Washington to argue for more auto production after Pearl Harbor.

Wilson's argument was that the auto industry had accumulated inventories amounting to about $75,000,000 in the last few months of restricted auto production, and the industry hoped that it could now assemble that inventory into finished automobiles.

"No, Charley," Bill Knudsen replied. "We've got no rubber supplies coming after Pearl Harbor. There simply are no tires to put on new cars."

Reporters heard this argument through a door in the war production headquarters then located in the Social Security building at Fourth and Independence Avenue, Northwest. "Iz" Stone, who was hard of hearing, placed his hearing aid outside the door behind which the automobile industry leaders were meeting with Knudsen. As they talked, Stone relayed the conversation to a small group of other reporters standing in the corridor.

Knudsen had thought the "no tire" argument would be a simple, no-nonsense reply for Wilson and that this would end the great debate that had raged for weeks about getting the auto industry finally and fully into the war production effort.

But he misjudged Wilson, who had one more argument ready.

Let us, Wilson proposed, assemble the new cars anyway and sell them to the dealers without tires.

Knudsen was too smart to fall for that. Again he said, "No, Charley." Knudsen was well aware that if the automobile companies unloaded cars without tires on the dealers, the dealers quickly would have mobilized political pressures that would have obtained the release of scarce tires from local tire-rationing committees.

It was not an easy decision for Bill Knudsen to make after a lifetime of devotion to the automobile industry which had made him rich. It was not easy for the automobile executives to take, and some of them never forgot Knudsen's action. After the war, which Knudsen finished as a three-star general in uniform as the War Department's troubleshooter in the plants of its suppliers, he never went back to work for General Motors or for any other automobile company.

It was clear to me then, and it is clear to me now, that the United States was not even halfway ready for all-out war when the Japanese struck with such fury and success at the undefended naval base of Pearl Harbor in Hawaii.

Like every other American who was alive that day, I can remember well what I was doing that Sunday afternoon when the news came of the Japanese attack. I was listening to the broadcast of a football game being played by the Washington Redskins against the Philadelphia Eagles in Griffith Stadium.

At 2:26 P.M., Eastern time, an announcer broke in to say that the Japanese had bombed Pearl Harbor in Hawaii. I did not wait for an assignment from *The New York Times* Washington bureau. I got in my car and drove directly to the White House, where important officials were beginning to come and go somewhat frantically as the slumbering giant woke up and prepared to go to war.

We had known that negotiations with the Japanese had reached a crucial stage that weekend and might be broken off at any moment, but none of the reporters knew that our intelligence had cracked the Japanese codes and were reading all their go-to-war messages. Nevertheless, even the intelligence officers were taken by surprise when carrier aircraft hit the Pacific fleet, defenseless at its moorings in Pearl Harbor.

On that night, there were many newsmen huddled against the cold under the north portico as Roosevelt met with his Congressional leaders to ask them for a declaration of war and to inform them in generalities about the success of the Japanese surprise assault.

Mrs. Roosevelt was having a dinner at the White House that night. One of the guests was a Montana wheat farmer, Tom Campbell, and another was Edward R. Murrow, the CBS broadcaster already famous for his "This Is London" broadcasts.

When Campbell came out after dinner, he told us the Japanese had sunk all our Pacific battleships at their moorings. We telephoned the news to our offices, but publication was withheld by our publishers, alerted by their old friend, Secretary of the Navy Knox, lately the publisher himself of the *Chicago Daily News*. It was very important that the Japanese not know how unbelievably successful their attack had been or they might follow it up with an amphibious assault against Hawaii, which we would have been almost powerless to resist.

Murrow, who in the best tradition of responsible American reporting could keep a secret, never mentioned on the air that he'd been to dinner at the White House, that he had heard the same damage reports Campbell had given out, and later that same evening he had talked privately for a few minutes with FDR himself. Murrow was that kind of conscientious and patriotic reporter.

At noon the next day, Roosevelt delivered his "date that will live in infamy" speech to a joint session of Congress. The Congress promptly declared war upon Japan with a single dissenting voice. Democratic Representative Jeannette Rankin of Montana cast the "no" vote, just as twenty-four years before she had voted against the American entry into World War I.

When the Japanese struck against Pearl Harbor, organized labor narrowly averted a catastrophe from which it might never have recovered.

The railroad unions, seeking a pay rise, had been threatening a nationwide strike to begin as midnight ushered in December 7, and they long ago had worked themselves through all of the complicated machinery of the Railway Labor Act that serves to delay if not prevent strikes in this industry. But there was no railroad strike on December 7 because Wayne L. Morse, then dean of the University of Oregon Law School and later to be a United States Senator, was able, on FDR's instructions, to mediate an eleventh-hour compromise settlement between labor and management.

It is hard to imagine the high pitch of the public outcry against organized labor if the nation had been paralyzed by a nationwide railroad strike on the same day that the Japanese bombers appeared at dawn (Honolulu time) in the skies over Pearl Harbor. At the very least, the unions would have been accused of conspiracy with Japan, and the anti-labor sentiment thus unleashed might well have destroyed labor's influence for many years.

Roosevelt was not simply a passive, titular Commander-in-Chief. No President before or since has played such a direct role in military planning and execution. FDR helped to shape the "grand design" for fighting the war on all fronts and his role in strategic planning often was dominant.

Unlike President Lincoln, who despaired of his military and civilian advisors in the darkest days of the Civil War, Roosevelt was blessed in the high quality of his generals and admirals, who understood both the military and the political implications of the big decisions on which they were required to give advice to the President. You could go for generations without finding a soldier to match General George C. Marshall, a sailor like Admiral Ernest J. King, or an airman like General Henry H. (Hap) Arnold.

Though it was the Japanese, not the Germans or the Italians, who struck the first blow against the United States, Roosevelt and his military leaders decided promptly that the war in Europe had to be won first, and that it would not take too long thereafter to knock the Japanese out of the war, especially if the Russians joined the ground fighting in Asia.

This "Europe first" strategy was challenged by "Asia Firsters," who packed some considerable political punch at home because of the national desire to remember and avenge Pearl Harbor. Some of this Pacific sentiment found echo in the United States Senate, especially among recent isolationists, some was stimulated by the Pacific commander, General Douglas MacArthur, already a hero in the public eye though his forces had been mauled by the Japanese before FDR arranged to rescue him by submarine from the Philippine Islands. MacArthur's worldwide reputation as a master military man even withstood the known fact that he had left his air force on the ground to be destroyed in the Philippines many hours after the surprise Japanese attack upon Pearl Harbor thousands of miles eastward. The country was short of heroes in those dark days, so MacArthur's bubble never burst.

As Washington buckled down to war, Roosevelt concentrated on winning, and showed his disinterest, for the time being, in most domestic affairs. He said at one of those informal, continuing twice-a-week news conferences in his oval office that Dr. New Deal had changed his title and function to Dr. Win the War, and he intended to concentrate on survival before any additional domestic reforms could be considered. Some New Dealers were unhappy.

Within a few hours after Pearl Harbor, the President summoned labor and management into an emergency meeting in Washington to hammer out a no-strike, no-lockout agreement to be supervised and enforced by a War Labor Board. Secretary of Labor Perkins and Utah's Senator Elbert Thomas were named co-chairmen of the group that included the highest leaders of labor and management.

Agreement was easy on the no-strike, no-lockout pledge and on creation of the War Labor Board, but management maintained hard and fast reservations against empowering this government board ever to impose a union shop in any plant. This last condition, vital to management philosophy, was the sticking point on which the whole conference stalemated. Failure seemed inevitable until Mrs. Perkins reported the impasse to the President. He seized upon the language where labor and management were in agreement, completely ignored the vital reservation entered by management, and thanked the conferees for their "agreement," wishing them a Merry Christmas as they headed home.

The management men were furious, and Roger Lapham, later to be mayor of San Francisco, said to me that it was "like being raped in Macy's window at high noon."

In *The New York Times* the following day, my story began: "President Roosevelt today *decreed* agreement between labor and management. . . ."

Though born under such difficult circumstances, the War Labor Board did function and work pretty well for the remainder of the war. Its power to force a union shop upon an unwilling employer was used, but sparingly, and there was no public outcry, no organized campaign by management to eliminate the power Roosevelt had given the board.

Harry L. Hopkins, fifty-two when the war began, was always frail, so emaciated and haggard that his very survival seemed in doubt, but he remained Roosevelt's closest confidant in war as he had been in peace. Amidst loud and angry denunciations from his Republican and conservative Democratic enemies, Hopkins moved into the White House, occupying "the Lincoln bedroom," which seemed a special sacrilege to his GOP opponents.

But Hopkins had special qualities that FDR liked. His mind was tough and incisive. He could keep a secret when that was indicated or do some judicious planting of news stories if that were indicated.

Hopkins sat in on war planning at the highest levels in Washington and elsewhere, and served as Roosevelt's "legs" when war conditions made impossible widespread travel by the crippled President.

I had easy entrée to Hopkins' bedroom-office on the second floor of the White House, and I saw him fairly frequently to seek out background on some of the big military and political decisions of the war.

It was from Hopkins that I learned in great detail about Roosevelt's unrelenting campaign to open a second front in Europe to smash the German armies with a frontal blow in order to relieve some of the terrible pressures on the Soviet Red Army, which was being bled white. Roosevelt and Hopkins kept up the pressure on British Prime Minister Churchill, who did not share their enthusiasm for a cross-channel landing.

Time after time the Allies met and promised the Russians a second front at an early date. Then complications would develop, or seem to develop. The enterprise would be postponed again and again until the tired Russian leaders began to wonder if their allies were truly friends or were willing, simply, to fight to the last Russian.

In fairness to Churchill, he subscribed reluctantly to these agreements and he constantly feared the worst if Allied armies were to attempt an amphibious cross-channel landing in western France. Churchill always argued for alternate plans, for a blow at the "soft underbelly" of Europe, perhaps through the Balkans, or against the southern coast of France, less heavily defended.

It was in Churchill's whole upbringing that he should feel this way. After all, Britain felt safe from Europe's land armies, even Hitler's *Wehrmacht*, behind the channel. Crossing the channel, Churchill reasoned, was much more difficult than simply smashing over a wide, wide river.

The "Torch" landing in the French colonies of North Africa in

November, 1942, was one of the substitutes for the second front promised to the Russians, and it had been Roosevelt's inspiration, as Hopkins told me at the time.

In *The New York Times Magazine* of November 22, 1942, under the headline "We Have a Blitzmaker, Too," I wrote:

> As the full story unfolds, Franklin D. Roosevelt's feat in outguessing the dictators becomes more and more spectacular. The North African venture, which caught the Axis totally unprepared, stamps the President as the equal, if not the master, of Hitler and his associates in the use of the psychological blitz.

My view of FDR's strategy and its success was not universally held. One of the critics—privately anyway—was Wendell L. Willkie, with whom I was dining along with other campaign train associates on the night that the American armies stormed ashore in Morocco and Algeria. Willkie dismissed the whole North African venture as a sideshow, and said it would never satisfy the Russian demand for a second front. It wasn't just a sideshow, but it didn't satisfy the Russians.

One of Willkie's first wartime assignments for FDR had been to London during the blitz to carry a word of cheer to the British and to assure Prime Minister Churchill that the loyal opposition as represented by Mr. Willkie was as pro-British in its sentiments as was Mr. Roosevelt. This sentiment was not truly representative of the Republican party as a whole, but Willkie cheerfully undertook the mission because he had long been a champion of the Allied cause.

I was with Willkie immediately after he got the assignment from Roosevelt in the White House, and Willkie showed me the handwritten note he was carrying from Roosevelt. It was the now famous note that quoted from Longfellow's "Sail On, O Ship of State" and concluded with these lines:

> Humanity with all its fears,
> With all the hopes of future years
> Is hanging breathless on thy fate.
> Our hearts, our hopes, are all with thee,
> Our hearts, our hopes, our prayers, our tears,
> Our faith triumphant o'er our fears
> Are all with thee—are all with thee!

It was to this message that Churchill later responded, "Give us the tools and we will finish the job."

In discussing Willkie's trip to London, Mr. Roosevelt suggested the recent Republican Presidential nominee would also want to talk with Averell Harriman, who only recently had been assigned by the President to London to expedite American military aid shipments.

"You'll like Averell," said Mr. Roosevelt, "he contributed to *our* campaign [meaning his own and that of other Democrats], you know."

FDR stopped abruptly, and blushed. Then he said to Willkie he had not meant to make the political campaign contribution remark, but he had been thinking of Harriman's help to the Democrats in 1940.

"Oh, that's all right," Willkie replied. "Harriman did contribute to *our* campaign. Harriman gave me money for my pre-convention campaign before I got the nomination, but then he contributed to your election campaign."

Willkie told me that story himself and I never forgot it. Some time later after Harriman became Ambassador to the Soviet Union he was quite critical at a news conference of Willkie's public advocacy of a second front by the Western Allies in Europe to help out the Russians. Harriman made me angry, so I said acidly, "Well, Ambassador Harriman, at least Mr. Willkie didn't contribute to both campaign funds in 1940."

After the news conference, Harriman demanded of me the source of my information about his contributions to both sides.

"FDR told me," I replied. I thus gently skipped over the fact that my information was secondhand. But never again, in my presence anyway, did Harriman criticize Willkie.

My rebuke to Harriman followed still another Willkie wartime mission for FDR, one that took him to London to see Churchill, to Moscow to confer with Stalin, and to China to talk with Generalissimo Chiang Kai-shek. I never learned much about Willkie's reaction to the Generalissimo because he fell under the influence of Madame Chiang. This non-secret mutual admiration society fed the gossips of China and America for a long time.

I was toastmaster at a dinner for Willkie in the Carlton Hotel in Washington on November 7, 1942, the night of our invasion of North Africa. It was my job to introduce Willkie to his old friends from the campaign trail.

I recalled an old story that had been a favorite of the former Chinese Ambassador, Hu Shih, about the boy from Canton who had been sent to America to study medicine, financed by the contributions of all his neighbors, who had graduated with the highest honors and who had now come home to his native Canton to practice and to teach. The neighbors gave the young doctor a large banquet, and the young man was called to speak after the most flowery of introductions.

As the story went, the doctor carried an obviously lengthy manuscript and his listeners settled back in their chairs for a long speech.

"I know that properly one should deliver the prepared manuscript first, and only after that yield to questions from the floor," the young man began. "But I also know that there is one question on the mind of every man here, so I shall dispose of that first.

"What they say about American women is not true."

To this I added, "And now I present Mr. Wendell Willkie."

Willkie spoke for perhaps an hour, giving us not even a hint of his romance with Madame Chiang. It was a marvelous summary, an eloquent description of his journey to the far corners of the earth and his meetings with all the principal Allied commanders, civilian and military.

The news of my brash introduction of Willkie quickly spread around Washington. On the following Monday, Arthur Krock looked me squarely in the eye and inquired caustically, "Would you have introduced the President of the United States that way?"

My answer was swift, and short.

"Sure, if Wendell Willkie had been the President," I responded.

Roosevelt's first trip abroad was in 1943 to liberated Casablanca, where he met with Prime Minister Churchill. Both had hoped until the last minute that Stalin might join them, but the Soviet dictator pleaded inability to leave Moscow while the battle for Russia hung in the balance. Neither Roosevelt nor Churchill would dispute that excuse; indeed, the farthest Stalin ever went during the war was to Teheran in Iran the following year and to Potsdam in Germany after the war in Europe had ended and the war in the Pacific was being fought to a finish.

It was at Casablanca that Roosevelt first said the Allied strategy for the war could be compressed into two words: Unconditional surrender. Some have complained this was a costly spur-of-the-moment phrase uttered by Roosevelt, and that Churchill failed to dissent because (1) it was public and (2) he and FDR had not thought through the tragic implications of such an inflexible demand.

In any event, most historians think "unconditional surrender" probably protracted the war in both Europe and Asia. I am inclined to agree with them.

Roosevelt and Churchill tried at Casablanca to resolve the differences between General Charles de Gaulle, head of the exiled Free French movement, and General Henri Giraud, who had more recently defected from the Vichy French army to join with the Americans in the battle for North Africa.

The initial Allied arrangements with Giraud had been made without seeking or obtaining De Gaulle's agreement, and he would not give assent later. De Gaulle considered himself alone the master of France, most of it occupied by Germans and still to be liberated by the blood of American and British armies.

De Gaulle was proud, haughty, arrogant, and a tough nut to crack. During much of the Casablanca conference he flatly and bluntly turned down the combined appeals of Roosevelt and Churchill that he compromise his quarrel with General Giraud in the best interests of all the Allies.

This battle of wills with De Gaulle became one of Roosevelt's favorite stories, an anecdote he told again and again. I heard him tell it several times.

"De Gaulle was unbending," Roosevelt said, "and he claimed many reasons or excuses.

"Once he could not meet with Giraud, De Gaulle told me, because he [De Gaulle] constituted a modern-day version of St. Joan of Arc . . . and another time he said he couldn't because he was the reincarnation of the Old Tiger, Clemenceau.

"Finally, I said to him," Roosevelt went on, " 'See here, General de Gaulle, I never knew Joan of Arc but I did know the Old Tiger, and I can hardly conceive of two people being more different.' "

I carried the anecdote back to the *Times* Washington bureau and told it to Krock.

"For the first time," Krock said, "I am truly disappointed in Roosevelt. He should have hit De Gaulle harder than that. After De Gaulle told him in two separate breaths that he was both Joan of Arc and Clemenceau, Roosevelt should have told him, 'General, go fuck yourself.' "

Roosevelt roared with laughter when Krock's rejoinder was repeated back. Krock's advice was in effect the attitude adopted by

Churchill and Roosevelt toward De Gaulle for the remainder of World War II. De Gaulle never forgave them during or after the war, and it created troubles between him and the Western Allies for as long as the French leader lived and ruled his country. His almost dictatorial powers as President of the Fifth Republic gave De Gaulle opportunities that he seized to undermine and weaken the North Atlantic Treaty Organization, and to keep Britain out of Europe's Common Market.

I do not agree with my colleagues or with world statesmen who classified De Gaulle as a great man. I feel he epitomized the old saying: If you had De Gaulle for a friend, you didn't need an enemy.

CHAPTER
6

During the war years, they had to change the old White House rule that the flag flies from the White House flagpole only when the President is in residence. And even that change came only after White House officials had been reminded by an observant reporter.

On one of Churchill's early wartime visits in 1942, the Nazi submarines assembled in packs off the North American Atlantic coast, hoping that they might bag Britain's indispensable leader as he headed home by ship. It was important therefore that his departure be kept secret.

One morning Steve Early summoned the White House press corps to his office to tell them "off the record" that Churchill and Roosevelt had left town together, but this was to remain secret. Early asked the newspapers not to indicate in any way that the President was not in the White House but had left Washington.

"Well, Steve," observed Tom Reynolds, who by now had left the UP and joined the newly founded *Chicago Sun*, "I'm willing to play the game that Roosevelt is still here. But don't you think somebody had better tell those people who already have lowered the flag over the White House to show the President isn't here?"

Early, who had a low boiling point, was outraged. He grabbed the telephone on his desk and chewed out the White House chief usher for lowering the flag and thus telling anyone familiar with Washington customs that Mr. Roosevelt had left town. Nobody had told the poor chief usher about the new system.

Quickly the flag went back up the flagstaff, but the lowering had already been observed by others besides Reynolds. In the late afternoon, as I rode in a cab in downtown Washington, the cab driver informed me that Churchill probably had left town that day.

"What makes you think so?" I asked him.

"Drove by the White House this morning and the flag was down, indicating Roosevelt wasn't there," the cab driver responded. "This afternoon I saw the flag was back up, so the way I figure it is that Roosevelt saw Churchill off from someplace near Washington and then came back to the White House."

There was voluntary censorship of newspapers, magazines, and radio stations throughout the war, supervised by Byron Price and a small staff in the Office of Censorship. They did a pretty good job of keeping out of print and off the air information that might be valuable to the enemy.

Another White House wartime visitor was Madame Chiang Kai-shek, wife of China's chief of state and generalissimo, whose visit had long been discouraged by FDR and his aides because of the fear she would use all her feminine wiles to plead the case for an Asia-first policy.

There was a deep pro-China strain in much that Roosevelt did, perhaps because of his family's ancient China ties, but by 1943 the discouraging reports of Chiang's unwillingness to fight had diminished some of his enthusiasm for the Chungking government.

Roosevelt agreed to the visit of Madame Chiang only because he was forced to do so. But once she was here, all the stops were pulled out.

The American-educated woman, one of the famous trio of Soong sisters, was a beautiful and persuasive lobbyist for her country. She won over the entire country, starting with a joint session of Congress and later at one of FDR's oval office press conferences which drew a crowd of 172 men and women reporters jammed into that comparatively small room.

I covered that press conference for the *Times*. In those days—

before radio and television coverage—we were permitted to report what was said only in indirect form unless specific permission was given by the President to place a word, a phrase, a sentence, or a paragraph in direct quotation marks.

I had been covering the White House regularly for approximately six months when Madame Chiang arrived. Her charms worked on me too. This is how I described the confrontation with FDR in the *Times* of February 20, 1943:

> The high point of the conference, in which Mrs. Roosevelt sat as a silent participant, was the matching of the President's charm and persuasiveness against that of Mme. Chiang Kaishek on the China aid question.
>
> China needs munitions, she stressed. The country has the manpower and even trained pilots, but lacks airplanes and gasoline with which to fuel them. Flashing her most brilliant smile, she added that President Roosevelt had solved so many problems and come through so many crises with flying colors that she was certain she could safely leave to him the problem of working out ways and means to increase the flow of aid from this country.
>
> #### PRESIDENT STRESSES PROBLEMS
>
> The President replied that he thought Mme. Chiang was 100 percent right, but he asked reporters to look at the old map again to realize the transport difficulties blocking substantial air reinforcements to China. You cannot fly them directly across the Pacific, he said, and you cannot fly them in from Russia.
>
> He stressed that once the planes reached a base from which they could be flown to China they still must be supplied with gasoline and the other things needed to keep planes in combat. There is no other one thing that is being studied by the strategists and military people more than that of getting the wherewithal to China. We're doing the best we can, he added, and he expressed the belief that we try to increase the shipments as fast as we can.
>
> The United States is just as keen to knock out Japan as China is, said the President, and he announced his intention to speed up the aid so that China could become a large and important base of operations against the common enemy.

Eschewing any policy of inch-by-inch or island-by-island reconquest of the territory taken by Japan in the Pacific, he pointed out that if we took one island a month it would require fifty years to reach Japan.

The President conceded that if he were a member of the Chinese Government he would want to ask: How soon and how can aid be speeded up?

His answer was that we would do it as fast as the Lord would let us and with as much speed as we could bring to bear on the problem.

MME. CHIANG IN ACCORD

When reporters asked Mme. Chiang if she had any ideas about how United States aid could be speeded, she rose to endorse what the President had said and to add her observation that the Lord helps those who help themselves. The reporters laughed at her sally.

The *Times* desk man who wrote that last subhead, "Mme. Chiang in Accord," could not have been more wrong, nor could I have been less correct when I described as a "sally" her observation that the Lord helps those who help themselves.

It was a knockout blow aimed squarely at Roosevelt's chin. And she meant it to be just that.

The look on the President's face was that of a man who has just been hit and hit hard, but who did not know how to respond, under the circumstances of being both a gentleman and the host.

It was the one and only time in all of Roosevelt's news conferences that I ever saw him bested. He didn't like it, and he never forgot it. And in later years Mme. Chiang may have had real cause to regret a pyrrhic victory.

A few months before I went to war myself, I played a role in one of Roosevelt's off-the-record trips from Washington to the Southwest, into Mexico where we met with President Manuel Avila Camacho at Monterrey, and then back into Texas where Avila Camacho returned the visit at Corpus Christi. We were off the record except for the two meetings with the Mexican President, the first face-to-face conference of Mexican and United States Presidents since October, 1909, when President William Howard Taft and Mexican President Porfirio Diaz exchanged visits at El Paso and at Ciudad Juarez. Mexico played no important role in the war and nothing FDR said or did could persuade her President to step up Mexican participation.

Roosevelt was gone from Washington from April 13 to April 29, 1943, but off the record all of the time except when visiting with the Mexican President. This is not to say his trip was secret; it simply could not be reported in the newspapers or on the radio. Everywhere we went, including six military bases in South Carolina, Alabama, Georgia, Tennessee, and Arkansas, and many war plants in other states, we were seen by tens of thousands of persons.

Every mile of railroad track was guarded by soldiers and there was some grumbling from the political opposition that the security provided for Roosevelt was too heavy and too expensive.

For those who missed seeing the President or noting the heavy security measures in force, there was still another revelation of the secret. It was Roosevelt's little Scottish terrier, Falla, almost as well known at first sight as his master. Whenever the Presidential special train stopped to take on a new crew or water, it was "a water stop" also for Falla, and many hundreds spotted and recognized him as he made his way friskily along a station platform in some small or large city.

While thousands talked among themselves about seeing their President, or knowing he was around, not a word was being published in the newspapers of the time. Those unfamiliar with the rules of wartime censorship wondered why their local papers had suppressed the news of the President's visit. It was, I suppose, both essential and unavoidable. But it was hard to explain to the newspaper-reading rank and file.

I made the entire trip by the sheerest chance, and so did five other "specials" in addition to the three wire-service reporters. "Specials" are those correspondents who work for individual newspapers such as the *Times* or the New York *Herald Tribune*.

I had heard that Roosevelt was about to make the trip when a UP executive from New York, assuming that I was in on the secret, inquired of me where FDR had gone.

I asked the UP man, my former boss Earl Johnson, what made him think Roosevelt had gone anywhere.

"Well, Merriman Smith [UP's White House reporter] drew five hundred dollars in expense money yesterday but said he couldn't explain what for," Johnson replied.

Bert Andrews, then bureau chief of the New York *Herald Tribune*, and I promptly tried to force our way into this trip. Our effort was to persuade Roosevelt to take along some regular White House correspondents as well as the wire-service reporters.

Andrews and I first asked Early if the President was about to make a trip. The press secretary was evasive, but didn't lie to us. We then told Early we'd like to raise again the question of White House regulars traveling with the President. Steve said resignedly he'd take it up with the President again, but he doubted if it would do any good.

"If you need any arguments," I said, "we'll be glad to supply them."

"Do you guys want to see the President about this yourselves?" Steve asked.

"Sure, if we could," Andrews and I agreed.

In a few seconds, Steve ushered the pair of us into FDR's office and the President looked up from his desk with a smile.

"These fellows want to bring an old chestnut out of mothballs," Early told the President. "They want to talk about White House regulars traveling with you on these off-the-record trips you've taken from time to time."

Andrews and I did not think this the best possible opening for a salesmanship job, but there was little we could do about it, for FDR promptly launched into one of his famous filibusters. Once again, and for the umpteenth time, he told about his meetings with De Gaulle at Casablanca, and the general's fondness for fantasy in comparing himself in one breath to Joan of Arc and in another breath to Clemenceau. On and on the President talked and we were certain any minute another secretary would appear to tell us our time was up.

Finally we dared to interrupt the President and to raise with him the question of the forthcoming trip. We asked whether Mr. Roosevelt might reconsider taking along some "specials" as well as the wire-service reporters.

Mr. Roosevelt replied he couldn't take along "all the reporters in Washington who would want to go . . . that would take two or three trains and it would destroy all the secrecy."

"No," I told the President, "we're not asking for all the reporters. Just the White House regulars."

The President asked how many that might be, and I replied eight or nine in addition to the wires.

"I've got an idea," said the President, "Let me talk to Steve about it, and you fellows come back and see me tomorrow morning."

The next morning we were back in FDR's office. The President said he had thought over our request and decided he would take "six regulars."

"But," FDR smiled, "you two fellows have to pick the six."

Probably we should have said "no thanks" then and there because we had no mandate from our colleagues to choose among them. But Andrews and I both wanted to make the trip, so we told the President we would pick the six correspondents.

Andrews and I went off to lunch together at a seafood restaurant on Washington's Potomac River front. We had no trouble at all with the first two names: Andrews and Lawrence. The other four were harder. But we chose Dewey Fleming of the *Baltimore Sun*, Raymond P. (Pete) Brandt of the St. Louis *Post-Dispatch*, Roscoe Drummond of the *Christian Science Monitor*, and William Murphy of the *Philadelphia Inquirer*. None of these six papers had supported Roosevelt for a third term but the President liked the chosen reporters individually.

When the Office of Censorship and the White House jointly sent secret advisories about the trip, and the fact that six "specials" would go along, the White House then explained in response to questions that the six had been chosen by Messrs. Andrews and Lawrence.

There was an uproar and screams of outraged jealousy all over town. Andrews and I obviously had only four friends left in town —the four we had chosen. We were in danger of being hanged if we showed up in the National Press Club bar. We escaped Washington without being manhandled, however, and made the trip with Roosevelt. He was a charming traveling companion and invited us to dine with him in his rear car on two occasions. He censored our copy personally, in his own handwriting, to make certain no essential security information was disclosed about the war plants we visited.

Soon after this, I decided it was time to report the war from abroad.

The choice of an initial war assignment for me posed a seemingly big question for the editors and publisher of the *Times*. My assignment changed more than once before I got underway.

First our publisher, Arthur Hays Sulzberger, had picked up a tip from the British Middle East commander, Field Marshal Wilson (a giant of a man known as "Jumbo"), that the Allies were going to hit in the spring of 1943 at the soft underbelly of Europe through the Greek islands and on into the Balkans. At once I drew the assignment, got myself accredited to Wilson's forces in the Middle East, and prepared to leave Washington. But a last-minute physical examination showed I was walking around with pneumonia. I was pulled off the story, and someone else was sent while I recuperated.

At about the same time, our correspondent in Australia and New Guinea, Byron (Barney) Darnton, was killed, mistakenly strafed by the machine guns of an Allied plane while crossing a body of water in a small boat.

I was chosen to replace Darnton as the correspondent with General MacArthur's forces in the Far East. About the same time though, my colleague, Frank L. Kluckhohn, who had been with General Eisenhower's armies in North Africa, was barred from returning to Eisenhower's theater.

Because I thought the main theater was Europe and would remain so for a long time, I had never been too enthusiastic about the Australian post anyway. So one day I suggested to Krock that perhaps MacArthur, who hated Eisenhower, might accept Kluckhohn as a correspondent in the Far East if for no other reason than that Eisenhower had banned him.

If Kluckhohn could go to Australia instead of me, it would serve two purposes. It would get Kluckhohn out of Krock's hair in Washington, where Kluckhohn seemed likely to remain if Eisenhower didn't relent, and it would keep me from going to Australia and make possible an assignment in Europe, perhaps the one Kluckhohn had just vacated.

My plan worked like a charm, and Kluckhohn soon was headed for duty with General MacArthur.

This was not the first time Kluckhohn had been in trouble in the North African theater. On an earlier occasion the British general Harold Alexander had become angry with Kluckhohn and had placed him under house arrest for a ten-day period. The news of Kluck's punishment by General Alexander was passed along to us in the Washington bureau but with the admonition from New York that we were to do nothing about easing the penalty.

Roosevelt really hated Kluckhohn and I simply could not keep this news secret from the President.

I telephoned his secretary Grace Tully, told her of Kluckhohn's troubles, made certain that she understood that the *Times* was not asking for any clemency, and then asked if she might find her way free to inform me of the President's reaction. In about thirty minutes, Miss Tully phoned from the White House and said she had informed the President of Kluckhohn's house arrest.

"What was the President's reaction?" I inquired.

"Oh, I couldn't possibly tell you over the telephone," Grace responded. "Come to the White House right away."

At the White House, one of the police guards at the front reception desk handed me a small manila envelope bearing my name. Inside was a small white piece of stationery bearing the printing "The White House, Washington," and on it this scrawl in the President's handwriting:

Dear Bill

I am "so sorry"—my sympathy—Try a habeas corpus.

The initials "FDR" stood out big and bold beneath the message. Below was the date, March 31.

Here in the middle of a great war, the President had stopped long enough to write this chit, to convey again his dislike for Kluckhohn.

How can I be so sure it was dislike?

Two or three days later, Mr. Roosevelt held another of his regular news conferences, and during the conference motioned with his eyes for me to stay behind after the other reporters had left.

"What did you do about Kluckhohn and the habeas corpus?" the President inquired.

"Nothing," said I. "I don't care if he never gets out of jail."

"Ah, that's just the point," Roosevelt said, chuckling with glee over his own joke. "You see, under French law the prisoner can not be released once a proceeding like that is started until the judge reaches a decision. And those courts in North Africa are so jammed now it would take years before Kluckhohn's case could be heard."

He threw back his head and laughed uproariously. For a few minutes anyway, the cares of war were forgotten.

With Kluckhohn on his way to Australia, the search for another job for me went on, and the next assignment was a great one: London, where the blitz was ending and from which almost certainly the great invasion of Europe would be launched.

So off I flew to London on one of the old-fashioned Pan American flying boats, *Yankee Clipper*, severely restricted to a forty-four-pound baggage allowance.

This baggage allowance could not be altered even by the intervention of an old friend, James V. Forrestal, then Under Secretary of the Navy. There were simply no exceptions to the forty-four-pound rule, no matter how long I planned to stay in London nor how well known the shortages of necessities in wartime Britain. So, though they couldn't raise the allowance, Pan American sent an expert to my New York hotel room to help me pack. It was at the end of July and I didn't need to wear my topcoat, which was in fact a military trench coat, and so several suit jackets were fitted into the topcoat, and the pockets were jammed with soap, scarce nylons for the girls of Britain, and cigarets. Carrying my coat, my weight on the scales that night was fifty pounds more than it ought to have been, thanks to the good packing job Pan American had done.

The first stop overseas was at Shannon Airport in Ireland. Ireland was neutral, so war correspondents and military officers all pretended for the moment that they were civilians so as to escape the internment neutrals were required to enforce against belligerent personnel of both sides in wartime.

The Irish were not fooled for a moment, as one of their officials went out of his way to make clear at Shannon.

"Oh, yes," he said, "Mister Jimmy Doolittle passed through the other day."

Doolittle's fame as the leader of the B-25 raid from an American naval carrier in the far Pacific against Tokyo was still resounding around the world. Now Doolittle was in Britain to command our Eighth Air Force of heavy B-17 and B-24 bombers against the Germans.

London, I thought, would be a fine place to work. But my smug self-satisfaction soon was shattered.

To London from New York came a cable from Publisher Sulzberger inquiring whether, on second thought, I might not prefer the post of chief correspondent in Moscow to the London job. The opportunity to report on the Soviet Army and the Russian people at war in this grave time just after their victory at Stalingrad was really more than any twenty-seven-year-old correspondent could dream about. I cabled my acceptance to Mr. Sulzberger at once, adding, "Thanks for that nice trip around the world."

This was my joke about all my previous unfulfilled assignments —to Cairo, to the Greek islands, to the South Pacific and the Far East, and then to London.

But in wartime, getting assigned to the Soviet Union and getting there were two entirely different things. One took a lot longer than the other.

The biggest headache was getting a Soviet visa; next in difficulty was getting outfitted; and finally there were travel arrangements to be made with the American military air transport command. The route was a long, roundabout one by way of North Africa and the Middle East because the German Army and Air Force had closed the European continent to unarmed civilian aircraft. Only a few over-the-North-Pole flights were carried out by British military air transports, and they, of course, were very crowded on the London-Moscow leg. The Russians, with their penchant for secrecy, never encouraged the polar route anyway.

I was given the Moscow assignment in early August, 1943, and went to work immediately on the things I had to do to get there.

This of necessity curtailed my active journalistic career in London, but not quickly enough to keep me from sending, and the *Times* from publishing, a most inaccurate and important story. And the worst of it was that my hunch had been just the reverse of the story that was published. I had been talked out of my own hunch, which might have given me a brilliant scoop.

During the brief period I worked in London, Ray Daniell, the bureau chief, began to introduce me to some of his best news sources, including the Foreign Office.

At the Foreign Office I started off theorizing that it had been a few months since the Casablanca summit conference, and much had happened, including the fall of Mussolini, so it seemed to me that it now was time for another strategy conference between Roosevelt, Churchill, and their principal lieutenants. But the British Foreign Office spokesman, an old-timer named Ridsdale, was very persuasive in discouraging my speculations, with the result that I not only discarded my own hunch, but wrote from London, on August 5, 1943, a story that flatly said just the reverse of what I had thought would happen:

> Informed sources asserted tonight that Anglo-American war strategy had been developed sufficiently ahead of time to make unnecessary another Roosevelt-Churchill meeting in the near future, even though the imminence of Italy's fall was well ahead of schedule.
>
> Best sources have not ruled out the possibility of another conference of the President and Prime Minister during the

next few weeks, but they regard it as unlikely in view of the
comprehensive strategy worked out at the January meeting
in Casablanca and the Washington session in May.

Well-informed persons said that the fall of the Mussolini
government at the time of the Sicilian invasion was well
ahead of schedule because Mr. Churchill and Mr. Roosevelt
had expected his collapse only after Italy herself were invaded. These sources added, however, that the United Nations plans were sufficiently flexible to take advantage of the
windfall and move ahead without further considerations
between the top officials. Since the Atlantic Charter meeting
at sea in August, 1941, the President and Prime Minister have
conferred every four to seven months.

MEETING WITH STALIN POSSIBLE

Keeping in mind the latest mission to Moscow of Joseph
E. Davies, sources did not rule out the possibility of a conference between Mr. Roosevelt, Mr. Churchill and Premier
Stalin in the next few weeks or months, in view of the recent
general successes of the armies. But also observers professed
ignorance of the time and place.

Persons who doubted the necessity of another conference
at present pointed out that the two Governments had been
drawing up special terms for Italy's unconditional surrender
for several months. They asserted that this demonstrated
most conclusively that the Allies were not surprised or
unprepared for Italy's withdrawal.

If Mr. Roosevelt and Mr. Churchill should meet in the
next few weeks it would indicate that the war had developed
far more than had been anticipated at the time of the Casablanca or Washington conferences.

If Mr. Roosevelt and Mr. Churchill do not confer in the
next few weeks, it is believed certain here that they will get
together in the next few months to work out the final strategy for knocking Germany out of the war.

The worst thing about this story is that it was published in New
York on the very night that Churchill and Eden left London for
Quebec, and Roosevelt set out for the Canadian city with a large
group of my fellow correspondents in Washington.

My facts were 100 percent wrong; my timing was even worse. From Quebec there came cables from my newspaper friends conveying sentiments such as "having a wonderful time, wish you were here."

For the Foreign Office, Ridsdale could not have been more apologetic, and swore that he simply had been uninformed. I asked of him only that in the future he not be so persuasive if he didn't know what the hell he was talking about.

The wait in London for a Soviet visa seemed as if it would never end. Daily telephone calls to the Russian Embassy were never encouraging; always the refrain was the same "Zaftrah budyet," which translates roughly as "Perhaps tomorrow it will be." It is about as firm and precise a pledge as the Latin American official chorus of "mañana."

Diplomatic relations between the United States and Soviet embassies in London were perhaps better than in most capitals, so as time went by I appealed for help to my old friend, John G. Winant, a former liberal Republican governor of New Hampshire who had come into the New Deal to help set up the new Social Security system for FDR. He had replaced Joseph P. Kennedy as FDR's Ambassador to London. His opposite number, highly placed in the Soviet hierarchy at one time, was Ivan Maisky.

Winant inquired of Maisky if there were real problems affecting my visa, and the Soviet Ambassador agreed to cable the foreign office in Moscow for instructions. After several days of delay, Maisky told Winant what the problem was, and Winant then told me.

The Russians had nothing against me officially or personally, Winant said, but there already was an outstanding visa for entry into the Soviet Union held by another *New York Times* correspondent, Cyrus L. Sulzberger. The Russians were well aware, Winant went on, that Cyrus Sulzberger long had been contending that *The New York Times* ought to have two accredited correspondents in Moscow, but they were not willing to grant this privilege.

Being young and brash, the solution seemed simple to me. I told Ambassador Winant to have the Russians cancel the Sulzberger visa. Then I told my managing editor, Edwin L. James, what I had done. Cy Sulzberger, of course, was annoyed that I had acted without consulting him but I explained to Mr. James that I felt it was wiser to have a correspondent in residence in Moscow rather than leaving the post vacant while Cy carried on his seemingly unsuccessful fight to get two correspondents there.

Within days after Winant passed the word to Maisky that *The New York Times* had agreed to the cancellation of the Cyrus Sulzberger visa, mine came through, and I could head for Russia and the big war being fought on the Eastern Front.

Winter was approaching and I was knowledgeable, if Hitler had not been, about the severity of winter in the Soviet Union. I knew that the heaviest kind of foul-weather gear would be required. How to get it in England where everything was severely rationed was not so easy.

Larry LeSeuer, then of CBS and recently back from Moscow, urged on me the heaviest kind of leather coat lined with sheepskin. Together we figured out that the only source of supply for such a coat would be the tradesman who made flight jackets for the Royal Air Force. I approached this firm boldly and told its officials of my assignment to spend a considerable time in the Soviet Union and my need for an ankle-length lined leather coat. In fact, I helped their designer sketch exactly what I wanted, including a hood that would fasten tightly around my head with leather drawstrings.

The leather coat makers were sympathetic, but where, they asked, would they get the authorization for the use of leather and furs for such a coat?

Like all war correspondents in London, I wore an Army officer's uniform, with the simulated rank of lieutenant (a rank that had bearing only because it permitted us to eat and drink at the junior officers' mess and decided how we were supposed to be treated if taken as prisoners of war). I told the coat makers not to worry at all, I would sign the authorization. I did and that was the end of the whole affair.

Elsewhere in London I obtained a set of fur-lined flying boots and from the tailors on Saville Row a couple of suits made of the heaviest tweed available.

With my visa stamped in my passport, and the heavy clothes ready, the next job was transportation, and that turned out to be easy, thanks to a fortuitous visit about that time by General C. R. Smith of Military Air Transport Service (MATS), the peacetime head of American Air Lines, and his public relations officer, Rex Smith.

Before the war, Rex Smith had been an editor of *The Chicago*

Sun. He was always eager to help a correspondent who needed to move swiftly anywhere in the world.

Air Corps Captain Cecil Holland, from the *Washington Evening Star,* took over the processing of my travel plans. The plans to move me swiftly ran into a bureaucratic hitch. I had not been given a clearance by the Middle East command at Cairo and this would take time, perhaps a week. But not with Captain Holland at the controls. Orders from Army GHQ in London were essential really only for the trip aboard the unlisted "ghost train" that traveled every night from London to the great air force base at Prestwick, Scotland, jumping-off place for MATS flights out of the British Isles. Instead of waiting for Cairo to clear me, orders were written which said that I was to proceed via military rail transport to Prestwick, thence to obtain transportation "for a secret and unannounced destination."

As a reporter, I had the lowest (No. 4) priority and my route took me across the top of Africa where the war had piled up backlogs of Priorities No. 2 and No. 3. I was subject to bumping wherever I landed, including Marrakesh in Morocco, Algiers in Algeria, and Cairo in Egypt. But my orders read "Secret," and so was my destination. So no one dared bump me and I whizzed across the entire route to Cairo and beyond to Lydda in Palestine, to Habbaniya on the outskirts of Baghdad, and finally to Teheran, Iran, where there was a considerable delay waiting for a Soviet air transport that would take me on to Moscow.

Before I left London, I was not unaware of the problems of an American correspondent in Moscow, restricted in his movements by Soviet authority, denied normal contacts with Russians, and with his copy heavily censored by the press department of the Soviet Foreign Office.

While I weighed these difficulties, I also reached the naïve conclusion that no one had ever tried as hard as I would to be the best possible correspondent of Russia. I talked about these problems and plans with my old friend and London chief, James (Scotty) Reston. I told Reston that I knew there would come times of loneliness, frustration, and therefore depression.

To Reston I proposed that I cable Arthur Sulzberger before I left London, telling him it was my wish to make a career of being Moscow correspondent, that I hoped therefore he would keep me there for a minimum of five years. He was to disregard any future complaints or requests for relief from me.

Scotty was too wise to laugh. That would only have made me mad, and probably would have meant that I would send the cable to Arthur Sulzberger instantly and without further consideration. Instead, Reston urged the most careful reconsideration of so fateful a decision before I committed myself in writing.

"Wait until you've been in Moscow," Scotty said. "Then if you still feel the same way, send the telegram as you wish to the publisher."

Reston saved me from myself. I had not been in Moscow more than five or six days when I knew it was no place for a free man, especially a reporter. As it was, I stayed for sixteen months, fifteen days, and four hours. A self-imposed five-year sentence would have been equivalent to life.

CHAPTER
7

I flew to Moscow from Teheran, spending the night in the oil city of Baku and stopping only briefly in shattered Stalingrad, so recently the scene of the most decisive battle of the entire Soviet-German war and perhaps of World War II. We came in low over the ruins of Stalingrad where every inch of ground had been contested in the coldest of winters, and the wreckage below left no shadow of doubt about the ferocity of this struggle. Stalingrad was the high-water mark of the German invasion, and now the armies of the *Wehrmacht* were reeling westward and homeward, destroying what little was left of the Soviet cities they had occupied in triumph two and one-half years earlier.

My arrival in Moscow preceded by only a few hours the coming of the U.S. Secretary of State, Cordell Hull, and the British Foreign Minister, Anthony Eden. The Allies were assembling for the first time at the foreign ministers level since the war against Germany had begun. As I said, I got there just in time to cover this Moscow conference, but I would have been better off covering it from London. Indeed, it was from London that the *Times* did cover the story, as Scotty Reston got from the British and diplomatic circles in Britain far more information than was available to any reporter in Moscow.

In Moscow, we simply had no sources of information—reliable or otherwise—on a story like this one and my inability to keep up with Reston on a story in my own backyard made me frustrated and unhappy in my very first few days in Russia. It perhaps colored my point of view for the rest of my long stay in that unhappy country.

We didn't know it then but it was at Moscow that the final arrangements were made for the Big Three (Roosevelt, Churchill, and Stalin) to meet about six weeks later at Teheran. We didn't know it either when they actually met in Teheran, where a handful of reporters were on hand largely by accident.

From the U.S. viewpoint, the major accomplishment of the Moscow meeting was an agreement that the Soviets would accept China under Chiang Kai-shek as one of the four major powers around which the United Nations could be formed. The communique was silent about the war with Japan, for in this one the Russians, still hard pressed by the Germans, were neutral. But Cordell Hull left the Soviet capital with a feeling Russia would be in the war against Japan as soon as the Germans were finished, and that it was in our own interests to quickly mount the long-promised Allied invasion of Europe.

There was something of a holiday mood in the Soviet capital those days because the Red Army had turned westward and was driving the Germans from key points in the Soviet Union. The Russians began dramatic, colorful fireworks displays to mark the liberation of their cities and territories from the German occupier.

On October 16, in a dispatch, I noted that Moscow's big guns had been fired twice in the last week—twenty salvos from 124 guns when the Germans were cleared from the Taman peninsula, and a few days later twenty-four salvos from 224 guns when Zaporozhye was recaptured.

These were, I wrote, "morale builders of the first magnitude as smiling Russians looked skyward at the green, red, blue and white flares" lighting up the sky and the snow-covered buildings below. "The military clock in Russia has been turned back two years."

During these talks, Stalin had a friendly comment for the first time on the war effort in North Africa, which until then had been discounted by the Soviet press as an ineffectual substitute for the real second front the Red Army needed.

"This is not a second front," Stalin said, "but it is something like it."

Secretary Hull had brought the new Ambassador, W. Averell Harriman. Harriman, a rich New York businessman, had given up a life that included mostly polo and skiing to embark on a public service career that was to last more than thirty years. He was to sit in on all the Big Three talks during and after the war, and later serve as Truman's White House advisor on foreign policy and as his Secretary of Commerce. He was governor of New York for four years in the 1950s, and then served ably under Presidents John F. Kennedy and Lyndon Johnson.

With the Ambassador as his official hostess was his attractive daughter Kathleen, a friend to the unhappy correspondents in this city where foreigners were given the cold shoulder by the Russian government and where rank-and-file Russians, for the most part, simply were afraid to associate with any foreigners, even members of the Communist party.

There were perhaps thirty American correspondents in Moscow, most of them quartered in the Metropole Hotel, which was about a block from the Kremlin, a block from the Bolshoi Theater, and a couple of blocks from the U.S. Embassy chancery. We were perhaps a mile from the British Embassy across the Moscow River from the Kremlin. The British Ambassador, Sir Archibald Clark Kerr (later Lord Inverchapel), befriended the correspondents, supplying them with a little news and Scotch. Both were in short supply in Moscow. He was "Archie" to all of us and we shared many more secrets with him than we did with the American Ambassador.

At the Metropole I settled down in a spacious suite, numbered 373, and person by person acquired a small staff to look after my needs.

The routine was a deadly boring one.

Outside the press office of the foreign department, we had access to few Soviet officials. Occasionally, I could see Maxim Litvinov, who was on the skids but remained an Assistant Foreign Minister. He had had a brilliant career first as Soviet Foreign Minister and later as the first Ambassador to the United States. But even to see Litvinov, I had to go through a side door of the Soviet Foreign Office. His comments were always guarded but they were invaluable to me because I was talking to one who had been part of the Soviet power structure.

Among U.S. officials the most helpful was Harriman's deputy, George Kennan, the best-informed American about the Soviet Union, the history of Russia, and its culture. He had an absolutely charming wife, Annalisa.

Most rank-and-file Russians avoided any contacts with us, unless they were encouraged to seek us out by the Soviet secret police.

My work day began at 10 A.M. and lasted until well after midnight. It began when the secretary came to my Metropole suite to translate *Pravda*, the Communist party organ, and *Izvestia*, the government newspaper. *Pravda* means "truth" and *Izvestia* means "news." An old saying in Moscow was: There is no truth in *Pravda* and no news in *Izvestia*. But both were our principal sources of news during my long stay in Russia, except when we were taken on carefully conducted tours of the fighting front, well behind the advancing Red Army.

Most people probably thought that the Moscow correspondents, like war correspondents everywhere else, covered the actual fighting with some risk to life and limb, but I never heard a gun fired in battle during my tour of duty in Russia.

Besides my English-speaking secretary—and there was a succession of these of indifferent abilities—my other regular employee was a tall, thin widow named Lydia who served as my courier, trudging through the snowy or sun-baked streets of Moscow to carry messages to be censored at the Foreign Office and thence to the Central Telegraph Office where they were transmitted to the *Times*.

At midnight, I made the trip to the Foreign Office in the darkness of the wartime blackout to listen to the daily war communiqué on the radio. I would write my story there, wait for it to be censored, and then walk to the Central Telegraph Office to file the dispatch. Because we were six or seven hours ahead of New York, depending on the season, I could usually rely on a telegram leaving Moscow by 1 A.M. reaching New York for publication in the newspaper of the same morning.

On those lonely post-midnight walks from the Metropole to the Foreign Office, to the Central Telegraph Office, and then back to the hotel, one scene leaps back to mind after many, many years: Hordes of women, most of them old enough to be grandmothers, working through the night with their sharp pointed sticks and shovels to clear Moscow's main thoroughfares of ice and snow. Though their instruments were crude, they were damned good at it, and I once cabled a short story saying they were more efficient and swift than New York's snow-removal battalions with all their modern mechanized equipment.

For Russian women, full liberation came early. They had equal rights, equally low pay with men, and their sex did not keep them from assignment to the hardest manual labor performed in sub-zero weather all through the long black nights.

Women fared no better in the rationing of short food supplies, so my courier Lydia, who also did my marketing for me, was grateful for the several loaves of bread I could give her weekly from my ration as chief correspondent for the *Times*. By Russian protocol, a chief correspondent of a foreign newspaper ranked equally with an ambassador who headed a diplomatic mission, so my monthly personal allotments were the same as those given to Ambassador Harriman, though he did, of course, get extra supplies for diplomatic entertaining.

It was in Russia that I learned to cook—in order to survive. Before we bought our own supplies and cooked them on small individual electric burners in our own rooms, we found that the government-run restaurant in the Metropole was cheating us on our rations.

I remember some of the monthly ration quantities:

> 15 eggs
> 11 pounds of meat
> 30 loaves of wholewheat bread
> 4 pounds of sugar
> 30 bottles of vodka

For the rationed items, purchasable in a store maintained for foreigners, the prices were dirt cheap, but fifteen eggs do not go very far if you do any entertaining, and neither does eleven pounds of meat.

John Hersey, of Time-Life, and I liked to entertain small groups of diplomats for Sunday morning brunch of bacon and eggs, preceded by lots of vodka and followed by champagne. Unfortunately, whenever we threw one of these affairs, we had to buy on the "open market," where eggs brought $2 each and bacon was $60 a pound (at the official five-to-one rate of exchange). Hersey and I liked to boast about our $250 breakfasts, personally cooked over the electric burners called *plitkas* glowing on the floor of my apartment. Sometimes we had as many as four burners going at once.

We never went hungry in Russia, but dining in restaurants without ration coupons was frightfully expensive. A small dinner at the Aragvy or one of the other small restaurants maintained for foreigners might cost $500 in American money. Such entertainment was restricted to a truly important visitor like President Roosevelt's son Elliott, who flew in on Air Corps business, or Eric Johnson, the president of the United States Chamber of Commerce and an old friend.

The American Embassy maintained a small commissary, and thanks to Secretary Hull, a few diplomatic regulations were bent so the American correspondents might buy a few items there, like four cartons of American cigarets per month.

Another delicacy was peanut butter in large cans such as a restaurant might use. One can contained the ration for all the correspondents, and it was my job to divide it up. I was a kind of self-appointed supply sergeant. I had negotiated the original deal with Secretary Hull, whom I had known in Washington. My colleagues knew well my passion for peanut butter, so they always supervised the division of the large can right down to the last spoonful lest I tip the scales in my favor. Once the peanut butter had been divided, deals were often struck for individual shares. I might give a bottle of vodka for somebody's peanut butter, and I was always willing to part with a couple of pounds of sugar for a bottle of Scotch whiskey.

Ambassador Harriman was always good for a drink or two of Scotch, and the British Ambassador, Archie Clark Kerr, might slip you a bottle on occasion. The ships sailing into the Soviet Union were loaded with war material, and there was always a shortage of Scotch. Russian-made vodka was not as available as one might imagine. Much of the vodka we drank was brought up by the American Embassy by train from Teheran. Iranian-made vodka tasted better than the Soviet product, and so did the rich gray No. 1 Iranian caviar. As the expense account auditors at the *Times* can testify, I developed some expensive tastes in Russia, and if, at times, I felt deprived of my freedom and fun, I pampered myself.

In Moscow, we were fed only the Communist party line, in the newspapers, over the radio blaring from loudspeakers at every corner, and in all our talks with Russians. Luckily, foreigners were allowed to listen to shortwave radios and I listened daily to the chiming of Big Ben on the BBC as the news was given. This made me homesick for London, and so did a cable from Reston after I had been in Russia only a few weeks asking if I would like to return to land with the American troops when they crossed the English channel and invaded Europe. "Of course, and when shall I leave," I cabled back, but, alas, there were so many delays getting someone else accredited and visaed and into Moscow that the Americans were well into Germany before I could get out of Russia. I have always regretted missing D-Day in Normandy and all the battles that followed.

In Russia, of course, we continued to cover the war by communiqué and by lifting some of the more graphic descriptions of battle from the dispatches of the Soviet correspondents. Night after night we watched the flares announce a new Soviet victory, and day after day we petitioned the Soviet Foreign Office to allow us to go to the front. They never said no, but they never said yes, either. When we did travel to any liberated city it was at least several days after the Nazi armies had retreated.

After about two months in Moscow, I made my first trip inside the Soviet Union, to Kiev, fifteen days after it had been liberated by the Russians in the western drive that had carried the Red Army 315 miles in a single year. Kiev, the capital of the Ukraine, was a great prize whose capture had been saluted with flares on the eve of the November 7 anniversary of the "October Revolution," the Soviet Union's national day corresponding to our July Fourth.

It was on November 22 that the British and American correspondents were flown in an American-built Douglas DC-3 transport from Moscow to Kiev. When we landed at Kiev we drove into a city without lights, without running water, and almost without people. Its pre-war population of more than a million had dwindled to about 75,000 cold and hungry people. Almost none of the survivors were Jews.

My first impression of ancient Kiev was that it had retained the features that made it the oldest city of that region, and that the most amazing fact about the damage done to Kiev was that it had not been damaged more extensively. It had escaped with far less destruction than had Stalingrad and Kharkov and other major cities over which the German and Soviet armies had fought, and it seemed that perhaps the Germans had been taken by surprise by the speed with which the Russians moved into and recaptured Kiev, at dawn on November 6, 1943. Bridges across the wide, frozen Dnieper River were smashed, of course, and so were the factories and all the municipal services such as power and water plants. Most of the damage seemed to have taken place in September, 1941, when the Germans first took the city from the retreating Red Army.

Famous landmarks remained. One was the great cathedral of St. Sophia, built in the Byzantine style of the eleventh century, and in it, comparatively undamaged, remained the image of the Holy Virgin done in colored mosaics by Greek masters.

At that time, Nikita Khrushchev was a leader of the Ukrainian Community party, but if we met him we didn't notice him then or remember it later. But we did meet the men who were already struggling to rebuild their city and restore its factories, hotels, and universities. The Soviet bureaucrat at the city or regional level always impressed me as both competent and likable, and so did the Red Army leaders I met in the field. It is perhaps an overstatement, but I have said many times that I never met any Russian five minutes from Moscow that I didn't like, and vice versa.

As we entered our hotel in the heart of Kiev, we saw the bodies of two civilians, obviously Nazi collaborators, hanging from an improvised gallows. Both were fully clothed, except for their shoes, which were probably being worn by some Red Army man. I never saw a corpse—Soviet or German—on any battlefield in Russia with its shoes on. Shoes were in such demand in the Soviet Union and commanded such high prices even in peacetime that no one could afford the luxury of allowing a dead man to rest in his shoes.

There was something quite unusual about the dress of one of the men hanging outside the hotel. He was wearing an overcoat, and it looked like a warm one. The hands of both men had been tied behind their backs with wire, but when we arose the next morning the overcoat had been removed from the corpse, though his hands were still manacled behind his back. This had to be the work of a Russian Houdini! Nonetheless, the central fact was emphasized. Overcoats also were in short supply for the living, and could not be left with the dead.

The Russians had curious ideas about entertaining foreign guests even in the midst of wartime shortages. A simple meal would never do, it had to be a banquet, with the tables groaning from the weight of gray caviar and elaborate pastries prepared especially for us. There was always plenty of vodka too, and wartime toasts to victory and in salute to our mutual leaders called for "bottoms up" drinking. I got pretty drunk on a number of occasions, and so did my colleagues.

Many was the time we would gladly have settled for more simple meals, but our hosts would not hear of it. One occasion was on the way back to Moscow from this first trip to Kiev. We were flying at very low levels, perhaps 100 feet, to avoid any German fighters. As the morning wore on, the DC-3 began to ice up, and we made a hazardous landing at the military airport at Kursk. It was Thanksgiving Day back home and we made this known to our Russian guides as we left the plane and sought shelter in the huge underground dugouts that the Germans had prepared while there. We remained there for many hours, without food or water, while our guides were off in downtown Kursk talking to the general commanding the front. By evening we were pretty hungry, and one of the Russian-speaking correspondents finally persuaded the Red Air Force officers on the airfield to let us join their simple mess. The airmen were reluctant to have foreigners eat a simple meal, but I assure you that food never tasted better. We ate until we were satiated.

We had just finished this meal when our guides returned from Kursk shouting that the commanding general for this front had learned it was a great American holiday and had commanded the correspondents to be his guests at a banquet.

It was now after 9 P.M. and we had, as I said, just eaten and drunk more than we could handle. Some correspondents felt we should say "no thanks" to another meal downtown, but others felt that we should not be rude to the Russian general who had laid out a banquet for us. We climbed into the body of an open truck and drove a dozen frigid miles into Kursk where we found a banquet table that would have done honor to any visiting monarch. We had been required to wait so very long so they could gather together food of such quality and in such quantity as to do honor to the Americans and their strange holiday of Thanksgiving.

By the time we had toasted the general, the victories, Stalin, Roosevelt, and Churchill—all in "bottoms up" fashion—I was drunk beyond caring at all, and slept happily in the rear of the cold truck as it bounced back to the military airfield.

We made the short flight back to Moscow the next morning, and that night Bill Downs, then of CBS, set fire to his room with his ever-glowing electric heater. He burned himself pretty badly trying to put out the fire in the heavy drapes with his hands. We had to get an American Embassy doctor to treat and sedate him. The Russians sent an enormous bill for damages.

CHAPTER
8

I grew up in the generation between the two great world wars—
a generation which had a natural skepticism and inherent disbelief
of all wartime atrocity stories. In our most formative years, we had
found out that the propagandists for the Western Allies, including
our own government, had fabricated some of the most lurid tales
of German behavior to arouse their people to wartime fervor. It
was not true, as I had been led to believe, that goose-stepping
Germans sliced off the breasts of Catholic nuns in Belgium or
tossed small babies into the air so they could be caught and killed
on the points of bayonets.

So by the time I headed off to war in 1943, I was unsure just
what to believe of all the stories I had heard and read coming out
of Europe about Hitler, his SS troops, and the Nazi armies as they
marched east across Poland, Czechoslovakia, Austria, and into the
Soviet Union.

I had no doubt that Hitler had treated the Jews badly, forcing
many of them to flee to the sanctuaries of the West, including the

United States. But I was not prepared for, and my mind did not at first accept, the systematic extermination campaign that Hitler and his minions had conducted.

I could not believe that the Hitler regime, employing many thousands of Germans, had participated in the murder of millions of Jews, Slavs, gypsies, political opponents, and those who might be mentally retarded. Hitler's boast that he would create a purely Aryan "master race" was as factual in intent as were his other aggressive aims set forth in *Mein Kampf*.

In Russia and in liberated Poland, I found out that the Germans had committed all the violent deeds and unspeakable atrocities with which they had been charged. There were no limits to the brutality and bestiality of the Germans, and I do not distinguish necessarily between those who were members of the Nazi party and those who claim they were not. Unlike so many who, in 1972, can find excuses for the vast majority of the German people, including some who lived within a few miles of the death camps, I do not believe many of the protestations of innocence. I do not believe the wind always blows in one direction and that the stench of death was not to be sniffed in the air.

Unlike my government, I have not made peace with the Germans, whether they live in the East or West. In my opinion, they have not atoned yet for all their sins.

I heard my first World War II atrocity story on my initial trip inside Russia, standing in that bleak deep ravine known as Babi Yar, which is northwest of Kiev.

In Babi Yar, we were told that the Germans had machine-gunned 50,000 to 80,000 Jewish men, women, and children in late September, 1941, and two years later—when Kiev's recapture by the Red Army seemed imminent—the Germans had forced Russian prisoners of war to burn all the bodies, thus completely destroying any evidence of the crime.

We listened to three Russian soldiers who said they had been prisoners of war who had participated in burning the corpses and then were lucky enough to escape from the Germans while other POWs who also had helped burn the bodies were shot by their German captors.

We walked through the deep ravine searching for evidence that would help to prove the story that had been told us. We did find a few isolated bones, including a skull and some matted hair, a shoulder bone, and an arm, and some gold bridgework that had rested in the teeth of one victim here. There also were spectacle cases, handbags, and other belongings left in Babi Yar.

As I have said, Babi Yar was the first site of an alleged atrocity that I had ever visited, and my skeptical mind simply rejected the Russian claims that more than 50,000 Jewish people had been murdered here.

In the dispatch that I sent from Kiev on October 22, 1943, I reported the enormous crime of which I had been told and the small amount of supporting evidence I had been able to find to verify it.

There was a note of disbelief in what I wrote. So and so had said such and such, but your correspondent couldn't prove it.

This is what I reported, as it passed through the Soviet Foreign Office censorship:

> On the basis of what we saw, it is impossible for this correspondent to judge the truth or the falsity of the story told to us. It is the contention of the authorities in Kiev that the Germans, with characteristic thoroughness, not only burned the bodies and clothing, but also crumbled the bones and shot and burned the bodies of all prisoners of war participating in the burning, except for a handful that escaped, so that the evidence of their atrocity would not be available for the outside world.
>
> If this was the Germans' intent, they succeeded well, for there is little evidence in the ravine to prove or disprove the story.

My colleague from CBS, Bill Downs, who had seen some other atrocity evidence, believed it all and we had some furious arguments about how the story should be reported.

Our guide on this tour of Babi Yar was Pavel F. Aloshin, chief architect of Kiev and the man charged with rebuilding those parts of the city that had been destroyed in the 1941 fighting and to a lesser extent in the surprisingly swift recapture of this Ukrainian capital on November 6, 1943.

Aloshin, who said he had first heard the story of Babi Yar from a boastful German architect, told us how on September 28, 1941— nine days after the German Army took Kiev—all Jews in the city had been told to report to the Lukyanovka district.

The Jews, who confidently expected evacuation but not death, were told to bring with them their most valued possessions they could carry. These Kiev Jews obviously disbelieved reports they had heard of German atrocities, and they came to the Babi Yar area bearing their valuables. They expected evacuation, but instead were ordered into the ravine, where they were directed to give up their valuables and also to remove parts of their clothing. Then, according to the story told Aloshin and now repeated to us, the helpless Jews were directed in groups to mount a platform where machine guns were fired at them. Their bodies, he said, were tossed into the ravine and were buried there, including some who had been wounded but not killed.

There were other correspondents besides me who were skeptical and we asked the Soviet authorities if there were any witnesses still in Kiev who might provide testimony about some of the crimes alleged against the Germans.

On the following day, we were escorted back to Babi Yar, accompanied by Mr. Aloshin and Mikola Bojan, the Ukranian poet who was also a vice commissar of the Ukrainian Soviet Republic. There we heard stories about the destruction just recently of the disinterred bodies of the Jews and of their possessions, stories related by three former POWs who said they had taken part in these events. The witnesses were Efim Vilkis, Laonid Ostrovsky, and Vladimir Davidoff.

Vilkis, an Odessa-born Jew who had worked as a freight loader in Kiev, was the principal witness, but Ostrovsky and Davidoff interjected remarks from time to time that confirmed or added to the account that Vilkis gave to the foreign correspondents.

Vilkis said that he had been a prisoner of war in a German concentration camp just across the road from Babi Yar. On August 14, 1943, he said, all prisoners in his camp were lined up and 100 of them were selected by the German authorities for an undisclosed task. Many of them feared they were about to be killed when the Germans herded them across the road and into the ravine of Babi Yar. The POWs, he said, were told to strip themselves to the waist, to remove their shoes and hats, and then were shackled together with leg chains. All three men showed wounds on their legs they told us had come from the shackles placed there by the Germans.

Vilkis said they worked at digging in the ravine under the command of SS troops headed by a major general whose name he did not know. The initial digging of several days uncovered nothing, but then they were directed to dig in another place by a German officer whom Vilkis said claimed to have participated in the original shooting of the Jews. Now they began to uncover bodies.

As the work of disinterring the Jews continued, Vilkis said, other prisoners were sent to an old pre-war Jewish cemetery nearby and told to return with stone grave markers. These markers, he said, were used to form crude stoves. According to Vilkis, the prisoners then carried the bodies of the Jewish men, women, and children they had dug up from the ravine and placed them on the marble foundations. More than 100 bodies comprised each layer, then there was a layer of wood, and another layer of bodies.

When the first stove was filled, Vilkis said, gasoline was poured on the firewood and the bodies, but the fire that was started did not burn well because of lack of draft.

Vilkis told how the Germans then sent another group of prisoners back to the Jewish cemetery, this time to tear down and bring back the iron railings around the graves. Back in Babi Yar, these railings were used as grates on which the bodies were placed, thus providing the draft needed to make the fires burn more efficiently.

Even so, said Vilkis, each pyre took two nights and one day to burn, and the destruction of the evidence continued from August 19 to September 28, 1943.

For the POWs impressed into such labor, Vilkis said, it was a horrid, gruesome experience, and some became ill and others went mad during the long days of work. The ill and the mentally deranged were killed by the Germans as a warning to other prisoners not to become ill themselves. Every day, he said, three to five prisoners were shot.

Vilkis gave us what seemed at the time a highly melodramatic story of how some of the prisoners, including himself, had escaped.

When the corpses of the original Babi Yar victims had been burned, and most evidence of the crime had been destroyed, Vilkis said the prisoners then were directed to build still more crude stoves.

It was clear, he said, that the Germans now meant to silence by death the men who had carried out the body-burning operation in Babi Yar. So an escape plan was hatched.

Vilkis said that in going through the clothing of the disinterred Jews, the prisoners had found a few keys including one that a prisoner who had been a locksmith before the war was able to use to open the door of the dugouts in which they were housed at night and also to loosen their leg shackles.

By this time, the number of prisoners working in Babi Yar had been increased to about 300, and they made their break for freedom on the night of September 28, breaking out of the dugouts in groups. German sentries outside fired their machine guns into the escaping prisoners, Vilkis said, and only a very few—he could not guess the number—managed to get away. With Ostrovsky and Davidoff, Vilkis said, he had found a hiding place in a cement factory not too far away. There they remained in hiding until Red Army troops crossed the Dnieper River and came into Kiev on November 6.

For me, the Vilkis story was hard to believe. It had obvious holes that defied credulity. The absence of general supporting evidence made it impossible at that time to break down my built-in skepticism.

Many, many months passed between Babi Yar and my next atrocity story, and in the interim, I remained doubtful because of the lack of supporting evidence for the stories we had been told about what happened in Babi Yar. I accepted the fact that nearly all of the Jews were gone from Kiev, but where and how they had departed remained a mystery.

My next experience, in early 1944, was at Katyn Forest near Smolensk, where the bodies of 11,000 Polish officers and men were in the process of being taken from mass graves. This experience moved me several steps nearer to a belief that the Germans were guilty of the atrocities charged against them.

Long before I got there on January 22, Katyn had become a worldwide *cause célèbre*. When the German Army occupied this area of the Soviet Union, the Germans claimed to have uncovered the graves of these Polish officers and men. They assembled an "international" commission of alleged disinterested experts which blamed the crime on the Soviet armies that had captured these Poles originally during the fighting in 1940.

The German charges were a shocker for Allied public opinion, especially for those people who had no love for the Soviet Communist system in general, and who opposed Lend-Lease or any other collaboration with the Russians to defeat Hitler. These Westerners thought it would be far wiser in the long run if the armies of Hitler and Stalin could destroy each other.

When the first German charges of a massacre against the Russians were made public, the Polish government in exile, made up of pre-war Polish authorities, who hated the Russians as much or more than they did the Germans, asked for an investigation by the International Red Cross of the graves at Katyn. Angrily, the Soviet Union broke off diplomatic relations with the London Poles, asserting that they had implied the Russians might be guilty of the crimes charged against them by the Germans.

If the London Poles expected to return to Warsaw after the war, this was perhaps the gravest mistake they ever made. From this time forward, the Russians were intent on keeping the government in exile out of Poland.

In fairness to the London Poles, they had some reason to raise questions about what had happened to their former officer corps taken prisoner by the Red Army when it was in collaboration with the German Army. After the German strike against the western boundaries of the Soviet Union in June, 1941, the Russians always answered such inquiries about Polish POWs vaguely by saying they had been evacuated before the Germans hit to safer areas of the Soviet Union well to the east. But no Polish official had been allowed to visit these Polish prisoner camps.

It was therefore a diplomatically sensitive story when the correspondents in Moscow first were told in January, 1944, they would be allowed to visit Katyn. The first word we got from the Foreign Office was that we would make the trip by automobile or truck from Moscow to Smolensk, that we would need to dress warmly, and that we should carry with us our own food and drink in sufficient supply for three days.

One of us mentioned the forthcoming trip to Ambassador Harriman at the U.S. Embassy one night and his immediate reaction was that his daughter Kathleen, a part-time correspondent for *Newsweek* magazine in which the Harrimans had a financial interest, might like to make the trip with us. Harriman asked the Soviet Foreign Office if Kathy could go.

Though we had expected to leave any moment by automobile or truck for Smolensk, the Russians now began to stall about when the trip would begin. They continued to delay the trip for two or three days. Suddenly there was word the trip to Smolensk had been rescheduled, Miss Harriman would make the journey with us, and we would be taken by a special train provided by the Soviet Foreign Office for very important persons on rare occasions. Our

VIP obviously was Kathy Harriman; otherwise we certainly would have been rattling along the miserable roads of the Soviet Union in a truck. It was, as I wrote at the time, "probably the most unusual press junket in the history of the world—and certainly of the Soviet Union."

The train was made up of well-heated, well-lighted, plush-carpeted compartment sleeping cars and a bright, cheery dining room whose windows were curtained in pastel green. Food was plentiful aboard the train, and when we reached Smolensk near the eastern bank of the Dnieper River after an eighteen-hour trip from Moscow, our Soviet hosts insisted that we eat two breakfasts before we moved into a convoy of cars for the trip to Katyn Forest, ten miles to the west of Smolensk.

After we drove through pine, fir, and birch trees, we came to a well-guarded road down which our driver proceeded approximately one quarter of a mile to huge piles of freshly turned sandy soil near which were pitched three tents.

These excavations were mass graves that had been opened and from which more than 700 bodies already had been exhumed, according to Soviet authorities. In any event, I saw more bodies than I could count, and in some graves there were three and four layers of bodies.

Red Army men with shovels loosened the dirt around the bodies and other soldiers wearing rubber gloves carefully picked up the bodies and placed them on wooden stretchers.

Rows of well-preserved good-quality black boots protruded from the dirt, and some of the corpses were still wearing fur-lined heavy winter overcoats.

It had been the German charge that the Russians murdered these Polish officers in March, 1940, and it now was the Soviet claim that the Germans had committed the murders a couple of months after they plunged into the Soviet Union in June, 1941.

With us that day in Katyn were members of a Soviet investigating commission which included medical authorities, Red Army men, the Metropolitan Nikolai of Kiev and Galicia representing the Russian Orthodox Church, and Alexei Tolstoi, one of the foremost writers in the Soviet Union. He was a distant cousin of Leo Tolstoi, author of *War and Peace.*

Our principal guide was Dr. Victor I. Prozorovsky, director of the Moscow Institute of Criminology and Medical Research, who was of medium height, with black hair and a black Vandyke beard, wearing a white smock, a white cap, an orange rubber apron, and red rubber gloves.

Inside the tents we were to watch eleven teams of doctors performing postmortems on the bodies that had been taken from the mass graves. With their dissecting knives, the doctors laid open the brains, hearts, and other organs of the dead Poles, explaining to us that the bodies were unusually well preserved because of the sandy loam in which they had been buried. One correspondent remarked the slices of brains placed before us looked just like Spam.

Some of the bodies wore small metal tags which Soviet officials explained had been put there by the Germans when the bodies had been excavated a year earlier for the German investigation of this same crime.

One Pole on the postmortem slab bore the number 808, and we took notes while a Soviet interpreter gave us this medical report:

> The body of a male, middle height, good physical condition, without any defects in physique. Member of a Polish unit, but no marks of rank on coat or uniform. Fully dressed. Right foot had fallen off.
>
> One-half centimer below the base of skull is a large bullet hole; size is nine millimeters in diameter. No exit hole found yet. Epidermis is dirty, yellowish color; partly mummified. No documents found in pockets, which had been slit open.

But there were documents and other interesting items in the pockets of other prisoners.

We were shown a letter dated June 20, 1941—two days before the Germans invaded the Soviet Union—said to have been written by the Polish prisoner, Stanislaus Kuchinski, to his wife in Warsaw but never mailed. There were notes in Polish currency and even an occasional American $50 bill in the pockets of other prisoners according to our guides.

The Soviet commission members gave us a hard sell on German guilt, but they also ran into some difficult, pointed questions from the correspondents.

If the Germans had killed the prisoners in July and September, 1941, as now was claimed, we asked how come some of the prisoners were dressed in heavy fur coats. The writer Tolstoi replied that the prisoners were wearing all the clothing they had had when they were captured by the Red Army in 1939 because they had assembled expecting to be transferred elsewhere when they were killed by the Germans. Vladimir P. Potemkin, now the Soviet Commissioner of Education, and a former Ambassador to Italy, added his conclusion that the nights were very cold in September in the Smolensk region.

After we left the forest, the commission held a hearing to listen to some Russian residents of the area who earlier had been witnesses for the Germans and against the Russians in the German inquiry. These witnesses all had been heard by the Soviet commission previously, and now they were to tell their stories again just for our benefit.

When we first asked the right to question these witnesses ourselves, our request was refused. Then when I suggested that we go back to the train if we could not question the witnesses, the Soviet authorities reluctantly agreed to our asking questions. Nothing of major significance developed from our questions.

The first witness was Parfen Kiselyoff, seventy-three, unshaven and wearing a quilted jacket, who said he had signed a German document stating that the Russians had killed the Poles, but only after he had been tortured and beaten by the Germans. He said the Nazis had threatened to pull out his veins and crucify him on a tree in the same forest where the Poles were buried. The other witnesses told similar stories.

To the correspondents who had seen a number of mass graves in the Soviet Union, one interesting fact here was that all of the executions apparently had been performed individually by firing an automatic revolver at point-blank range into the back of the head. The practice in most German executions, according to our experience, had been to machine-gun the victims.

My feeling at the time was that both the Germans and the Russians were capable of committing these murders in cold blood. I knew the brutality of the Soviet secret police and had no illusions about our wartime allies.

The evidence certainly was contradictory, and I was not qualified to judge whether the exhumed bodies had been in the ground since March, 1940, or only since August-September, 1941.

But there were two highly important bits of evidence that in my view pointed to murder of these Poles by the Germans and not the Russians.

So many of the Polish officers wore big, quality, well-preserved leather boots to their graves, and others were dressed in warm fur-lined overcoats.

Never before in all my travels in the Soviet Union had I seen corpses wearing shoes, to say nothing of good boots or fur coats. These items were in such short supply for the living they were never buried with the dead.

On this basis, I decided that it was the Germans, not the Russians, who had murdered the Polish officers at Katyn. Not all my colleagues agreed, but in any event, it was not the kind of speculation that the Russian censors would permit to be transmitted from Moscow to our newspapers. And we did not argue the case while English-speaking Russians were in our vicinity.

Whatever doubts about Russian versus German guilt might have lingered after the trip to Katyn were to be removed entirely after my visit in late August, 1944, to a German extermination camp near Lublin, Poland.

This was the first time Western observers had ever seen a Nazi death camp. Our visit came well ahead of the Western Allied push into the more famous death camps at Dachau and other places inside Germany.

But at Lublin all my skepticism about war crimes and atrocities vanished. Now I knew that the Germans were fully guilty of the most bestial crimes. Under a Lublin, Poland, dateline of August 27 (delayed), I reported to the *Times*, "I have just seen the most terrible place on the face of the earth—the German concentration camp at Maidanek, which was a veritable River Rouge for the production of death, in which it was estimated by Soviet and Polish authorities as many as 1,500,000 persons from nearly every country in Europe were killed in the last three years."

Most of these victims were Jews, and I said so in the written dispatch I submitted for censorship to the Russian authorities back in Moscow. But for some reason, the Russian censors eliminated the description of the victims as mostly Jewish. A few days after publication, my managing editor, Edwin L. James, cabled to ask why if most of the victims were Jewish I had not said so in my story. This was my first realization that the Russians had eliminated this fact from my story, and I descended hopping mad on the press office officials. I got a rather lame and halting explanation from the press officer on duty that some anti-Semites around the world might feel that if the victims were Jews, the murders were justified. This reflected, of course, the basic anti-Semitism of so many Russians which still has not been entirely eliminated, as we have witnessed during 1970 and 1971 in the mistreatment of Soviet Jews who wanted to emigrate to Israel. Finally, the Soviet official allowed me to cable Mr. James that the reference to the Jews had been contained in my original dispatch and had been censored from it by mistake.

The scene at the Maidanek camp near Lublin had been a shocking one in every horrible detail. Here for the first time I saw the shower-bath execution chambers into which the Germans poured a gas-producing chemical bearing the German-language label "Zyklon B." I saw used and unused cans of this gas. Nearby were the furnaces where the bodies were cremated. Built of brick, this huge crematorium looked and was operated not unlike a small blast furnace for a steel mill. The coal fuel was fanned by an electrically-operated blower. Each furnace held five bodies at a time, and there were five openings on each side—on one side the bodies were placed inside the furnace and the ashes were removed from another side, to be used as fertilizer on the cabbage patch below. We were told that it took fifteen minutes to fill each furnace and about ten to twelve minutes for the bodies to burn. It was estimated that the battery of furnaces had a capacity of 1,000 bodies a day.

Near the furnaces we saw a large number of skeletons, including more than a score that we were told represented persons who had been killed by the Germans just before the Russian and Polish armies smashed into the Lublin area. They had lacked the time to burn these bodies before the prison camp was overrun.

We saw a concrete table near the furnaces and asked its purpose. We were told the Germans placed the bodies of their victims there just before cremation and searched their teeth for gold fillings and bridgework. No body would be accepted for placement in the furnace, we were told, unless it bore a stamp saying the mouth had been searched for gold.

This death camp had such a high production rate that it was not possible to burn all of the victims' bodies. Many were in mass graves nearby. I saw three of the ten mass graves that had been opened, and counted myself 368 corpses in states of partial and nearly complete decomposition.

I called this a "River Rouge" of death because it reminded me of the great highly mechanized Ford plant near Detroit on the Rouge River which had become a symbol of American mass production. Death was highly mechanized by the Germans, and they looted their victims before and after killing them.

At the camp, I visited a wooden warehouse perhaps 150 feet long, forty feet wide and thirty feet high. There I walked on literally tens of thousands of shoes of men, women, and children spread across the floor like grain in a half-filled elevator of my native Nebraska. There were shoes for children of one year or less, and there were shoes for adults and older people. They were all sizes, shapes, and colors, and one pair at least had come from the United States for it bore the stamp "Goodyear welt."

In downtown Lublin, in a warehouse, the clothing and personal effects of those killed at Maidanek had been sorted and prepared for shipments to Germany. The Red Army had captured a German officer, Herman Vogel, of Millheim, and he admitted to us that as head of the clothing warehouse he had shipped in one two-month period alone eighteen freight-car loads of clothing to Germany. He admitted that he knew that these articles came from the people killed at Maidanek. Vogel was one of six persons captured by the Red Army and being held for trial for their part in the death camp who were questioned on that August day by the visiting British and American correspondents.

According to several witnesses, the peak death-production day for Maidanek was November 3, 1943, when for some reason not made clear the Germans executed a total of 18,000 to 20,000 prisoners by a variety of means, including shooting, hanging, and gassing.

We were told that Jews, Poles, Russians, and others from a total of twenty-two countries had entered Maidanek to die, and I believed the story I heard, backed up as it was by the evidence I could see.

Much of what I reported from Poland that day met skeptical eyes and minds in the United States, people who were not convinced of the German guilt because they had not seen the evidence personally as I had seen it. Evidently *The New York Times* felt it necessary to reassure its readers that my account could be accepted at face value. In an editorial a few days after my dispatch from Lublin had been published, the *Times* stated that I was "employed by this newspaper because he is known to be a thorough and accurate correspondent." Never before or since have I seen the *Times* so describe one of its reporters.

The *Readers Digest* reprinted my account from Lublin under the heading "Lest We Forget." But in the angry post-war quarreling over the political aims of the Communist government of Russia, I think we did forget that it was the Germans who committed these crimes against humanity.

After Maidanek, I no longer entertained doubts of any kind about German atrocities and the complicity in these atrocities of literally many thousands of Germans. Gone was all the skepticism built up by my generation during the post-war years. I can still see those bodies lying on stone slabs waiting to have their teeth examined for the gold they might contain, and I can still remember those piles of shoes, of clothing, and other possessions ready for shipment back to Germany.

Once after the war, a U.S. military policeman inquired if I was a German because I was dressed in civilian clothes and traveling in an Army jeep in Germany. My face went red with anger and I barely restrained myself from smashing him in the face. I whipped out my passport, and demanded an apology from the somewhat astounded soldier. I was not a German.

CHAPTER
9

By their arbitrary censorship and their rigid limitations on travel, the Soviet authorities made life difficult for the foreign correspondent during most of the war. We were always in danger of expulsion if our conduct displeased them in the slightest. Any correspondent who took home leave risked denial of a return visa if he spoke critically of the Soviet system in his absence from Moscow.

We won a few minor concessions by argument with the censors, but these were possible only when the censor spoke and understood English well. Some of the censors could barely read the language of the dispatch they were censoring.

But there was one notable victory achieved by the British and American correspondents over the Soviet bureaucracy. And this single victory was won by a sit-down strike, backed up, for once, by total solidarity.

The issue was whether a handpicked few or all of us would cover the arrival in Russia of the first U.S. heavy bombers carrying out the "shuttle bombing" raids that had just been agreed upon by the two governments. In the end, we all went, as the Soviet press authorities capitulated to our "all or nothing" demand.

The time was early June, 1944, just days ahead of the Anglo-American landings that opened the second front on the western coast of Europe.

The strike strategy was hatched in an all-night session in my suite at the Metropole. I called the meeting upon learning that the Russians had chosen a handful of correspondents to cover the bombing mission when all of us had been promised by the American authorities that we could cover the story. I was not in the first group selected, but was quickly made a member of the chosen few when I protested to Major General John R. Deane, then commanding the U.S. Military Mission at the Moscow Embassy. General Deane, a fine soldier and a nice guy, was in no mood to tangle with the *Times* being left out of this story of such importance to the American people. It was the first, and nearly the last, example of direct cooperation between the Soviet and American military forces, which until then had been fighting separate wars.

But my indignation over my initial exclusion was not cooled by my belated inclusion in the Soviet plans for the trip. I fought through the night for solidarity among the correspondents, which was hard to get because the AP and UP hesitated to defy the Russians.

Finally there was agreement among all of us, and at 7 A.M. the entire group of more than twenty correspondents made their way to the Moscow airport. We were met by Soviet press department officials who insisted only half a dozen of us were authorized to go. We said "All or nothing." When the DC-3 was brought to a gate for boarding, all of us climbed aboard the airplane and took seats.

Then there was a long argument about whether we would all go or whether the uninvited correspondents would heed Soviet requests to leave the airplane. We all sat tight, and the Soviet officials conferred with headquarters by telephone. Finally they came back and agreed, in principle, that all of us could go, but there was not enough room on the aircraft in which we were then sitting, so one correspondent would have to volunteer to come later in the day on another aircraft the Russians promised to provide.

One of our British colleagues said that would be satisfactory to him, so he left the plane, and the rest of us flew off to Poltava, in the Ukraine, to await the arrival of the American bombers from Italy, which were scheduled to hit targets near Budapest on their way north. The Russians kept their promise of later transportation to the British volunteer and he joined us in Poltava in time for the arrival of the shuttle bombers.

The fliers who conducted this first mission into Russia described it as a "milk run," meaning the opposition from Nazi anti-aircraft and fighters had been minimal and that the bombs had been dropped squarely on the railroad-marshaling yards near Budapest.

The base was typically American with its messes, post exchange, and barracks, and was a sight for sore eyes to Americans who had been too long in Moscow. We overstayed our leave by a couple of days, and indeed ignored a telegraphic request from General Deane that we come back to Moscow by the night of June 5.

We didn't go back, so we missed all the excitement, the cheering, and the demonstrations when the second front was opened on June 6, 1944, and the news of it reached Moscow. General Deane was right, we should have been in Moscow for that historic celebration. But in our enthusiasm over seeing an American base and American airmen again, we simply did not want to leave Poltava.

My most interesting trip inside the Soviet Union was one arranged in July, 1944, only after Marshal Stalin personally overruled Foreign Minister Molotov and gave permission to four correspondents to travel into the Urals and Central Asia with a visiting United States dignitary, Eric Johnston, then president of the United States Chamber of Commerce and of the Motion Picture Producers Association.

Johnston was an old friend of mine and had been planning this trip to Russia for a long time. Many months before, during a visit to London, he had promised Harrison Salisbury, then of UP but later of *The New York Times*, and me that he would ask the Soviet authorities to let the two of us make some of the trip with him.

Johnston, accompanied by his aide Joyce O'Hara and Kansas publisher William White, the son of William Allen White, had come to Moscow in late June to get a firsthand look at the war and to discuss the motion-picture business with the Soviet Foreign Trade Commissar, Anastas Mikoyan. He found Mikoyan an agreeable host, and Mikoyan approved Johnston's request that four American correspondents travel to Siberia and other eastern regions with him. Invited on the trip were Robert Magidoff, who represented the National Broadcasting Company in Moscow but on this trip also would file for AP; Richard E. Lauterbach of Time-Life; Harrison Salisbury of UP; and myself for the *Times*.

Although Mikoyan was Johnston's host, he was not *our* host in the Soviet capital. The technical host for the newsmen was Foreign Minister Molotov whose ministry included the press office. Molotov's subordinates said we couldn't go because it would be unfair to other correspondents wishing to go to the Urals but who were not included in Mr. Johnston's party.

This was just a short time after our successful strike for solidarity in covering the American shuttle bombing raids, so once again we went to our colleagues seeking unanimity. And once again our colleagues agreed. They all signed a petition to the Soviet Foreign Minister asking that the chosen four be allowed to make the trip as Mr. Johnston had requested and Mr. Mikoyan had agreed. Molotov still said no.

The four correspondents decided to ask Johnston to carry the case to Stalin himself. Johnston's first meeting with Stalin was scheduled in the Kremlin that night.

Johnston at first was not eager to make a federal case of our plight. He thought it might be wiser if he talked it over with Ambassador Harriman. Harriman, we forecasted, would not support our claim and we urged Johnston to move ahead even so. When they went to the Kremlin that night, we didn't know whether Johnston would raise the question or let it slide. The correspondents, all of them, assembled at the Embassy to drink some of Harriman's Scotch, to see the Humphrey Bogart–Ingrid Bergman movie *Casablanca* for the umpteenth time, and to await the return about midnight of the Ambassador and Johnston from the Kremlin.

When they came back, both Harriman and Johnston were grinning.

"For the benefit of the four American correspondents who are wondering if they can travel with me tomorrow," Johnston began, "go home and pack. Marshal Stalin says you may go."

There were whoops of victory, and then we learned how Stalin had interceded in our behalf.

At the outset of his talk with Johnston, the Soviet dictator said he hoped the Johnston trip would promote better understanding between the Soviet and American peoples. Johnston said he shared the hope, and he added that in the United States the best avenue for promoting better understanding was through the press.

"Therefore," Johnston wondered, addressing himself directly to Stalin, "would it not be a good idea if four American correspondents accompanied me to the Urals and to Siberia tomorrow?"

"Of course," was Stalin's response.

Johnston was both amazed and befuddled. He had a speech all prepared about the many virtues of the American press which he had intended to make at this point—he was not prepared for Stalin's ready acquiesence.

"Does that mean they can go?" Johnston asked.

"Yes, yes," Stalin replied.

Johnston still wasn't quite ready to take yes for an answer. He looked at Molotov sitting at the table farther down and remarked, "I'm not sure that Mr. Molotov agrees."

Stalin turned in his chair, smiled, and also looked directly at Molotov.

"I always agree with Marshal Stalin," Molotov responded.

We raced from the Embassy back to the Metropole to pack, and an hour or so later, the Foreign Office press department called me to say "We are happy to grant Mr. Lawrence's request to travel with Mr. Johnston."

"Yes, I know," I told the press department official by telephone. "Will you please thank Marshal Stalin for me?"

At dawn the next day, we flew off from Moscow in a DC-3 provided by the Soviet government just for this group. Our pilots were excellent, our male steward served first-class meals, and our tour took us to such fabulous and little known cities as Magnito-gorsk, Sverdlovsk, Omsk, Novosibirsk, Alma-Ata, Tashkent, and even ancient Samarkand whose streets had accommodated the hordes of Genghis Khan.

In the Urals, for the first time in eleven months, I was out of the blackout—lights blazed at night as factories, some of them new and many of them relocated from parts of the Soviet Union over-run by the Germans, poured out war material in this sanctuary halfway between Poland and the Pacific, an area that was bomb-proof because it was beyond the range of German bombers.

We met Red Army men, skilled industrial technicians who man-aged the Soviet war production plants, and leaders of the Com-munist party in every city. In a few, we could see slave laborers— men and women—at work while under heavy guard, looking not unlike members of a black work crew sent to the roads from any Southern prison in the United States.

We saw the great strides that had been made in industrializing the Urals and Siberia and heard of even more ambitious post-war development plans that would increase the steel-production capacity of the Soviet Union from its pre-war base of 22,000,000 tons annually to 60,000,000 tons after the war, a projected total at that time second only to that of the United States. At Magnitogorsk, for example, the Russian plant had been modeled on the U.S. Steel Corporation plant I had seen so often at Gary, Indiana.

At Chelyabinsk, we saw the first models of the new Stalin tank, with heavier armor plate and heavier fire power than the American-made Sherman. Six years later when we first faced this tank firing at us in Korea, it remained a superior tank to anything the Americans had on hand to turn back the North Korean invaders. I remembered in Korea that we had long ago fully briefed the American military on the new Soviet tank.

We spent a couple of days at Novosibirsk, the site of the elimination of the last Russian czar and his family right after the Revolution, now a thriving Soviet regional capital. We stayed at the *dacha*, or summer house, of the Siberian Communist party secretary, Mikhail Kulagin, whom we all called "Mike." The *dacha* was a pleasant, roomy, comfortably furnished house on the eastern bank of the River Ob, one of the great rivers of the world and one of the few that flows from south to north, emptying finally into the Arctic.

We found Mike to be a hard-working, affable, but no-nonsense kind of man, during working hours at least, and his working hours certainly were not circumscribed by any five-day, forty-hour week. As secretary general of the party in Siberia, he obviously was a man of considerable power which he did not hesitate to use. One minor use of power, it might be noted, was in the selection of artists to entertain us as we sailed one evening aboard a tidy little yacht on the Ob, listening to the world-renowned Leningrad string quartet as we headed north and to a Red Army chorus of singers and dancers as we returned.

Foreigners instantly liked Mike, and that might have been one cause of his undoing at the hands of the suspicious Stalin and his secret police force after the war ended. I never knew whether Mike was executed or died naturally, but he was in disgrace when his life ended. It was only after the rise of Khrushchev and his denunciation of Stalin's crimes that Kulagin was posthumously rehabilitated.

Posthumous rehabilitation is a comparatively new invention, even for the Soviet Union, but it is one of their ways of rewriting history to remove evidence after death that a Soviet citizen was persecuted unjustly while alive. There were many such rehabilitations once the bureaucrats were prepared to admit the enormity of Stalin's crimes against his fellow officials and party members.

By the time we reached Magnitogorsk, Eric Johnston, who suffered from stomach ulcers, had appointed me his "drinking deputy" for protocol purposes. In most situations, the Russians went along amicably with this substitution. I liked to drink and had an enormous capacity for it, and there were innumerable toasts to be offered and accepted at the official lunches and dinners given for Johnston as an honored guest of the Soviet Union.

No man and no occasion tested my drinking capabilities more than did Kulagin. After working hours, he was a hard drinker too. July, 1944, was a time when the Red Army was moving westward toward Germany and the Western Allies were breaking out of their beachheads on the western shores of Europe. It was a time of unprecedented common endeavor and friendship, and relations on the surface never were better between Washington and Moscow.

In short, there was lots to drink about, so we did. In the course of one luncheon, I had told Kulagin about a drink the Red Army had invented to mow down Western correspondents. Its contents were 50 percent vodka and 50 percent champagne, and it was called *Katoosha*, after the highly mobile, multi-barreled rocket-gun anti-personnel weapon the Russian armies used with such success against the Germans.

The correspondents long ago had learned, though, that the only way to withstand the deadly effects of the *Katoosha* was to treat it with great respect, to sip it as one might a very long drink, and not to rush into battle with a succession of *dudnas* or "bottoms up" drinking such as the Russians insisted upon after very special important toasts had been offered.

Kulagin challenged me at dinner on the day I told him about the Red Army drink, of which he claimed no previous experience or knowledge. Bringing Robert Magidoff of NBC along as his interpreter, Kulagin approached my place at the dinner table and said he now would like to try the *Katoosha* about which I had informed him at lunchtime. He reached for two large glasses, and indicated I should now prepare the drinks for both of us. I did.

"To victory over the German invader," proposed Kulagin as his first toast.

I know that meant "bottoms up," so I drained my glass containing at least six ounces of the lethal mixture. So did Kulagin.

"Please," said Kulagin, meaning that he wanted another drink. I complied, and I also knew now what my cue was.

"To Marshal Stalin," was the toast I proposed, and once again we drained our glasses quickly.

Once again Mike said "please," and once again I filled the glasses with vodka and champagne. The next toast was inevitable.

"To President Roosevelt," was the Kulagin toast, and once again we swallowed quickly the entire contents of the glasses.

When Mike again said "please," I protested through Magidoff that Kulagin and I had best take it easy, that we were dealing with truly overpowering drinks that had best be sipped slowly over an evening of conversation. Instead, we had now downed three of them in less than five minutes. I submitted that to continue would mean total and complete unconsciousness in a matter of a very few minutes and I urged Mike to desist.

The Siberian Communist party leader smiled, and said he was willing to accept my words of caution, but first there was one toast that had not been offered and without which the evening could not be complete. He proposed therefore that we drink to our personal friendship. If I would now mix and drink that toast with him we could end our friendly socialist competition.

With hands that already were shaky, I mixed the deadly concoction, and I handed one of the glasses to Mike.

"To the friendship between Comrades Lawrence and Kulagin," he said, slipping into the easy form of address used between fellow citizens of the Soviet Union.

This one too had to be "bottoms up."

Within a very few minutes thereafter, Kulagin suddenly slumped unconscious at his seat at the dinner table next to Mr. Johnston and his aides moved his prostrate body into a bedroom not far from the dining room.

Now the Russians and Americans crowded around me to congratulate me on my great "victory," and in the excitement I accepted a few "bottoms up" toasts in straight vodka to celebrate the triumph. Minutes later, fully clothed, I was stretched out on a twin bed across from that of Mike, snoring in thunderous tones.

When we flew off the next morning for the fabled city of Alma-Ata, near the Soviet-Chinese border, I had one of my worst hangovers ever. Kulagin shook hands formally with all of his departing guests except me. I was kissed squarely on the lips for the first and last time by a man.

My last trip of any importance during my stay in Russia, one from there to liberated Poland, was made at the end of December, 1944, about two months before I was to return home. I got permission to go first from Boleslaw Bierut, who then headed the Lublin Poles.

When the Soviet press office indicated there might be some question about my going, I pointed out that champions of the Polish government in exile, headquartered in London, would find any barriers placed in my path as added evidence the Lublin Poles weren't independent, as the Russians claimed. Finally, they said I could make the trip, along with several other correspondents including the author Lillian Hellman, then visiting Moscow, and my old friend from Time-Life, Dick Lauterbach. We went by train from Moscow, via Kiev, to Lublin, traveling for four days in cold sleeping cars for a journey that by air would not have required four hours even in those days of propeller-equipped small transport aircraft.

At Lublin, it soon became apparent that we were part of the window dressing for the establishment on Polish soil of the Lublin provisional government headed by President Bierut and the Soviet handpicked premier Osubka-Horowski. Also on hand was a great Soviet military leader, Marshal Rokossovsky, hero of many a great victory over the Germans who in the immediate post-war period was to revert to Polish citizenship and become the Polish Minister of Defense. As I usually did on field trips in the Soviet Union, I was wearing my uniform as an American war correspondent. The American correspondents stood near Marshal Rokossovsky on the reviewing platform as the Soviet-trained Polish Army marched in review down the main street of Lubin.

It made our Soviet conducting officers and press censors very unhappy, but the Lublin Poles agreed that the correspondents might file dispatches via Radio Lublin to reach the outside world. Never before had we been permitted to transmit news stories from anywhere in Russia except Moscow, and only then after the most careful scrutiny by officials of the Soviet press department. The permission to file by radio had not been anticipated and we had made no advance arrangements with our offices to monitor the Lublin shortwave transmitter, but during that first day in the temporary Polish capital we sent repeated warnings to all who might be listening advising that news transmissions would be made later in the day and requesting that such stories be relayed to the nearest office of the newspapers and wire services we worked for. In my case, the radio was monitored by the U.S. Information Service office in Cairo, and the dispatches were forwarded quickly to the *Times'* London office and from there to New York for publication.

We also persuaded the Lublin Poles to take us to "the front," to the eastern bank of the Vistula River opposite Warsaw, where the Red and Polish armies had ground to a halt in the face of strong German resistance just a few weeks before.

This was one of the great political and military controversies of the war, and another cause of bitter disagreement between the London Poles and the Soviet authorities.

As the German Army reeled back from the Soviet onslaught to the east of the Vistula, the London Polish authorities gave the order for an uprising of Poles in Warsaw. The strategy was for Poles to liberate their capital themselves before the Red Army got there, and this would be regarded as a coup and a great military-political victory for the London Poles over the Russians and their satellite Lublin Polish committee.

But the London Poles miscalculated gravely. The Germans were not so weak that the Warsaw Polish resistance forces could win a victory alone, and when the Red Army either could not or did not push across the Vistula, there were loud cries of double cross as the Germans systematically wiped out the Warsaw rebel forces and began methodically to destroy Warsaw building by building.

When I reached Praga on the eastern banks of the Vistula in the company of Polish officials and Army officers, this German destruction of what remained of Warsaw was still in progress, weeks after it had begun. The Vistula was the barrier between the opposing armies, but it was evident to me that now the job of preparing the Red and Polish armies for another great offensive was nearing its end.

I made my way with the other correspondents to a front-line artillery observation post at the bank of the Vistula, barely 1,000 feet from the most forward German machine-gun position on the west bank of the river, and from there I watched an occasional exchange of artillery shells and heard, from the other side, the sounds of dynamite blasting as additional buildings were being destroyed. These buildings were being destroyed by the Germans who moved on foot from building to building planting their explosive charges.

This was a part of my story in the *Times* of January 15, 1945, bearing the dateline "With the Lublin Polish Army, at the Vistula River opposite Warsaw, Jan. 4 (Delayed)":

> Words are inadequate to picture Warsaw's tragedy, to depict the scene that lies before me. An estimated 770,000 of the city's prewar population of 1,300,000 have been killed by the Germans. Fully 75 percent of this once beautiful capital has been systematically destroyed and there are signs that the Germans intend to complete the job before they are finally driven out.
>
> Before me, as far as the eye can see even with the aid of a powerful telescope, only the hollow shells of buildings remain. Street by street, block by block, building by building, Warsaw is being destroyed.
>
> In 1939, the Germans, using their artillery and aerial bombs, succeeded in destroying about 10 percent of the city before it capitulated. In 1942, when they liquidated the ghetto, destroying Jews by the tens of thousands, and burning the ghetto district, 15 percent more of the city went. Now, in the wake of August's unsuccessful uprising led by underground soldiers loyal to the London Exile Government and led by General Bor, the Germans have wiped out 40 percent more of the west bank part of the city.
>
> I have looked at Warsaw when crouching on a five-story apartment building not far from the river bank and when lying on my stomach in a dug-out at the very edge of the Vistula.
>
> A few columns of smoke are curling skyward in the vicinity of the Prudential Life Insurance seventeen-story "skyscraper" which stands as Warsaw's dominating building, although I am told that three stories of that building have been knocked off by artillery fire. Every building I can see is gutted.

The Polish soldiers I met here had been freshly trained by the Russians and had not yet been blooded in major conflict. Now they were spoiling for a fight and were taunting the Germans on the other side of the river. I was told that a few days before I came to Warsaw, these Poles had posted a huge eighteen-by-eighteen-foot picture of Corporal Hitler on the side of an apartment house near the river bank, telling the Germans in a large-lettered German-language caption easily distinguished through binoculars: "That's your enemy; shoot at him!"

Off the record, officers of the new Soviet-controlled Polish Army briefed us about the forthcoming offensive to retake Poland's capital, or what remained of it. Lieutenant General Stanislaus Poplawski, a native of Poland and commander of this Polish force, proudly wore a Distinguished Service Cross awarded by President Roosevelt and had memorized the citation that came to him in both the Russian and English languages and bearing FDR's signature. He asked us to carry back a message to the President, which he dictated through an interpreter:

"You say to President Roosevelt that when I received the DSC I was deeply moved. Although it was far away he managed in some way to learn about my military successes and he gave me this decoration to repay me for them. I wish for President Roosevelt many years of life and successful work for democracy."

By February 1, I was back in liberated Warsaw, and a little less than two months later, I had a chance, in Washington, to talk privately with President Roosevelt and to tell him, so soon after the Yalta conference, of my own experiences in Russia and more recently in Poland. I had not seen the President since mid-1943 and the visible evidence of his physical decline was obvious during those few minutes in the White House oval office. I, who treasured him as a friend as well as a President, would never see him alive again.

CHAPTER
10

I finally persuaded the *Times* to let me leave Moscow, without waiting for the arrival of Cy Sulzberger who had a visa but who kept putting off his own trip into Russia. Once again, Cy was trying over Soviet objections to establish the principle that the *Times* was entitled to two correspondents in Russia, and once again this battle was being fought at my expense. Just as I had waited in London to get a visa to Moscow while Cy carried on the same losing battle, now I was waiting to go home.

Finally, in desperation I telephoned my managing editor, Edwin L. James, in New York and he consented to my departure at once without waiting for Cy. There was a special American plane about to leave that would take me directly home to Washington, and I had long ago befriended this crew when they came to Moscow on an earlier special mission. This time they were there to deliver the ashes of Soviet Ambassador Oumansky, who had been killed recently in an air crash in Mexico.

As we headed out of Moscow for Teheran, the big C-54 transport also carried John Hersey of Time-Life and nine American prisoners of war who had recently made their way to Moscow from eastern Germany. It was to be a record flight, fifty-six hours and nine minutes to Washington via Teheran, Cairo, Casablanca, and the Azores.

In Washington, I learned that my draft board had canceled my essential occupation classification. But Mr. James hadn't informed me before I left Moscow. I had a day-long series of physical tests and the doctors found that my feet were unquestionably flat and I was unfit for infantry service.

Arthur Krock decided to send me to the United Nations organizing conference in San Francisco, where my experiences in the Soviet Union and Poland might be helpful. The political fate and independence of a new Polish government was very much an issue in the Western world then, and it was possible I could make a contribution to the *Times'* coverage of the U.N. meetings in San Francisco.

But after only a few days back in the United States, I found myself unhappy at the thought of remaining in my own country while the war was still going on. The war in Europe was coming to an end and the fighting in the Pacific, then in progress on Iwo Jima, was moving toward a climax. I won assignment to a *Times* team covering the war from Admiral Chester Nimitz' theater with headquarters based on Guam.

Before I left I talked to President Roosevelt and James Forrestal, then the Secretary of the Navy. Forrestal provided me with letters of introduction to his top Navy commanders.

On Easter Sunday, April 1, 1945, I headed west for San Francisco. Admiral Nimitz' forces on that day made an amphibious landing on the island of Okinawa.

Frankly, it was the first time I had ever heard of Okinawa, an island I was to know almost inch by inch before the eighty-two days of fighting for it were over. The conversion of the island into a vast and unsinkable aircraft carrier on which big B-29 bombers could be launched against the Japanese home islands was a crucial factor in our ending the war in the Pacific when we did.

Our final stop (for twenty-four hours) in the continental United States was San Francisco, where Mayor Roger Lapham was getting ready to act as host to diplomats from around the world at the U.N. founding sessions. Lapham, in his sixties, bright and blue-eyed and full of the perpetual enthusiasm of youth, had been a highly successful steamship operator who had engaged in rough and tumble public debate with the radical Australian-born Harry Bridges, leader of the International Longshoremen's Union. Later, Lapham had been made a member of the War Labor Board and it was in that capacity that I had met him.

I had left Washington on short notice, and had not obtained an adequate supply of hard-to-get Scotch. During my day in San Francisco, I lunched with Lapham at the Pacific Union Club on Nob Hill. I asked him where I might be able to buy a case of Scotch.

Lapham said he had acquired a considerable reserve, which would be necessary when the diplomats came to town. He agreed to sell me a case from his own cellar. I carried the whiskey out to the airport in the mayor's automobile.

When the aircraft crew found out my large box contained Scotch, they readily agreed to load it on the plane, and thus supplied, we headed west out over the Pacific to Pearl Harbor, where it had all begun with the Japanese sneak attack three and one-half years earlier.

I was a new boy in an old war, and I needed to get acquainted quickly with the Army, Navy, and Air commanders who made and carried out the big decisions here.

My letters from Secretary Forrestal would help, but I needed even better contacts than they would provide initially. The Air Force lent me a small apartment during my brief visit in Hawaii, and I was soon contacted by *The Honolulu Advertiser*, which wanted to send out a reporter to interview me.

Because I was so recently returned from Moscow, the big question in the Pacific zone was, "Will the Russians enter the war against Japan one day?"

I didn't really *know* the answer, but thought I had some clues after the Big Three meeting at Yalta. Also, as a result of my long stay in Moscow, including off-the-record talks with Soviet Deputy Foreign Minister Litvinov, I was able to assemble some guesses.

I told the Honolulu reporter I was sure Russia would enter the Pacific battle once the Germans had been defeated. I observed that Russia now had a non-aggression treaty with Japan, which was due to expire soon. And I said that I thought the first clear-cut test of Soviet intentions might come if and when she renounced renewal of that treaty with the Japanese.

Quite honestly, I had no idea when or whether that event might take place, though it was a reasonable conjecture. But only that.

My interview forecasting Russian entry into the Pacific war was front-paged the next morning in Honolulu. It was read with some interest in military circles around the island, especially in the intelligence community.

At noon of the same day, the Russians in Moscow gave formal notice to the Japanese that they were renouncing their non-aggression treaty. It was an unbelievable coincidence, and a great break for me.

Suddenly, and undeservedly, I was no longer a new boy, but rather an expert on the Pacific war. The telephone at my apartment at the air base rang constantly. One military leader after another wanted an opportunity for him and his intelligence staff to talk with me.

One invitation came from former Governor Harold E. Stassen of Minnesota, who had resigned to join the Navy, and now was serving as "flag secretary" for Admiral William E. (Bull) Halsey, the colorful and controversial commander of the Third Fleet. Commander Stassen wondered if I would lunch with Admiral Halsey's staff at Pearl Harbor?

This was exactly the opportunity I had hoped for, and I leaped at the chance to meet Admiral Halsey and get acquainted with his officers. Bull Halsey gave me my first orders in the Pacific.

"Take off that necktie," he commanded when I showed up in a smart tropical-weight war correspondent's uniform the next day. "This is no-tie country west of Pearl Harbor, and you might get started right now."

Thanks to my lucky guess about Soviet intentions, I made some friends that day who were to be quite useful in the next few months before the war in the Pacific was brought to its climax by the atomic bomb. One of the groups I met with was an intelligence outfit called JIGPOA (an alphabetical concoction that meant Joint Intelligence Group, Pacific Ocean Area) whose members included some ex-Washington newsmen like James Free of *The Chicago Sun.*

When I got to Guam, I found the forward fleet headquarters of Admiral Nimitz and the GHQ for Army Air Force heavy bombers commanded by General Curtis ("The Cigar") LeMay, whose only concern was "bombs on the target."

LeMay had recently undertaken what appeared to be a dangerous experiment, bombing Japanese cities from B-29s at very low levels. It would have been suicidal over German cities, but it worked against the Japanese. God knows we needed it because at high altitude the bombers had missed their targets completely, even when the targets were large cities. Now with the recently developed napalm bombs, a fleet of bombers at low level could wipe out large areas of any Japanese city made of wood and paper.

I had been on Guam only a few days when my *Times* superior, Bruce Rae, asked if I would like to fly a low-level mission with the B-29s. It was to be the second fire-bombing attack upon Tokyo itself.

I will not pretend that I had no misgivings about undertaking such an assignment, but I had been so long in Russia, so long a war correspondent without hearing a gun fired that I now thought to myself that Rae's suggestion provided the test I needed of my own courage and willingness to undertake the risks any war correspondent ought to face.

So I said yes, and negotiations were started with LeMay's Twentieth Air Force for me to fly on the long twelve-hour mission on one of the B-29s based on Guam itself.

While we waited, the news came from Warm Springs, Georgia, that President Roosevelt had died and Vice President Harry S Truman had succeeded him. I hadn't known Truman well while I covered the Senate, and I could not have been more wrong about his capabilities. My first fear was that without Roosevelt we might still lose the war. But Truman took over smoothly and we never faltered on the road to final victory.

My first bombing mission against the Japanese home islands left Guam on the evening of April 13. I flew with a B-29 group commanded by Brigadier General Thomas S. Powers. Our goal was Tokyo and this was only the second of the low-level attacks carried out against the Japanese capital. The Guam-Tokyo round trip took about twelve hours and I flew that night in a super-fortress bearing the name *City of Binghamton*, home town of the aircraft commander, Captain Joseph J. Semanek. This was a large attack of approximately 350 airplanes. I flew in one of the last aircraft to reach the target, perhaps one hour after the bombing had begun.

Captain Semanek, his crew, and I enjoyed a routine and smooth flight as we droned across the Pacific from the Mariana Island group toward Mount Fuji, a landmark that served as a guiding point for the aircraft homing in on Tokyo.

As we swept in over Tokyo Bay after midnight, fires set by the earlier planes were visible for miles and a heavy cloud of smoke hung over the target.

Approximately eighty Japanese searchlights swept back and forth across the sky seeking us out. Just as we came in over the target, at about 6,000 feet, the searchlights found us and we were illuminated by a searchlight cone for ninety seconds.

When our bomb-bay doors came open to release our cargo of napalm fire bombs, our speed was slowed to 200 miles an hour. As the bombs dropped, we were hit by anti-aircraft shells three times just before we flew into the heavy cloud of ascending black smoke.

I was standing in the nose of the B-29 as Captain Semanek kept the aircraft on a steady, straight course until the bombs were dropped. Just after we were hit, we were caught in a thermal updraft that suddenly jolted us upward perhaps 2,000 feet.

The incendiaries dropped by the airplanes ahead of us looked like millions of fireflies as they neared the ground. In a few seconds, fire spread among the dry wooden buildings of the densely populated capital, and a few minutes later, the entire city seemed to be consumed by red flames.

There was a stiff breeze blowing, and though our aiming point was well away from Emperor Hirohito's palace, the fires roared through Tokyo in that direction and actually burned structures on the palace grounds.

We burned approximately eighteen square miles of Tokyo that night. To me, who had never seen a fire raid before, it looked like all the lumberyard fires I had ever seen put together.

Once the bombs had dropped, we moved through the smoke cloud and turned back out over Tokyo Bay. Captain Semanek and his crew began to assess the damage to our plane from antiaircraft fire.

The bomb-bay doors had been damaged and would not close when the hydraulic switch was thrown. This created a major drag and slowed our air speed so much that we couldn't fly the 1,500 miles back to our home base.

We had two possible alternatives: Ditch in the Pacific some distance out from Tokyo in an area regularly patrolled by American submarines waiting to rescue the crews of downed aircraft. This would be a hazardous but not necessarily fatal undertaking since many crews had been saved after exactly the same maneuver. The other possibility, if the damage was not too great, was to fly back to Iwo Jima, the island recently captured at such heavy cost. There were airfields on Iwo Jima on which a B-29 could make an emergency landing.

Between the cockpit of a B-29 and its bomb-carrying compartment was a long tunnel through which one could crawl wearing his parachute and rubber life vest. I crawled back to inspect the damage.

As we flew east over Tokyo Bay, one of the crew members volunteered to be lowered on a rope to see if he could help force the closing of the bomb-bay doors. Down he went, and bracing his feet against the fuselage, he managed to pull the bomb-bay doors until they closed. We made it home without further incident.

A few days after the raid on Tokyo, I was sent to Okinawa.

Marines and soldiers battled side by side to clear this Japanese island, which our commanders had decided would provide magnificent airfields for basing more heavy bombers to carry on the air war against Japan.

The Japanese resisted fiercely and we paid a high price in dead and wounded men and damaged ships. This was the closest we had come yet to the Japanese home islands and it provided the final days of glory for the *Kamikaze* corps of pilots who dove their bomb-laden aircraft into American ships.

Navy men called the air route of the attacking Japanese aircraft "Bogey Highway." A thin picket line of destroyers and destroyer escorts stood in an arc around our anchorage to detect the approaching Japanese and warn the fleet and the transports crowded into Hagushi anchorage on the western approaches to Okinawa. Most of the Japanese suicide attacks were made in the half-light of early dawn or evening and the ships in the anchorage "made smoke" by puffing out dark layers of smoke from their engines to cover the ships as they lay at anchor.

Soon the picket line became the main battleground for the suicide aircraft, and the little ships bore the brunt of the attacks that might better have been directed in full force against the supply ships that lay at anchor on the eastern and western sides of Okinawa.

It was one of the grave disadvantages of the Japanese *Kamikazes* that their pilots were destined to die without ever having a chance to report their success or failure. If the Imperial Headquarters had only known how well their suicide pilots were succeeding, they might have expended even more aircraft and men against our fleet.

As it was, Japanese air attacks sunk twenty-eight of our ships and damaged another 225 big and little ships ranging from battleships down to destroyer escorts during the battle of Okinawa. Even a well-lighted hospital ship was purposely rammed by a

Japanese bomber in total violation of the Geneva conventions, bringing death to men already wounded and to medical corpsmen as well.

It has been estimated that more than 1,000 U.S. naval personnel were killed or wounded in these battles at sea.

The Japanese lost about 1,900 aircraft, most of them flown by suicide pilots. It was a last desperate gasp by a nation that was losing the war and could ill afford to sacrifice so many trained pilots, but it was terribly expensive for the United States too.

On the ground, the main line of Japanese resistance was the Naha-Shuri-Yonaburu line. Our progress was slow into this heavily fortified mountain terrain, honeycombed with caves which gave shelter to an enemy that had decided to die rather than surrender.

We took few prisoners on Okinawa, and the enemy took even fewer. But I remember the Roman holiday atmosphere surrounding the capture of one Japanese taken alive from a cave who agreed to talk if we would allow him to marry the woman who had hidden out with him and been taken prisoner at the same time. At the XXIVth Corps, a Japanese shrine was erected and a marriage ceremony performed while the fighting went on in other parts of the island. Then the Japanese and his new wife had a one-night honeymoon before the intensive questioning began. The naval censors kept this story out of print all during the war. It would have enraged the families of men who had been killed or wounded on Okinawa.

Finally, an end run by the Marines broke the Naha-Shuri-Yonaburu line. Marines, led by one of their most decorated heroes, Colonel Chester (Chesty) Puller, staged an amphibious landing in the Naha area that brought us in behind the enemy and forced his retreat. Through some mistake, the Navy's press boat, satirically called the "U.S.S. Never Run," had put me ashore ahead of Puller's troops and I was waiting on the beach when he came wading ashore along with Homer Bigart, my rival of the New York *Herald Tribune.* Bigart and I saw a lot of action together on Okinawa, and later in the Korean War of 1950, and I never knew a better war correspondent.

Even after the main line cracked, Japanese defenders had to be blasted out of cave after cave before the island could be secured safely. Sometimes on mountains that contained many caves, our aircraft would literally spray a hill with napalm and we would ignite it with a well-placed phosphorus shell. The GIs called these "Jap

Barbecues" and they certainly were an easier way to eliminate the enemy than the costly cave-by-cave approach.

From the time we landed on April 1 until the island was declared secure eighty-two days later, the Japanese were without hope of victory, reenforcements, or rescue, but they fought down to the last inch of dirt on the southern tip of the island. Many of the highest officers committed *hara-kari* in the final hours.

One week before Okinawa was secured, the psychological warfare experts tried a one-hour cease-fire to persuade the Japanese soldiers to surrender. It was only a limited success. We had dropped thousands of leaflets in the Japanese language setting a time for the cease-fire and urging surrender. Similar messages had been broadcast from low-flying aircraft by Japanese-speaking American officers.

I watched the exercise from the most forward position of the Seventh Division front below Gushican on June 17, an observation post that gave me a good look at the Army and Marine front-line positions as well. The cease-fire was in effect only on the Seventh Division front; elsewhere the fighting went ahead with undiminished fervor.

The cease-fire was signaled by five red smoke shells streaking across the sky leaving long trails as they fell back to earth, and, at that moment, every rifle, every machine gun, every artillery piece controlled by the Seventh Division stopped. Our troops took cover behind rocks. The Japanese soldiers milled about during this unexpected period of quiet. Japanese fire dropped, but did not cease entirely.

When the hour was up, the fighting resumed full scale, and the experiment, to put it bluntly, was far from successful. Fewer than a dozen Japanese surrendered.

When the fighting resumed, the Seventh Division went back to the kind of warfare that Colonel John M. (Mickey) Finn, commanding the Thirty-second Regiment, said was measurable only in terms of "so many rocks—so many more Japs."

"Until they are all dead or captured, there will be no rest for us," Colonel Finn said. "Those damned people just aren't human. They are beaten so badly, but they won't quit. They are in those caves and behind those rocks, determined to hold us up if they can until they are killed. We have got to go out and kill them, but, damn it, they are killing and wounding too many of my people as we do it."

The Japanese were blasted out of the caves by grenades and

demolition charges and rifle fire of American foot soldiers. Many of the cave mouths I visited were bloodstained. Occasionally, one could hear the moaning of the wounded inside before the cave mouth was sealed with a demolition charge.

Cries from the wounded were sometimes a trap by the Japanese to bring an American soldier into the caves. Helping them was entirely too dangerous; we let the Japanese die where they were.

The day before the island was declared secure, all the correspondents agreed to take a holiday. We begged some beer from a Seabee battalion, packed a lunch from the flagship mess, and set off in the press boat for the northern end of the island where the fighting had ceased. It was a day of total and complete relaxation as we swam in a quiet cove, ate our food, drank our beer.

As we made our way back to the flagship, we were met at the top of the ship's ladder by naval officers with the news that the Okinawan commander, Lieutenant General Simon B. Buckner, had been killed at the front that afternoon. He had been killed by a piece of rock blasted in his direction by an exploding Japanese artillery shell. We scurried to cover the story, interviewing some of the general's aides who had been with him when the Tenth Army commander fell on the eve of victory.

We had moved so slowly on Okinawa, and the Japanese had resisted so fiercely, it seemed that the Pacific war would last for many more bloody months and perhaps even for years.

After the Okinawa battle ended, I cabled the *Times*:

(1) The war with Japan may well last for years, instead of months as some optimists hope. However soon it is won the cost in life, blood and money will be high.

(2) Final victory over the Japanese can be achieved only by ground action. Large-scale bombing and fleet action unquestionably will reduce the enemy's power of resistance, but when his soldiers and sailors hole up in caves as they did on this island, they can be flushed out and killed only by foot soldiers supported by tank and flame throwers.

(3) There is virtually no evidence that the will to resist of the average Japanese soldier is weakening. The record number of prisoners taken in the final days of this campaign can be considered only a minor gain for our psychological warfare efforts when it is measured against the unabated fanaticism with which the enemy fought.

Because the war in Europe had ended, I was worried about any letup at home that might reduce full-scale concentration on the battles that seemed to be ahead of us in the Pacific.

My dispatch ended: "There are too many crosses in the seven divisional cemeteries on Okinawa to say that disposing of the Japanese is a one-handed job requiring only a 50 percent home-front effort now that Germany is out of the way."

While Okinawa was still being fought over, we made one more small amphibious landing in the far Pacific—on little Iheya Island, only 310 miles from the Japanese home islands. It was to be our last landing of the Japanese war, but we didn't know it then. I watched from a propeller-driven observation aircraft as the Marines stormed ashore on the morning of June 3, standing up as they moved forward. There was no opposition from the Japanese troops we had assumed would be on the island.

It took only a day and a half to search the tiny island and Colonel Clarence R. Wallace of Manitou, Colorado, the regimental commander, declared the island secure. From a nearby island, 156 Japanese soldiers watched the assault on Iheya, then took to boats themselves and rowed over to surrender.

As the campaign for Okinawa ended, General MacArthur and his top advisors, along with experts from Admiral Nimitz' staff and from the heavy bombers, were planning an amphibious assault for the fall of 1945 on the Japanese island of Kyushu. The island was the southernmost of the three main Japanese home islands.

After the Okinawa campaign, it was assumed that the Japanese would resist even more strongly on Kyushu. Intelligence officers estimated our casualties might be half a million in dead and wounded, and that there would have to be other landings on Honshu, where Tokyo lay. Eventually, we would have to deal with the Japanese Army on the main islands, preferably with help from the Red Army. We had learned that little could be expected from the armies of Chiang Kai-shek, who demanded much but made little effort in the common cause of defeating Japan.

Preparations for the big landings went forward. Marines and Army troops trained on many forward bases, but few of us in the Pacific knew that we were approaching success at home in the costly $2,000,000,000 "crash" program to build an atomic bomb. We didn't know what an atomic bomb was, and probably would have laughed at any scientific explanation of the theory. Our war was about to end, but we didn't know it.

CHAPTER

11

Air power—launched from land and aircraft carriers—won the battle of Japan even before the atomic bombs. But we didn't know it, and neither did the Japanese highest authorities, including the Emperor.

The first air strike against Japan by the tiny force of carrier-based bombers led by James A. (Jimmy) Doolittle in 1942 was more psychological than military. Doolittle's raiders did little damage to Tokyo, and none of the airplanes were able to fly safely to their bases in western China as had been hoped.

When the B-29s began their missions from China, and later from the Marianas, they flew at high altitudes—up to 30,000 feet—and encountered extremely stiff winds in the jet stream. Flying against the wind, the bomber would have been a sitting duck for anti-aircraft fire. With the jet stream, the aircraft speed was too great for accurate bombing.

Before General LeMay gambled with the low-level raids, I had heard that fewer than 10 percent of our bombs hit their targets.

But the Japanese people and cities were easy targets of destruction when the big bombers came in low with their cargoes of incendiary bombs. It was destruction on a scale never experienced by any other nation in history. Our own losses, in men and aircraft, were very small when compared with the heavy cost of land warfare.

From November 24, 1944, through the end of the war, the B-29s based in the Marianas flew 318 missions on which approximately 159,000 tons of bombs were dropped. Their targets were sixty-four Japanese industrial areas with a combined population of 21,200,000.

According to Air Force statistics, the incendiary attacks burned out 157.98 square miles of Japanese urban industrial areas and left dead or homeless an estimated 8,480,000 persons. Tokyo itself suffered under six heavy low-level fire-bombing attacks, and these left in ashes 50.8 square miles.

At the end of the war, our Air Force was composed of approximately 1,000 aircraft and about 10,000 men—and it was about to be doubled in size by a new force of B-29s being readied for use from Okinawan bases commanded by General Doolittle.

The last mission I flew with the B-29s against Japan was on July 29, 1945. It was unusual in several respects. First of all, it was the only mission in this war in which the B-29s carried a full ten-ton load of bombs from their bases in the Marianas, landed on Iwo Jima with their bomb load, refueled, and then took off again to hit a target at the northernmost end of Honshu Island. It was the deepest penetration of the Japanese home islands.

The most unusual feature of the raid was that LeMay told the enemy well in advance that our target, Aomori, was one of several Japanese cities that we proposed to destroy by fire bombing that night.

It was a big strike for the psychological warfare planners. Several hours before we hit Aomori, Japanese-language radio broadcasts and leaflets printed in Japanese announced the raids.

Never before in the history of warfare had an enemy been notified in advance that bombers would hit certain of their cities. The Japanese probably thought it was a trick and no efforts were made to evacuate the cities. LeMay listed twice as many cities as were hit that night by the B-29s, reasoning that after the first attacks Japanese workers would flee from any city on the target list whether that city actually was bombed or not.

On the Aomori raid, we took off from Tinian and flew into Iwo on the afternoon of July 28 along with more than sixty other superforts.

I still get nervous thinking about that landing on Iwo with ten tons of firebombs in the belly of the airplane in which I was riding. But we landed safely, and so did all the other planes in the group headed for Aomori.

Toward dusk, we took off from Iwo and headed north and west into a setting sun. Out of Iwo, we had the aircraft radio tuned in to the music broadcast by the U.S. armed forces radio when suddenly there was an interruption and the advance warning was given by LeMay. Aomori was listed first. The fliers had not known about LeMay's plans. They were surprised, disturbed, and angry with LeMay.

"Old LeMay has a lot of guts, sitting in Guam and telling the Japanese fighters we are on our way," said one airman bitterly.

I did my best to explain to the crew the psychological reasons behind LeMay's gamble, but I fear I did not satisfy them. Some frankly doubted my own sanity in undertaking the mission after I had been told it would be announced in advance.

Our fears proved unfounded. We came in over Aomori after midnight, a port city on Honshu's northernmost tip, 365 miles northeast of Tokyo, at a 250-mile-an-hour clip. We were led in by fires started by the lead aircraft that had been visible to us when we were still thirty miles away from the target.

If the Japanese expected us, they had no effective means of counterattack. We encountered no enemy fighters. We were fired on from land- and ship-based anti-aircraft guns, but were not hit.

It was a vivid demonstration to the Japanese populace that their military leaders could not protect them even when warned in advance.

We bombed at will, and hit all our targets, including the great yards, which turned out ships for Japan's shrinking merchant marine. The port area from which ferries plied the waters north to Hokkaido Island was leveled and made useless to the Japanese for the rest of the war. Warehouses containing precious food reserves for the Japanese military forces and civilian population were burned out.

We didn't lose a single aircraft on this mission and demonstrated beyond challenge our mastery of the skies above Japan, our ability to reach anywhere into the Japanese military-industrial complex.

For the crew flying the long mission back to Tinian, there was an exuberant feeling because we had hit the enemy and scored heavily even after we had tipped our attack in advance.

Now the stage was set for the use of the atomic bomb that had been secretly manufactured and tested in the desert flats of New Mexico in that same month.

With the war in Europe over, President Truman, Marshal Stalin, and two British Prime Ministers—Winston Churchill and Clement Attlee—had given the Japanese a final warning to surrender from their meeting place at Potsdam, Germany, in July, 1945. (The British were double-teamed at Potsdam because that summit conference took place during British elections, in which the victorious war leader, Churchill, was beaten at the polls.) The Japanese did not heed the warning. Nor would they, I think, have paid any more attention even if we had demonstrated the bomb on a Pacific island, which had been advocated by those opposing the use of a nuclear bomb against people and cities.

Even with hindsight, I have never joined those who criticize Truman because he ordered the attacks on Hiroshima and Nagasaki. There are those scientists and others who argue now and who argued before the bomb was dropped that use of the atomic bomb was immoral. Some contend it was unnecessary. I am not one of this group. Perhaps I am not because I would have been reporting the invasion of the Japanese home islands in a very few weeks. All of us who had been on Okinawa had no doubt that the casualties on Kyushu would be enormous, and that there would have to be other landings after Kyushu before the Japanese could be persuaded to surrender.

I think the atomic bomb provided the dramatic "excuse" that the Japanese Emperor needed to hurry his surrender, which may already have been inevitable but which would not necessarily have come swiftly enough to avert the Kyushu landings. Indeed, the war might have been protracted by the very act of landing on the Japanese home islands. The Japanese already had proved on Okinawa that they would fight almost to the last man rather than surrender.

Emperor Hirohito's offer to surrender came after the Nagasaki bomb went off on August 9, but it was not the unconditional surrender that Roosevelt and Churchill had envisaged in their declaration at Casablanca. The Japanese specified, and we agreed, that the authority of their Emperor would not be impaired. I was on Guam when this news came, a few hours after the Soviet Union formally had declared war on Japan.

There was nothing conditional about the GI reaction to the conditional Japanese offer. Our troops in the Pacific, getting ready for the assault on the home islands, literally went wild with joy. On Okinawa, men jumped to their anti-aircraft guns and machine guns and filled the sky with tracer bullets and bursting shells in a fireworks display unequaled at even the biggest American Fourth of July celebration. There were a few American casualties from this uncontrolled firing of weapons as shrapnel fell back to earth from exploding anti-aircraft shells. It took forty minutes for senior officers to get control of the situation and halt the firing.

One private, Tom Zuffelato of Torrington, Connecticut, summed up the reaction of every GI: "I got goose bumps all over."

The nuclear war age began on Monday, August 6, 8:15 A.M. Japanese time, when a super-fortress bearing the name *Enola Gay*, piloted by Captain Paul W. Tibbetts, Jr., of Miami, Florida, dropped a single bomb over the city of Hiroshima. It came floating toward earth on a parachute, and at about 1,900 feet above ground, it exploded with a blinding flash and a surge of power equal to 20,000 tons of TNT.

In a fraction of a second, perhaps 80,000 persons were killed or fatally wounded, and others suffered from burns and blasts that would mar them for life. Eighty to 90 percent of all the buildings in the city were destroyed by blast or fire. It was the mightiest blast man had ever set off in war. But even after this bomb went off, Emperor Hirohito hesitated to surrender unconditionally.

Three days later, at about noon on August 9, a second and even more powerful type of bomb was used against the port city of Nagasaki, killing perhaps 25,000 persons.

I got my first view of Nagasaki from a converted B-17 flying over the city on August 27 with a group of newspaper and radio correspondents assigned to the Strategic Air Force bomb damage survey.

Our flight to Nagasaki was made in that strange period between Emperor Hirohito's offer to surrender and the actual acceptance of that surrender on September 3 by General MacArthur on the deck of the battleship *Missouri* in Tokyo Bay. Technically, we were still at war and occasionally one of our airplanes was fired at.

From the air, the damage done Nagaski seemed almost unbelievable. In peacetime, Nagasaki's buildings had been jammed so closely together that it looked from the air like a sea of roofs.

I ad-libbed my report to the *Times* into a microphone as our aircraft circled Nagasaki, and my military censor, Lieutenant

Colonel Hubert Schneider, an intelligence officer based on Guam, sat close beside me to listen to my report. There were no military secrets that could be given away from an eyewitness description anyway, so Colonel Schneider actually assisted me in framing the report by providing military intelligence descriptions of Nagasaki's appearance before it had been hit.

A portion of my report to the *Times* sent by radio direct from the plane said:

> This correspondent, who has seen the worst damaged cities of Russia and Poland, was stunned by the sight of Nagasaki below him. About 50 percent of the town seemed to have been completely wiped out, and the destruction in that area was worse than any the writer had seen in Stalingrad or Warsaw.
>
> An arms factory is nothing but a mass of twisted girders. The wooden tinderbox houses which were jammed eaves to eaves have disappeared and all that remains are fragments that from a plane look about the size of match sticks. . . .
>
> On the sides of a rugged, tree-covered hill close behind Nagasaki whole sections of forest have been burned off.
>
> The winding Urakami River flows almost exactly through the center of the destroyed area. It was clear from the view we have had today that it [the river] was no barrier to the spread of fire and destruction.

When we first approached Nagasaki, there was not a single sign of life. As we circled for more than an hour, people came running into the streets and looking at our airplane as it passed back and forth over the city.

Down in the harbor area, we spotted a prisoner of war camp, which was not on any of our maps. We flew in low, dumping some food supplies we had aboard. The prisoners were shouting and waving their arms, and one group waved a tricolor emblem of the Netherlands.

The camp was in the middle of the great Mitsubishi arms works, a type of location expressly forbidden by the Geneva conventions. Eight prisoners died in the bomb blast, but another 200 Netherlands, British, Australian, and Indochinese captives escaped.

Two days after the Nagasaki trip, and while we still awaited orders that would allow us to go into Japan, we flew another unauthorized "armistice" mission to Shanghai and mistakenly landed our four-engined converted bomber on a highway near the city.

In this period of "war, no war," we decided to gamble that the Japanese wouldn't shoot at us or harm us if we landed. After our first landing on the highway, Japanese officers persuaded us to take off again and to land properly on a Japanese military airfield not far away. There we found it sticky going for a while, because the Japanese would not allow us to leave the airfield and proceed to the center of Shanghai as we wished.

Everything had started off splendidly and we thought we were doing fine. When we made the landing at the military field, we were met by a shining blue Chrysler automobile and driven to the headquarters of Major Nakamura, the field commandant, whose interpreter gave the name Lieutenant Hashimoto. On arrival at the major's headquarters we were served some chilled Japanese cider, which tasted faintly like cream soda.

We asked for transportation into Shanghai but Lieutenant Hashimoto kept mentioning some vague Japanese committee which he said desired to talk with us.

Hour after hour went by and still we sat on the airfield. The "committee" had not arrived. Lieutenant Hashimoto was meticulously polite, hissing through his big gold teeth, but each moment of delay there meant less opportunity to see Shanghai.

Finally we told Lieutenant Hashimoto that it was our purpose to go into Shanghai at once, and that his committee could find us if they wanted at the Metropole Hotel. There was another telephone call to the "committee" and Lieutenant Hashimoto came back to tell us, politely but plainly, that the formal Japanese surrender had not yet been signed, that a state of war still existed between our two countries, and that it was therefore necessary for us to wait at the airfield for the "committee."

At about this moment, an automobile pulled up outside the dingy office where we sat and four white-jacketed Chinese began to remove silver tureens of soup, covered dishes of other food, and quantities of china, glasses, and flatware. It turned out to be a four-course meal topped by steak so tender you could cut it with a fork. It had been cooked for us at the Japanese Army headquarters in the Astor House in downtown Shanghai and then brought to the airfield.

While we were eating and drinking, Lieutenant Hashimoto got another telephone call from the "committee," and he came

to the table to tell us we could now go into Shanghai. We thought
we were headed for the Metropole Hotel, but we wound up instead
at the Astor House, and the "committee," it developed, was the
Japanese General Headquarters. Japanese officers said flatly that
we were not free to move around the city without their consent
and protection. Our escort, Colonel John R. McCrary of New
York, argued for our release, and while he was still talking, the
correspondents simply slipped away, jumped into a car driven
by a Chinese, and headed for the Metropole Hotel. The Japanese
let us go without further argument.

At the Metropole, we found out we were the third American
airplane to land in Shanghai since the Emperor had surrendered.
The first two brought members of an American military mission
from Chungking to supervise the removal of American military
and civilian prisoners of war.

The word of our presence in the Metropole spread swiftly along
the grapevine, and English-speaking residents of many countries
poured in to tell us their stories. One of them took us to a huge
concentration camp at Chapei where there were approximately
3,000 Allied prisoners, including approximately 1,500 Americans.
One of them was the son of a colleague, Sir Wilmot Lewis,
Washington correspondent for *The Times* of London, and I sent
him a cable from Okinawa telling him that his son was alive and
well in Shanghai.

Most of these civilians were thin and undernourished, but all were
so happy at the prospect of freedom and rehabilitation that nothing
else mattered this evening.

The small band of correspondents walked the streets of Shanghai
surrounded by thousands of Chinese, but after our initial difficulties
we had no further trouble with the Japanese.

The city was almost undamaged and its shops were jammed with
consumer goods such as textiles, clothing, shoes, and even Scotch.
Prices in Shanghai currency were stratospheric, but an American
dollar brought a huge premium. Scotch was in short supply all over
the world, including Scotland, in 1945, but I managed to pick up
a case of pre-war Haig and Haig in Shanghai for 9,000,000
Shanghai dollars, or about $90 American.

We had a big party at the Metropole that night, drank a lot of
whiskey, and made some new friends. The crew especially had a
big night, and early the next morning, paid a striking farewell salute
to a White Russian countess by flying past the windows of her

third-story apartment on one of Shanghai's main streets. It was a bit breathtaking, but Captain Magnan was a good flier and we trusted him.

At the prison camp, we had laboriously copied down the names of literally thousands of prisoners, and these we radioed to American authorities as soon as we got back to Okinawa. Over at General MacArthur's headquarters at Manila, there was considerable official displeasure because we had gone into Shanghai without permission.

Once the Japanese quit bothering us, we were in the curious position in Shanghai of having been almost the last prisoners of war taken by the Japanese, and to the men and women in the prison camps, we certainly were welcome liberators.

C H A P T E R
1 2

On Okinawa, we were worried that we might not get a quick clearance to go to Japan from MacArthur's command, which had been given full authority to handle the surrender.

Our group was accredited to the Strategic Air Force, and we sought help from General James Doolittle, who had just arrived on Okinawa from the European theater and who would have led his Eighth Air Force heavy bombers against Japan if the war had continued.

Over a drink one night, in one of those Okinawa burial grounds found on nearly every hill, we asked General Doolittle to help plead our case with MacArthur's top commanders.

Doolittle explained that newcomers to the Pacific war weren't particularly influential with MacArthur's people. But he would try to help us.

Our misgivings proved to be exaggerated. Our two converted B-17 transports were among the first two dozen aircraft to touch down on Atsugi airfield near Yokohama when the American troop landings began. We were lucky because we not only had our own transport, but one of the planes had radio facilities with which we could transmit directly to the United States. We even had our own censor, Colonel Schneider, and we were able to make our own way from place to place without worrying about MacArthur's public relations office.

On August 28, 1945, at Atsugi airfield, General MacArthur arrived. He came down the ramp from his four-engined air transport *The Bataan*, puffing on his old corncob pipe. Meeting MacArthur was General Robert Eichelberger. MacArthur said it had been a long road from Melbourne in Australia to Tokyo "but this seems to be the end of the road."

That night, we commandeered a few dilapidated wood-burning cars and drove into Tokyo itself, walking around the Emperor's palace grounds and stopping for a drink at the Imperial Hotel before visiting Radio Tokyo.

As Air Force correspondents, our interests primarily were in the war that had been waged from the air. No story was of more importance than a visit to Hiroshima. But, correspondents were supposed to remain within the area occupied by American troops, and this was a small area indeed. However, we were determined to get to Hiroshima ahead of other correspondents, and we made our move by air on September 2, the day MacArthur accepted the Japanese surrender in formal ceremonies aboard the battleship *Missouri* in Tokyo Bay.

With Captain Magnan at the controls, we took off in one of the B-17s from Atsugi about the time that the official party was heading for the surrender ceremonies.

In the Hiroshima area, we spotted one usable airfield at the Japanese naval base of Kure. Japanese personnel crowded around the plane as it rolled to a stop, and fortunately we met some English-speaking American-born Japanese who had returned to the land of their ancestors just before war had begun. We told them we wanted to go to Hiroshima, and they managed to find us automobiles that would carry us twelve miles into the city.

Our Japanese guides had been in Kure the day the bomb had been dropped and they remembered a great flash of light turning to a purple mushrooming cloud followed by a great whoosh of wind. One said the trees bent almost to the ground in Kure.

As we headed for Hiroshima we did not know whether the residents would be friendly or hostile. Even worse, in our ignorance we did not have any real conception of the dangers there might be in the lingering radioactivity of the uranium bomb. It seemed a little silly even at the time, but all of the correspondents wore holstered .45-caliber automatic pistols, though we could have offered little resistance if the Japanese had decided to take revenge against us. Happily they did not. Equally happily, none of us ever showed any aftereffects from the radiation.

We were among the first few foreigners to walk in the ruins of Hiroshima and to talk with survivors on the city streets and in the hospitals, where it was estimated that approximately 100 persons still were dying daily. By that time, the Japanese said the death toll had passed 53,000 and it was predicted then that the final death toll would exceed 80,000.

Japanese doctors told us that they were helpless to treat burns caused by the intense heat of the exploding bomb and that some who had been considered only slightly injured on the day the bomb dropped later lost up to 86 percent of their white blood corpuscles, began to lose their hair, became nauseated, and finally died.

Viewed from the epicenter of the bomb blast, Hiroshima was a shocking, staggering sight, one that still haunts me. I'd seen a lot of bomb damage in Europe and more recently in Tokyo, but nothing had prepared me for this.

Much of Hiroshima had simply vanished, disintegrated from blast and heat. In the ruins from normal bombing, I was accustomed to seeing rubble, but here in the central city there was no rubble, except for a few concrete walls. And this was true of fully four square miles in a radius around the point of greatest impact. The ground had just been wiped clean, almost as if it had been gone over with a great vacuum cleaner. There were no identifying marks even for streets, except in a few places streetcar tracks remained. The trolleys were operating and the Japanese aboard them looked out at these strange Americans, the handful of correspondents, with more curiosity than hostility.

A twenty-three-year-old American-born Japanese naval lieutenant was my guide as I walked through the streets, occasionally stopping a resident to question him. One old man who was deaf recognized us as Americans and came over formally to shake hands with each of us. He then made the sign of the cross to show us that he was a Christian, and, through the intepreter, told us that all other members of his family had been killed.

It was a chilly, drizzly day. Most of the bodies had been removed, but a few remained on the outskirts, giving off the awful, sickening odor of death.

Even trees had been killed by the bomb. Birds that looked like buzzards were perched on the torn, twisted, leafless limbs.

Nobody I saw was smiling, for there was nothing here to smile about nearly a month after the Atomic Age began.

We talked with dying Japanese in the hospitals. We interviewed the doctors who were trying to cope with problems for which their medical education had not prepared them. Most of their patients were doomed to death, and they knew it.

In the later afternoon, we made our way by automobile back to Kure but it was too late by then to fly back to Tokyo that night. The correspondents, including my rival Bigart of the *Herald Tribune*, went to work on the stories we would transmit from Tokyo the next day.

When work was over, we assembled a meal from the emergency K rations we carried aboard the airplane, and invited our Japanese hosts to join us. The Japanese provided *sake*, beer, and a Scotch-type Japanese-made whiskey to drink with the food. They were friendly, and one of them kept singing "Old Black Joe." It was his favorite and the only American song he knew. We joined in discordantly.

Early the next morning, Captain Magnan crowded all of us into the nose of the B-17 so that it would lift off the short runway. We just barely made it into the air, cranking up the wheels of the plane just before they would have met the seawall at the far end of the runway.

When we got back to Tokyo, MacArthur's men were hopping mad. There was some talk we might be court-martialed for traveling outside the occupation zone and thus risking an incident with the Japanese. But to court-martial us would have meant taking action simultaneously against the most powerful news organizations —the Associated Press, the United Press, International News Service, National Broadcasting Company, Columbia Broadcasting System, American Broadcasting Company, the *Times*, and the *Herald Tribune*.

So MacArthur's men fell back on other ways to punish us. They simply cut off the supplies of gasoline that we needed to fly our planes. We countered that by getting a three-star lieutenant general, Barney Giles, flown in from Guam to requisition gasoline for us, which he did. Our job of reporting on bomb damage was considered that important by the Air Force commander, General Arnold.

CHAPTER

13

My transition to peace was not easy. Life in Washington under Truman was not as exciting or interesting as it had been when Roosevelt was President. Truman's first three years in office were not exactly his finest, once the war had ended.

As was always true while I worked for the *Times*, I returned directly to Washington from the Pacific battle area. I was never a member of the *Times*' foreign staff, but was simply on loan from Arthur Krock's Washington bureau. There was no debate about where I would be stationed once I got home. I was spared any duty in New York on the swollen, post-war city staff. Someone once remarked that the *Times*' city staff was big enough to cover the Second Coming of Christ. In short, good reporters did not find enough to do, and it was about this time that the *Times* city editor was provided with a microphone and loudspeaker so his voice could carry to the far reaches of his empire.

In the spring of 1946, the United Nations opened shop in New York City. By careful prearrangement, the *Times*' U.N. staff was not included in the city editor's domain, but made a part of the

foreign desk. The job of U.N. bureau chief long had been reserved
for Scotty Reston, who had won his Pulitzer Prize with a series
of exclusive stories on the U.N. preparatory meetings and the
debate between the great powers over the drafting of the U.N.
charter. Reston had played some role in the decision by the Rockefeller family to buy and donate the land on which U.N. headquarters was located, but when the final decision was reached to
put the U.N. in New York, Reston no longer wanted the job.

I became "acting" U.N. bureau chief when the first sessions began on the suburban campus of Hunter College, which was in the
northwest corner of the Bronx near the Hudson River and well
beyond the George Washington Bridge. I had to assemble a small
staff, recruited mostly from the city side, but we took our orders
from the foreign desk. Reston spent a good deal of time at the
U.N., writing interpretive stories or getting scoops from his own
sources in the diplomatic corps. Often Scotty and I wrote on the
same subject, but mine was the news version that usually was on
page one, and his was the analysis. Someone remarked that "Lawrence writes what happens; Reston explains what Lawrence meant."

My prize acquisition for the U.N. staff was a skinny, eager
young man from the city staff named Abe Rosenthal who had
waited in vain in the back rows of the city room for good assignments. I "borrowed" Rosenthal one day when Andrei Gromyko
took the first famous "walk" out of the U.N. and never surrendered
him back to his masters. He was a fine reporter, who won his
own Pulitzer Prize as a foreign correspondent, and about twenty
years later he came back to New York as metropolitan editor (the
new title given the old city editor's job) and a few years after
that he became managing editor.

The U.N.'s first big crisis was whether Soviet troops would
evacuate Iran now that the war was over in Europe. This was
difficult to handle since the U.N. charter obviously had been
written with a view that no action could or would be taken against
any of the Big Five permanent members—Britain, France, China,
the Soviet Union, or the United States. Unanimity was required
when any one of the Big Five was involved; there was no prospect
of action by majority rule. This was why each of the permanent
members had been given the power to veto any resolution of
the Security Council whether it involved one of the Big Five or
another member state.

But this did not prevent debate on Iran's demand that Soviet troops quit her territory—a debate led on the United States side by Secretary of State James F. Byrnes and on the Soviet side by Andrei Gromyko, then the permanent representative of the Soviet Union on the Security Council.

Jimmy Byrnes had been FDR's floor leader though he never had the formal title of majority leader. Byrnes was a master of the legislative system, and of compromise, talents that served him well in those ticklish first days of the U.N.

The Iranian case ended happily when the Soviet Union agreed to withdraw its troops, and carried out its promise. But meanwhile the Russians had been brought under the pressure of world public opinion, generated by the debate at the U.N.

During that same spring, the U.N. sought to bring the same kind of pressure to topple Generalissimo Francisco Franco as the leader of Spain, and to this end it called for an economic boycott against Spain. But the U.N. resolution, given its greatest push by Communist Poland and the Soviet Union, did not have any real teeth in it and Franco, who had been helped to power by the dead dictators Hitler and Mussolini, managed to ride out the storm. The Spanish experience was a clear indication that the U.N. could never be a very potent instrument for the settlement of world disputes beyond providing a forum for their discussion. But it was, as Winston Churchill once said, better to "jaw, jaw than to war, war."

My tour as acting U.N. bureau chief stretched into weeks and months, and it began to seem to me that I might be there forever if I did not take steps to move along to other assignments. In mid-summer, 1946, I therefore persuaded the managing editor to let me cover the "referendum" in Poland on whether its post-war parliament should have one or two houses, and whether the people of Poland approved of Polish demands for a western border of Germany that took in territories up to the Oder and Neisse rivers. My argument to Edwin James was that I had splendid news sources in the Polish government, which I had developed while a Moscow correspondent. The principal authority in the Warsaw government at that time was vested in the old Lublin Poles, though the London Poles were represented by Stanislaw Mikolajozyk, now Deputy Premier, who had been Premier of the government in exile.

Mr. James agreed I could go to Warsaw, and Thomas J. Hamilton was summoned from Washington to take over the U.N. bureau while I was away "temporarily." I never went back.

In Warsaw, a score or more of foreign correspondents had come in for the referendum, and the battered, destroyed city was ill prepared to receive them. There were about a dozen Americans and most of us wound up occupying the spare room of a suite assigned to a junior American Embassy employee. We slept on army cots that were put up every night and taken down every morning, but managed to get along well despite our cramped quarters.

I ran into my old friend and competitor of World War II days, Homer Bigart, and here I met for the first time Constantine Poulos, then a correspondent for the Overseas News Agency. Poulos and I formed a friendship that lasted through the years.

The staged referendum called simply for "yes" or "no" votes on the single-house parliament and on approving the new western boundaries. The government and the Communist party both wanted "yes" votes, so there was no doubt anywhere, anytime, that this first post-war Polish vote would be overwhelmingly in favor of the Communist regime. There was some talk of organizing an abstention campaign but the opponents of the government in power lacked access to the press and radio. They were therefore hopeless and helpless.

There was no need, therefore, to fake the referendum outcome, or to stuff the ballot boxes, but there were many rumors that the government did so. Bigart expressed the generally accepted view at the end of a long, hot day when he sat on his army cot in that sleeping room jammed with correspondents and said wearily, "My feet smell like a referendum return."

The Polonnia Hotel was not only a domicile for American diplomats, but its crowded corridors also provided the only Embassy available to the Americans in a city that had been destroyed house by house by the angry Germans inflicting revenge against the 1944 Warsaw uprising. Our Ambassador at the time, Arthur Lane, a diplomatic veteran, was so bitterly anti-Communist that he had lost all touch with what was going on in Warsaw. The Communists have always made life difficult for diplomats and correspondents, and have curtailed their ability to maintain social contacts. But Ambassador Lane, in his frustrated anger, cut himself off almost entirely, and did not make the attempt, as the British did, to meet and talk with Poles from the government when informal opportunity developed.

My own contacts in Warsaw were excellent. The press chief at the time, Victor Groz, was a veteran of the Communist army formed inside Russia, and he was of invaluable assistance to me in my efforts to get around Poland and to see members of the government. I had easy access to Boleslaw Bierut, then the acting President of Poland, with whom I had shared an apartment in the suburb of Praga on the eastern banks of the Vistula River before the capital had been taken.

I was, in short, persona grata with the leading Polish Communists, and my requests for interviews with officials were arranged quickly.

This was about the time that Winston Churchill made his famous "Iron Curtain" speech at Fulton, Missouri, but I wrote at the time that the "Iron Curtain" had been neither a barrier nor a screen for me.

The Polish Communists made no effort to deceive me. They admitted quite frankly that the parliamentary elections then scheduled for the following November would not in any sense be free as the Western democracies understood that word. There would be a single slate of candidates, these Poles admitted; of course, the government would control the outcome. But the officials then in power realized they could not impose all the rigidity of the Soviet system because the Polish peasant remained a rugged individual who reacted quite violently at times.

These Poles argued to me that the present system was the best that Poland could hope for at this time because certainly the Soviet government would not tolerate a free and possibly unfriendly government on soil so recently liberated with the blood of Russian soldiers. They seemed to have little faith that Stalin intended Poland to be a free, strong, and independent democracy. Instead, they believed Stalin wanted a Poland that was led by men not merely friendly to Moscow, but subservient to it.

One of the key and controversial problems between Washington and Warsaw at that time was the dual nationality of a group of Poles possessing both American and Polish citizenship. Some of these had been imprisoned, and Washington was angry because it could not talk with these prisoners, obtain their release, or even get an official list of their names.

Because my contacts with the Polish governmental authorities were so much better than his, I proposed to Ambassador Lane that he give me a list of American citizens whom he believed to be in Polish prisons, and I would intervene on their behalf. But Lane brushed me aside.

One morning in Warsaw, we heard by radio that there had

been a frightful *pogrom* in Kielce, a smaller city to the south of Warsaw, and that a large number of Jews had been put to death and a number of others had been wounded. Charles Arnot, then of United Press, had a Plymouth sedan, and he agreed to drive Bigart and me to the scene.

It was a horrible trip, a testimonial to the fact that anti-Semitism was still rife in a Polish community that had lost almost its entire Jewish population to the gas chambers and furnaces of the German occupiers. In Kielce, for example, there were fewer than 200 Jews in a city of about 50,000.

When we arrived, we found the bodies of forty-one Jews laid out at the edge of the city, men and women who had been killed because a small boy had circulated the age-old falsehood that he had seen evidence of a Jewish "ritual" killing of non-Jews for religious purposes.

There were two hoaxes that played a part in the *pogrom* that followed. One was the story of a nine-year-old boy who explained his three-day absence in the country by saying that during this interval he had been held captive in the Jewish headquarters in Kielce and there he had seen the bodies of fifteen non-Jewish children who had been killed by the Jews.

The boy's story was a lie, but it spread quickly through Kielce. In a short time it had fanned to white heat the latent fires of anti-Semitism always present in Eastern Europe.

At that point, armed bands began attacking Jews and laid siege to the Jewish central headquarters where the boy falsely had reported seeing evidence of the "ritual" murders.

Some of the slaughter of Jews occurred after several men in uniforms of the Polish Army went to the besieged Jewish headquarters and promised protection to Jewish leaders then holding out inside. They assured safe escort to these Jewish leaders, but when they came out of doors, the Jews were turned over to the mob and slain.

From Warsaw orders were issued for quick punishment of those responsible for the *pogrom*, and within a week, nine persons were sentenced to be hanged, while three others were given stiff prison terms.

Back in Warsaw, Ambassador Lane suggested to the foreign correspondents that we seek a statement from the Polish Roman Catholic primate, Augustus Cardinal Hlond. The cardinal was ready to talk to us, Ambassador Lane said.

We expected, of course, that Cardinal Hlond would condemn this outrageous slaughter of Jews, but he surprised and angered us by saying instead that Poland's rising anti-Semitism was "to a great degree due to Jews who today occupy leading positions in Poland's government and endeavor to introduce a governmental structure that a majority of the people do not want."

We could scarcely credit our ears or conceal our contempt for this Prince of the Church who seemed to be offering explanatory excuses for the brutal killings that had occurred in Kielce.

Wearing a red skullcap and his ecclesiastical robes with a jeweled cross around his neck, the cardinal did give lip service to sentiments of regret, but he offered a personal opinion that the killings "did not occur for racial reasons." He denied that Poles generally were anti-Semitic, and claimed that many had risked their own safety to give refuge to Jews when the Germans were hunting them down during the war.

"The fact that their condition is deteriorating is to a great degree due to Jews who today occupy leading positions in Poland's government and endeavor to introduce a governmental structure that a majority of the people do not want," said the Cardinal. "This is a harmful game as it creates dangerous tension. In the fatal battle of weapons on the fighting political front in Poland, it is to be regretted that some Jews lose their lives but a disproportionately larger number of Poles lose their lives.

The question and answer period that followed the cardinal's unexpected statement was a heated one, and the correspondents made little effort to conceal their contempt for the cardinal. I was outraged by him, especially by his declaration that only recently he had refused a request by American Jews to issue an appeal against anti-Semitism with the explanation that he did not feel the facts justified such a proclamation from the Church. Now, I hoped, the cardinal had become aware of the true facts which had cost so many innocent Jews their lives.

I never wondered afterwards about anti-Church campaigns in Poland.

Cardinal Hlond may have been a Prince of his Church, but he was not a true Christian.

From Poland I made my way to Paris, via Berlin and Bonn, and in Paris I found Secretary of State Byrnes who had just arrived to help negotiate final peace treaties covering the German satellites that had waged war against the Allies. Secretary Byrnes told me

Arthur Sulzberger had an "important mission" for me, and he authorized me to fly home on *The Sacred Cow*, the President's personal airplane that had just ferried the American delegation from Washington to the Paris peace conference. This was my first trip on a Presidential aircraft, and I was the only civilian aboard. It was a heady experience to have Army officers snap to attention and throw a salute as the doors of *The Sacred Cow* swung open displaying the Presidential seal and I made my way down the ramp during an intermediate refueling stop in Iceland on our way back to Washington.

Sulzberger's assignment was an important one indeed, a tour of all the Caribbean, Central and South American countries to investigate Communism in Latin America. It was to take six months, and I would touch down in every capital city, twenty in all.

I moved from Havana, where I spent a month in those long-ago pre-Castro days, across to Mexico City down through the Central American Republics, thence to the western coast of South America to Chile at the tip, over the Andes to Buenos Aires where Juan Perón still ruled, up the river to Paraguay, and then to Uruguay, Brazil, Venezuela, Trinidad, Haiti, and Santo Domingo.

Communism was flourishing but my chief impression was wonderment there were not more Communists considering the extremely low standard of living of most Latin American peasants. Life was beautiful for the very rich, there was almost no middle class, and then one encountered the deep poverty of the very poor. For the most part, the Roman Catholic Church allied itself on the side of the rich and fought social reform. Universal taxation was almost unknown and remained so for many, many years.

The chief villain blamed for all Latin American ills was that great "Colossus of the North," the United States. In many cases, we were not entirely without guilt. Firms financed with American capital extracted rich minerals and other products of wealth from our neighbors to the south and too often the return paid the exploited country was small.

As is so often the case, the rumors of Communist infiltration and control were usually greater than the available facts. Wherever I went I was told that the headquarters for Communist direction of the entire hemisphere were located in the next country, but when I got to that country, headquarters were said to be one more country ahead.

In those days, Havana was said to be a lively scene for Communist activity, but I found that hard to establish even though I spent nearly a month there. This was a long time before Castro.

The same was true of Mexico City, though there there were more admitted Communists among the intellectuals and artists. In Peru, Haya de la Torre, then in exile, was usually labeled a Communist under Moscow domination by his enemies, but my own impression was that he was a radical whose ideology was more nationalist than Moscow-oriented.

Chile had the most advanced Communist party, largely because of right-wing division and confusion. In the most recent election before 1946, the Chilean Communists had swung 50,000 votes, the balance of power, to the candidacy of President Gabriel Gonzalez Videla and he rewarded the CP with three cabinet posts.

In Buenos Aires, I had a long talk with Perón, who pictured himself as a solid bulwark against Communism and who should therefore get more sympathetic help and material aid from the United States. This was at a time when official Washington took a dim view of Perón and his dictatorship, an unfriendly policy that did not always have the backing of our then Ambassador George Messersmith.

After the tour, I estimated that Communist membership in the vast area between the Rio Grande and the southern tip of South America probably totaled about 300,000 to 400,000 members, but that the Communist party might garner as many as 1,500,000 votes if genuinely free elections were permitted.

"There seems little likelihood that the Communists are ready, or wish, to assume formal power in any Latin American country in the near future," I reported in late December, 1946. "Their importance, at the moment, is their consistent propaganda against the foreign policy of the Western democracies, and in support of the foreign policy moves by the Soviet Union."

It was another dozen years before Castro toppled the Batista dictatorship in Cuba and took over that country during the regime of President Eisenhower.

CHAPTER
14

The fabled Balkans with their rugged mountains, strong men, and beautiful women aren't the same under Communist rule as they were in the carefree days before World War II, but they still are adventuresome lands for a reporter to tour. I spent all of 1947 and the first few months of 1948 on assignment in Yugoslavia, Bulgaria, and Rumania, with an occasional side trip into Greece, and just once into Albania, into which few Westerners have been admitted since the war ended and the Communists took over.

I came to the Balkans in a time of trouble when civil war raged in Greece, conducted by Communist guerrillas and fomented by Greece's Communist neighbors. I left just before Tito's pursuit of independence from Moscow rule got him kicked out of the Cominform. I was the only Western correspondent on duty in Rumania when the Communists forced young King Michael to abdicate, and that country moved from a government of fellow travelers to one of outright Communism.

These were not the best of times for Americans in the Balkans, but I moved about in my bright red Pontiac with surprisingly little difficulty considering the poor state of relations between the United States and the Communist satellites. I was expelled from only one country—Bulgaria—and that was because the Voice of America had played up in an irritating fashion one dispatch of mine that reported the Bulgarians had moved to become a one-party state, just like the Soviet Union. What I wrote was demonstrably true beyond debate, but the Communist leaders in Sofia didn't like it anyway. So they gave me twenty-four hours to get out of the country, which I did.

When the Bulgarians expelled me I possessed an entry visa only for neighboring Yugoslavia, and I fully expected that Tito's men would be as unfriendly as the Bulgars. But surprisingly I was warmly welcomed back to Belgrade. Only later did I learn how much relations between Yugoslavia and its Communist neighbors had deteriorated in the months before the formal expulsion action against Tito by the Comintern.

The Red Army, with not a little help from local guerrilla forces, had freed these countries from Nazi occupation, and there was no doubt that Moscow was the master of all it surveyed in the Balkans when I arrived. Tito was the first to revolt along nationalistic lines, and, much later, the Albanian Communists were to side with the Chinese Communist party when the Moscow-Peking ideological split developed.

I had made my way to the Balkans by slow and easy stages. This was my first crossing of the Atlantic by ship, aboard the S.S. *America*, then the best of the American passenger flagships. My Pontiac had come along, costing almost as much in freight as my own first-class passage. The voyage was a fine one, enlivened by old friends like Mark and Willie Ethridge of the Louisville *Courier Journal*, and by new friends like the American Minister to Switzerland, Gilbert Harrison, and his attractive wife Nancy. My own roommate was an aging French wine merchant, the Baron de Luz, who worried because I consumed so much whiskey and stayed out so late every night.

Once ashore, I stayed quite awhile in Paris before I headed the Pontiac south through Dijon and the wine country to the Riviera and across to Italy. I paused only briefly on the Italian Riviera, then headed eastward through Milan to Venice and finally the unhappy city of Trieste, which still was the scene of much rivalry between the Communist Yugoslavs and the Western powers when I arrived. Once inside Yugoslavia, I put my automobile on a railroad flatcar and myself in a sleeping car for the final few hundred miles into snowy Belgrade. Little had been done to repair the roads since the Nazis had been driven out by a combination of the Red Army and the Yugoslav guerrillas, who were led by Marshal Tito and supplied with British and American weapons.

When I finally reached Belgrade, I found that my South American expense account, sent by mail just after I arrived in Europe, had attracted some attention in the home office in New York.

A cable from Mr. Edwin James, awaiting me in Belgrade, said, "Auditor complains your South American expense account includes $274 bar charges. What shall I tell him?"

This was a typical James message, laying the blame on the auditor and taking no position on the issue himself.

My first instinct was to send the message, "James, tell him I drink." But I noted the first message now was ten days or more old, and I decided to wait and see if there would be a follow-up. There wasn't, and we forgot the whole thing.

There was one other expense account exchange with James at the end of the Balkan assignment, after I had been back in the United States for a few weeks. It involved the shipping charges on my Pontiac, which I had sold to a colleague in Belgrade, Osgood Caruthers of the Associated Press, just before I came home in 1948.

James pointed out that the office had spent $425 to ship my automobile to Europe and that I had sold it before I returned. The auditor, James continued, suggested that I should bear all, or part, of the shipping expense, or what did I think?

I was livid with rage and responded angrily to Mr. James. Of course I had taken my own automobile to Europe, and of course the *Times* had paid the shipping expenses. I had driven it about 40,000 miles over Balkan roads and had then sold it to Mr. Caruthers.

"Indeed, if I had not sold it," I wrote Mr. James, "then the *Times* would have paid $425 to ship it home. It now occurs to me that you owe me $425, or part of it, or what do you think?"

In less than twenty-four hours, Mr. James sent a message to Washington saying, "Lawrence, let's call that car deal even."

James enjoyed the joke at the auditor's expense as much as I did. As a former chief correspondent in Paris for many years, he knew the expense account problems of a correspondent. But I always endeavored to stay on his good side. He was very fond of good Havana cigars and I never returned from any trip in those pre-Castro days without a big box of Uppmans. Sometimes I handed the cigars and my latest expense account to him at the same time.

In February, 1947, I found Belgrade to be a dingy, cheerless city. Its stores reflected the national poverty. There were few consumer goods for sale, and all prices were very high. It was a police state, and the streets were filled with uniformed soldiers. I lived in the Moscow Hotel, mostly populated by other foreigners but far from first-class.

I had been in town only about a week or so when Constantine Poulos of the Overseas News Agency drove in from Austria in a jeep he had somehow acquired from the U.S. Army in Germany. I had not seen Poulos since the Polish referendum of 1946 in Warsaw, and we had a joyful reunion. That night we did not bother to put the jeep into a locked garage, and the next morning it was gone, never to be seen again. The Belgrade police were politely disinterested in Poulos' complaint of a stolen car. Poulos soon got the point and quit complaining.

Poulos had been on his way to Greece to cover the Greek civil war then in progress in the northern parts of the country that bordered on three Communist neighbors, Yugoslvaia, Bulgaria, and Albania. Greece was not part of my territory, but the other Balkan countries were, and it seemed to me and to New York that it would be a good idea if I took a look at the border area in dispute and joined up with the United Nations Balkans Commission then meeting in Salonika and soon to head for Albania before it came to Yugoslavia and Bulgaria.

Poulos and I made our way south to Greece in the red Pontiac, which attracted a big crowd wherever we paused. The roads were in miserable shape, showing the wear and tear of tank battles during the war, and most of the bridges over rivers and streams still had not been repaired. So we detoured, and often forded the streams and rivers. Gasoline stops were few and far apart, so in the trunk of the Pontiac we always carried five jerry-cans which contained five gallons of gasoline each. I drove as fast as the condition of the roads would allow, and we made the Belgrade-Salonika journey in approximately seventeen hours including a delay at the Greek border.

In Salonika, we found Mark Ethridge and Paul A. Porter, both of whom had Kentucky backgrounds. They had taken over the U.S. leadership in Greece. Ethridge was the American member of the Balkans Commission, and Porter was a special envoy for President Truman in preparing the Greek-Turkish aid program that would be known as the Truman Doctrine.

Ethridge had his wife, Willie Snow Ethridge, with him, and Willie, a well-known author in her own right, was a born adventurer, absolutely indefatigable. Later at Easter time I was to drive Willie from Belgrade to Geneva, Switzerland, via Budapest and Vienna.

The war between the Greek regular Army and the guerrillas was being fought in the mountains around Salonika, and there were frequent clashes, usually at night when the guerrillas staged hit-and-run raids. On one occasion Willie had been missing for several hours and there were fears in some quarters that perhaps she had been captured by the guerrilla forces.

One of the Greek government officials reported this fear to Mark Ethridge one evening. "Those guerillas will just have to look out for themselves," he said with a big smile.

Poulos and I attached ourselves to the U.N. Balkan Commission inquiry team as it headed out of Salonika toward the Yugoslav and Albanian borders and on March 12, 1947, we were witnesses to the first refusal by a U.N. member state to allow a U.N. commission to enter its territory.

At issue was the Greek charge that the Communist-led guerrilla army inside northern Greece used the border area with Yugoslavia as a kind of privileged sanctuary for supplies, for training, and as a place of temporary refuge when the military pressure of the regular Greek forces grew too strong.

The U.N. commission team, headed by J. D. L. Hood of Australia, had heard charges that Dragos, Yugoslavia, was a key point in this privileged sanctuary. The U.N. team driving west from Salonika was determined to see for itself, but it did not reckon with Tito's willingness to ignore world opinion and deny entry to the U.N. investigators.

Poulos and I were the only two correspondents with the group of about thirty U.N. personnel who approached the border in the Dragos area in mid-afternoon on March 12, 1947. Ambassador Hood, through interpreters, requested permission at the frontier to enter Yugoslavia and displayed the visas for entry earlier granted by the Yugoslav consulate in Salonika. But the Yugoslav border guards refused to lift the barrier that blocked the road. Hood protested and argued loud and long that the U.N. had given his group a mandate to determine the truth or falsity of the Greek charges.

But the Yugoslav border guards wouldn't budge beyond making some telephone calls to higher authorities, whose names they declined to give. The Yugoslavs told the U.N. commission it could cross the frontier in the area near Bitolj, a bit more to the west, but a crossing at Dragos was not and would not be authorized.

Hood finally saw there was no chance of persuading the Yugoslavs to reconsider, so the U.N. group made its way back into a small Greek village where we spent the day before pressing on into Albania.

Poulos and I had a big story but there were, of course, no commercial cable offices or telephones available in this remote area of northern Greece. Happily, the Greeks with us saw a propaganda windfall for their country and the Greek Army agreed to transmit our dispatches via Greek military facilities. We had little hope even then of speedy movement because the military communications led into Salonika, and there would then be a relay via commercial channels to Athens and New York. I was therefore astonished a week or more later to learn that my dispatch datelined "The Greek-Yugoslav Frontier" had been front-paged in *The New York Times* of the following day, March 13.

Two days later, as we made our way along rough, winding mountain roads, we heard occasional bursts of automatic-weapon fire—presumably exchanges between the Greek regular and guerrilla forces—as we headed for Albania. The partisans controlled much of the territory through which we passed, and the decrepit old cars in which we rode flew flags of the United Nations as a signal not to shoot at us. At Sklethro we were told that the partisan forces had just been driven from the village and now were being pursued into the hills by truckloads of Greek regular soldiers.

At the frontier, we were given a warm welcome by Albanian officials, and it was there that we left our motorcade behind and boarded donkeys for the two-hour trip to Koritza. We traveled in a long line of forty donkeys through some of the most depressed villages I have ever seen, places of habitation that seemed literal combinations of pigsties and living places. These were so dirty, so ugly, so poverty-stricken that they would make a sharecropper's shack in Mississippi look good in comparison.

In Koritza, we heard Albanian witnesses charge that the Greeks had taken the initiative in much of the border trouble. This was an ancient dispute reflecting Greek demands on what they called Northern Epirus, land that the Albanians had refused to cede despite great pressure from the Greeks and from Americans of Greek descent. Seven Albanians were on trial for treason while we were there, charged with plotting to turn these territories over to Greece.

We spent only one night in Koritza, then moved back out aboard donkeys into Greece the next day.

It was the first, and so far as I know the last, U.N. mission to gain entry into Albania, which in later years moved out of Moscow's domination and into the political orbit of the Chinese Communists. While the Albanians and the Russians were allied there were always rumors in the Western world that the Albanians had given the Russians a submarine base they would be able to use with great effectiveness against the American fleet in the Mediterranean, but I never encountered an American who claimed certain knowledge of this Soviet base.

The Communist drive to take over Greece failed not only because of the vast American aid program, but also because of a split in the Communist ranks. Tito's Yugoslavia suddenly and surprisingly cut off its aid to the Greek guerrilla forces, and the partisan armies lost their control of northern Greek areas.

After I left Belgrade for Geneva in the spring of 1947, I found myself for a long period unable to get a visa for my return to Yugoslavia. I have always thought it was perhaps a reprisal for the stories I had written out of Greece, particularly at the time of the refusal to allow the U.N. commission to enter at Dragos.

In any event, I now shifted my attention to Rumania. In the summer of 1947, Rumania was a political rarity, a Communist country with a king still on the throne, and still tolerating an organized political party in opposition to the Communists. Over a six-month period these things were to change, and I was on hand to witness it all, unbothered by censorship or any restraint on my physical movements about the countryside. For most of the period, I was the only foreign correspondent in residence in Rumania.

I had a ringside seat as the Communists set out to transform Rumania into a totally dependent satellite, a process that took little more than eight months. When I arrived on July 4, the government in Bucharest was Communist-controlled, but not entirely Communist in its makeup. The Prime Minister, Petru Groza, was a farm leader, and not a Communist party member, and he thought he could outmaneuver the Communist party members on the local level.

The changeover came in stages. In mid-1947, there was terrible inflation in Bucharest, which got worse by the day as prices of commodities reached astronomical heights in an economy that was far more capitalist than Communist. The first test of the Rumanian man in the street was a suddenly imposed currency reform which in a fraction of a second wiped out the old currency and substituted new money. It came with dramatic swiftness over a weekend, and when the government got away with that, the stage was set for new tests of the spirit of resistance among the people.

A few days later, the emboldened government moved to arrest Dr. Juliu Maniu and five other deputies of the National Peasant party. Maniu had been a popular pre-war leader before Rumania went fascist and joined Hitler's war. Now he was a symbol of peasant resistance to Communism, and a man who worked closely with the American officials stationed in Rumania. Arresting Maniu was a step that even the Nazis dared not risk at the peak of their power in occupied Rumania, as I noted on July 18 in an uncensored dispatch to the *Times*. The trial of Maniu that followed a few weeks later was a fraud, conducted as it was by a judge who during the fascist period had been a judge serving Nazi justice and who now was just as willing to serve Communist ends. But there was no doubt that Maniu was guilty of most of the crimes with which he was charged. He had indeed collaborated with the American officials and had used their diplomatic channels to send and receive mail from abroad. He had kept the Americans informed of what was going on inside Rumania, and, without doubt, he hoped for substantial American aid if the time came when an uprising against the Communists and their collaborators might be possible.

During much of this time I was the only American correspondent in Bucharest, but occasionally was joined by Robert Low of Time-Life. Low and I developed easy access to Prime Minister Groza and quite often joined him for early-morning tennis at the Royal Tennis Club, still operating near the lake in Bucharest.

A tennis match with Groza would have been something to film, and hard to believe. A white-haired man of over sixty, he remained an active lady's man in the best Balkan tradition and quite often his companion or companions of the night before would accompany him to the tennis courts to watch our game. One of Groza's personal bodyguards, always armed with a German Luger pistol in his holster, usually served as umpire and scorekeeper. The guard never failed to rule in Groza's favor on a close call, and, even more appalling, he quite often reversed a score against the Prime Minister to announce that Groza was now ahead.

Once when Groza and I were double partners, we had fallen behind in games despite the best possible rulings given us by the guard serving as umpire. Now it was a last-ditch stand, and Groza urged me on to greater efforts.

"Let us stand as at Stalingrad," said the Rumanian Prime Minister, roaring with laughter.

It was funnier even than he thought, because I remembered from my days in the Soviet Union that it had been the Rumanian troops in the German armies that had first cracked on the Stalingrad front and allowed the Red Army to break through and finally to capture the Nazi forces of General Paulus.

Groza's cheating was harmless, and we got used to it. But the important fact was that the secret police knew that Groza and I were friendly, that I had access to the Prime Minister. It doubtless saved me lots of trouble with the police.

I had at the same time developed friends at King Michael's court, especially his private secretary, John Ionitziu, and occasionally I got to see the young King himself at the palace in Sinaia, or on the royal golf links near Sinaia. King Michael never told me anything of major importance, but through Ionitziu I could keep in touch with developments as the palace viewed them.

After Maniu's trial and conviction, the next step in the Communist march to absolute power was the demand made upon the young King on the night of November 7 that he appoint Ana Pauker, an outright Communist, as Rumania's Foreign Minister. At first, Michael was inclined to resist or at least delay, but his Communist leaders kept his feet to the fire so that Mrs. Pauker was present as Foreign Minister at the big party given by the Soviet Mission on this November 7 evening, the anniversary of the Russian Revolution.

One of my old friends from Moscow, Dongulov, was by this time the head of the Soviet information activity in Bucharest, and he proved a useful source of news and access to authority for me as I stayed on in Bucharest.

Dongulov also saw to it that the Rumanian Allied Control Commission extended my residence visa whenever it expired. He had been a censor in the Soviet Foreign Office when I was a wartime correspondent in Moscow, and we had made many trips together, including the entry into Leningrad when the German ring around that besieged city finally was lifted by Soviet forces. For a Soviet official, he was extraordinarily friendly and I had genuine affection for him.

After Mrs. Pauker moved into the Rumanian government there remained a single obstacle to total Communization of the Rumanian system. This was the King himself. And King Michael perhaps unwittingly contributed to the Communist plan by leaving the country late in 1947 to attend a wedding in Western Europe, and while there, becoming engaged himself. No obstacles were placed in the way of the King's return to Bucharest, but the government did not appear anxious to give approval to his wedding as required. The constitutional crisis was in full bloom by the Christmas holidays, when I joined British friends at a villa in the Carpathians near Predeal.

King Michael had indicated he might join our group for a brief visit between Christmas and New Year's, but he didn't show. It was customary for the King on New Year's Day to receive all diplomats at a reception, and we were interested at Predeal as to whether this custom would be continued into 1948. Rodney Sarrell, one of our group who was at this time the acting British Minister, and Iver Porter, his deputy, both wanted to attend if the King gave his usual reception.

Just before New Year's Day, I was delegated to telephone Johnny Ionitziu at the Royal Palace to ask whether there would be a reception. Ionitziu said he didn't know, but asked how long I planned to remain at Predeal. I told him my plans were indefinite, but I was in no rush to get back to Bucharest. He suggested that I telephone him on the following morning.

In mid-morning, on December 30, I telephoned Ionitziu about the reception again, and this time he said somewhat guardedly that perhaps I should return to Bucharest as soon as possible. I didn't know exactly what he meant but I told my friends at the British Legation that I thought we might go down the mountain that night.

The villa telephone rang shortly after lunch. It was my part-time associate in Bucharest, a Rumanian named Liviu Nasta, who spoke only halting English.

"The King has abdicated," said Nasta. "You must come."

We raced for the big red Pontiac. Porter was beside me in the front seat and Rod Sarrell sat in the rear as we drove down the snow-covered mountain roads. We had chains on the rear wheels as far south as Sinaia.

Night fell as we raced toward Bucharest along the winding mountain roads. Suddenly in the darkness my headlights picked up two horse-drawn carts using up much of the narrow road, but I was moving much too fast to try to apply the brakes so I simply swerved to my left and prayed to heaven we could avoid a collision. We did, but only by inches, and once again I pressed the accelerator to the floor board. In the back seat, Rod had opened a bottle of Scotch which he passed to me.

"You deserve a drink for missing those carts," he said.

Back in Bucharest, we confirmed quickly the official news of the King's abdication and I began to write and telephone my story without censorship to the Press Wireless office in Prague for relay to the United States. Seeking more details, I placed a call to the Royal Palace just outside Bucharest, but could not raise Ionitziu or any of the other officials known to me. And my telephone would not work after that call.

I drove to the apartment of Sam Buda, an American Legation employee, and used his telephone to finish telephoning the remaining information to the *Times* via the Prague Press Wireless office.

The next day I was surprised to find Ionitziu ringing the bell of my apartment in downtown Bucharest. He was one of the King's party who would be allowed to leave Bucharest for exile, but now he was risking his freedom to tell me the full story of the King's abdication which the Rumanian government had announced was entirely voluntary.

Michael had been with his mother, Queen Helen, at the Royal Palace in Sinaia for Christmas and had intended to remain until New Year's Day, returning only for the reception he gave annually for the diplomats. But Ionitziu told me that just after Christmas Prime Minister Groza had telephoned the King and asked him to return to Bucharest for discussion of an urgent state problem. The King agreed, but he and his staff were puzzled about the nature of the problem. They did not dream that the moment of supreme crisis had arrived.

The King drove to Bucharest on the morning of December 30, and took up residence in the palace of Princess Elizabeth on the outskirts of the capital. As he drove in, Michael observed and noted to Ionitziu that the area was heavily guarded by soldiers from the

Tudor Vladmirescu division, which had been formed from former Rumanian prisoners of war. They had been trained in the Soviet Union, where they had been held captive. Large numbers of secret police were plainly visible about the grounds of the suburban palace.

At about 10:30 A.M., Ionitziu told me that Prime Minister Groza arrived and laid before the King an act of abdication, offering no reasons or argument on the issue. The King clearly could sign or risk the consequences of the armed forces clearly evident just outside his palace window. King Michael didn't argue the abdication issue with Groza but he did seek and receive promises that the royal family and staff would be allowed to leave the country without hindrance.

At about one o'clock in the afternoon, Michael had signed the act of abdication. In mid-afternoon, Parliament was summoned to meet in special session, and at about 6 P.M., the People's Republic of Rumania was proclaimed.

A few days later, I was in a tiny crowd that watched Michael and his court board a royal train at Sinaia and head into exile. Many Rumanians wept in their homes but there was not the slightest overt sign of resistance.

I had a long talk with Groza, who insisted that the King's abdication was "a normal development," and that it was in accord with the Rumanian Communist recipe for "achieving results with a minimum of convulsions." Groza said the abdication could have surprised only those who were not familiar with Rumania's internal developments, and he boasted there would be "more surprises" for such people in the future.

Now the Communists had full control in Rumania without the anachronism of Communist rule exercised through a constitutional monarch. It was surprising that Michael had lasted as long as he had.

In neighboring Bulgaria meanwhile, the Communists also had liquidated the last of the opposition leaders during the same period that the red rule in Rumania was being cemented.

I had gone down to Sofia first for the trial and then the execution of Nikola Petkov, who, like Maniu, had been a stubborn, courageous fighter against fascism who had refused to compromise with the Communists. Petkov was hanged on September 23, and the Communist-controlled press of Sofia charged:

"Petkov and the gravediggers of the people's freedom grouped around him had prepared to cause the occupation of the country by foreign troops by the same powers who today have transformed Greece into a valley of people's tears and into a bloody battle-ground."

Not even all the Bulgarian Communists agreed that it was wise to execute Petkov, but the rulers from Georgi Dimitrov on down ignored all appeals for clemency.

My best friend in Bulgaria was an official of the Bulgarian foreign office, a man with a stranger-than-fiction history, by name, George Andreychine, who had been in and out of favor with the Communists for nearly half a century, often in Communist jails when he ran afoul of their plans.

Andreychine's story is hardly believable. He had been born in southern Bulgaria and was among a handful of young men chosen by the Bulgarian Tsar to be educated with his son. But young Andreychine turned radical and was tipped off by those friendly to him in the Bulgarian court to escape before he was found out. He made his way to Western Europe and finally to the United States, and there he became a leader of the International Workers of the World, a forerunner of the Communist party. As an IWW organizer, Andreychine took part in the strike of iron ore miners in Minnesota during World War I and was jailed in Chicago, along with others like Big Bill Haywood. When they were released from prison on bail, Andreychine jumped bond as did the others and fled to Russia, which recently had undergone the Communist Revolution. In Russia, Andreychine became Trotsky's secretary and was jailed himself when Trotsky was exiled by Stalin.

During his brief visit to the United States, Andreychine had been befriended by an anti-war Congressman, Charles Lindbergh, father of the famous aviator who was later to make the first solo crossing of the Atlantic by air. And Andreychine was moved out of his Siberian exile to serve as the younger Lindbergh's host and guide when the famous flier came to Russia during the 1930s. He later served as a Soviet liaison official with the foreign diplomatic corps first in Moscow and later during the war in Kuibyshev. When Bulgaria was freed of German rule by the Red Army, Andreychine had accompanied Dimitrov on a train across southern Russia and through Rumania to Sofia.

I had come to know Andreychine well while we were together with the Balkans Commission in Geneva during the early summer of 1947, and we had maintained our friendship during my occasional visits to Sofia. He was courageous enough to come to dinner with me and American Legation friends, notably Stanley and Sally Cleveland, but we had our best talks riding in the Pontiac along the Sofia streets and roads near the capital. He told me he could talk more freely in the automobile because he knew it was not bugged by the secret police.

I had loaned Andreychine Orwell's brilliant satire *Animal Farm*, which was a devastating ridicule of the Communist system in which the pigs, like the Commissars, were "more equal" than other animals. On one of these rides, I told him in jest the American government planned to print millions of copies of the Orwell book in Bulgarian and drop them from airplanes over his country.

"Your government isn't that smart," he said, his eyes twinkling.

We took another one of those automobile rides on the day Petkov was hanged.

"My wife says the Americans were the winners today," Andreychine said. "She said the Bulgarian government should have let Petkov live, and I agree with her."

A few months later Andreychine was scheduled to dine with me on the very same night I was ordered by the government to leave Sofia. After my expulsion notice had been broadcast, Andreychine telephoned to Stanley Cleveland at the American Legation to say that he would not be able to come for dinner.

"Bill will understand, I hope," Andreychine told Cleveland. I did.

And I understood also when Andreychine again disappeared into the silence of another Communist jail never to emerge alive. There was no trial, and no formal charges, but it was obvious the old IWW leader was too free a spirit for his Communist masters.

CHAPTER

15

Harry S Truman has to go down in history as 1948's Man of the Year because he won the Presidency in his own right at a time when nobody else thought he could. Defeat seemed inevitable for a divided Democratic party, whose left and right wings wanted to dump Truman before he was nominated. New York's Republican Governor Thomas E. Dewey was so sure of election that he and other Republicans took the White House for granted, and in the memorable phrase usually attributed to Washington lawyer Paul Porter, "snatched defeat from the jaws of victory."

I traveled thousands of miles with Truman in that hectic year but I must confess that right up to the end I had no premonition of his victory. In a curious way, I did sense and report a strong trend away from the Republicans in the Congress, but I could not and did not link voter dissatisfaction with the Republicans with the Truman-Dewey race.

William Warner, then a top aide of the Republican Congressional Campaign Committee, has always claimed I gave him the first tip-off that Dewey was in serious trouble. In the course of a state-by-state survey of Congressional races, I telephoned Warner in Washington from Indianapolis one day to report my tentative conclusion that the Republicans might lose as many as five seats in Indiana in November. I wanted to know if this agreed with his advance findings.

"That was the first time I knew we were in deep, deep trouble," Warner told me after the election. "I had no idea we might lose as many as five Republican seats in Indiana, but if we did, then we weren't going to elect a President either. If a Republican can't carry Indiana, he isn't likely to get to the White House."

As I made that pre-election survey on Congressional prospects, I really didn't bother to inquire much about the race between Truman and Dewey. Everybody knew that Dewey would win, or thought he would. Some of the pollsters were so confident they simply quit polling. When Dewey appeared, high school bands often played "Hail to the Chief," music reserved for the President of the United States alone.

Tom Dewey grew so arrogant about the imminence of his election that he would sometimes exclaim angrily that Truman ought to keep his hands off foreign affairs so as not to disturb the equilibrium of the world in the few months the President had remaining in office.

It has always been the theory of Edward T. Folliard, then the top political reporter of the *Washington Post*, that Dewey's arrogance finally forced the Lord to take a hand and punish the New York governor for his behavior. Folliard's reference was to an off-the-record news conference Dewey held in Albany, New York. It was about the time that Truman's plan to send Chief Justice Vinson to Moscow to negotiate with the Russians was prematurely disclosed and canceled.

"If that man will just keep his hands off foreign affairs," said Dewey in reference to the President.

"And that's when the Lord stepped in," Folliard said right after the election. "He wasn't going to stand for that kind of arrogance."

If the professional politicians were virtually unanimous in their choice of Dewey to win, there were some notable holdouts. One was Mrs. Earl Warren, wife of California's governor and Dewey's Vice Presidential running mate in 1948. Although some Dewey leaders already had leased houses and made other plans to move to Washington, Mrs. Warren sat tight, making no preparations at all to leave that gingerbread official mansion, in a kind of early Charles

Addams style, which California provided its governor. Somehow, Nina Warren detected a false note in all the Republican expressions of confidence.

Governor Warren, later to be Chief Justice, was very unhappy about the meaningless pap he was required to dispense as the Vice Presidential nominee, and he came to Washington once to complain to Herbert Brownell, the Dewey campaign chief, and other leaders that he was bored to death with his own speeches and wanted to strike out at the opposition.

"Don't rock the boat," Brownell told him. "We've got this election won, so don't try to change the strategy."

Warren kept saying nothing, and so did Dewey.

Truman meanwhile was pouring it on in his "Give 'em hell" campaign, blaming the Eightieth Republican-controlled Congress for nearly all the ills of mankind, including a rapid drop in the price of corn in the last few weeks of the campaign. The Republicans, said Truman, had stuck a pitchfork into the back of the farmer— he did not specify which part of the farmer's anatomy, except that it was his back. And Truman kept drawing the most amazing crowds, though the reporters, including me, explained this away as a kind of curiosity among the public to see their President.

Dewey never lost confidence in his own inevitable victory. On the final day of campaign travel, as the Dewey special train headed for New York City, the Republican candidate came back to the press car for one of his rare talks with the political reporters.

Dewey exuded confidence. He discussed some of the men he proposed to put into his cabinet. His tentative plan was to keep James V. Forrestal in office as his Secretary of Defense, the job Forrestal then held. Dewey confirmed his Secretary of State would be John Foster Dulles. The New York governor casually discussed plans for a post-victory holiday to make preparations for forming the new government, but he wouldn't tell us where he was going, except that "it will be someplace none of you fellows have guessed so far."

I shared all of Dewey's confidence in his certain victory. At the *Times*, Turner Catledge, then an assistant managing editor, proposed "an easy job" for me election night, broadcasting the returns over the *Times'* radio station, WQXR. Catledge thought it would take three or four hours beginning about 7 P.M., and that surely I could elect Dewey and sign off by 11 P.M. So did I, and I sailed into the broadcasting task without too much advance preparation and with no help at all. I was on the air for approximately seventeen hours, and, thank God, I got some volunteered help in the early morning hours from Orvil E. Dryfoos, son-in-law of Arthur Sulzberger and a future publisher himself. Truman was never behind, but it seemed incredible through that long night that he could hold his lead. But, I resisted all temptations to second-guess the returns, and, indeed, finally projected Truman to victory before the official figures showed his triumph. I finally quit talking around 11 A.M. on Wednesday morning, after Dewey had conceded and I had congratulated the President on his victory.

"You were right, Mr. President, and we were wrong," I told the WQXR audience. "We salute you, sir."

When the election returns were in, Alice Roosevelt Longworth, Washington's reigning political queen for all seasons, Republican and Democratic, said we should have known Dewey would lose.

"After all," said Alice acidly, "a soufflé never rises but once."

She had never liked Tom Dewey, and had ridiculed him in his earlier 1944 campaign for the Presidency as resembling "the groom atop the wedding cake."

Despite his arrogance, Dewey took defeat gracefully. He told about it at the annual white-tie stag dinner of the Gridiron Club in Washington the following month. It has always been the custom of the Gridiron Club to give a gold lifetime membership card to any retiring President of the United States, and that night the Gridiron broke a precedent and presented a similar gold card to Tom Dewey. After all, the Gridiron president said, "We elected you President, even if the people didn't. So as far as we are concerned, you are an ex-President."

Dewey smiled as he got to his feet, and said he supposed that many there had wondered how he felt on that November morning about 5 A.M. when the returns coming in from California, from Ohio, and from Illinois made it certain that Mr. Truman and not Dewey would be President for the next four years.

"I was reminded," said Dewey, "of the Irish wake when, as at many Irish wakes, the mourners consumed more liquor than they should, and indeed, one had become so drunk he had lost consciousness.

"The friends of the drunk thought it would be a fine joke if they would remove the corpse, and place their drunken friend in the casket.

"Well, just about 5 A.M., in the cold hours of the early morning, about the time I was hearing from California and Ohio, our drunken friend awoke to discover he was laid out in a casket.

" 'If I'm alive,' said the drunk, 'what in the hell am I doing here? But if I'm dead, why do I have to go to the bathroom?!!' And that's the way I felt election morning!"

The Gridiron Club roared its appreciation, and the evening was considered a great triumph for Dewey who had always been so cold and distant with reporters. I remember thinking that if he had been that human on the campaign trail he might then have been sitting there as President-elect, not an also-ran.

There was every reason that Truman should have lost. The Democratic left broke off to form the Progressive party, which nominated a ticket composed of former Vice President Henry A. Wallace for President and Senator Glenn Taylor of Idaho for Vice President. The conservative Democrats, having failed to nominate Georgia's Senator Richard Russell at the regular convention, split off to form a States' Rights party, usually called the Dixiecrats, and they nominated then Governor Strom Thurmond of South Carolina for President, and then Governor Fielding Wright of Mississippi for Vice President.

The moderate Democratic left, represented by the Americans for Democratic Action, also despaired of Truman's reelection. At the Philadelphia convention, the ADA leaders, including such notables as former Price Administrator Leon Henderson, pranced around in T-shirts urging the drafting of General Dwight Eisenhower in the belief Ike was some kind of Democratic liberal. He was later a quite conservative Republican President.

Ike cut off the 1948 ADA drive for him with a firm refusal to run, and the ADA tried without success to build up sentiment for Supreme Court Justice William O. Douglas as their Presidential candidate against Truman. Douglas turned down that bid as he also turned down Mr. Truman's request that he run for Vice President with him. The Vice Presidential nomination went to Senator Alben W. Barkley of Kentucky, largely because it was thought this was a worthless nomination, and that Barkley would be a worthy caretaker for the party in defeat who because of his age could be counted out of the Presidential nominating picture in 1952, four years later.

Most of the political reporters, including myself, made one long early trip with Truman on his whistle-stop train. Then we deserted him in late September to join up with the "surefire winner," Governor Dewey, and make friends with the prospective leaders of a new administration.

Although we didn't realize it, Truman had achieved a political ten-strike in his speech of acceptance—that famous call of Congress to meet in special sessions on "Turnip Day" after the conventions so the Republicans controlling the House and Senate now could enact into law their platform promises. Of course, the Republicans did no such thing.

Truman got another lucky break when the Progressive party convened in the full light of national newspaper coverage and regional television exposure right after the Democrats left Philadelphia. Old-line Communists had a viselike hold on the Progressive party and fuzzy-minded liberals like Henry Wallace, Rexford G. Tugwell, and Senator Taylor hardly knew what was going on in their name.

Wallace, who believed that Truman had been nasty to the Russians, thought there was a rich vein of votes in being pro-Soviet. His incredible Shibe Park acceptance speech was dedicated largely to the theme that the Americans ought to withdraw from occupied Berlin if this would make the Russians happy. It was about this time that Westbrook Pegler, the celebrated conservative columnist, dubbed Wallace "Old Bubblehead," and even midde-of-the-road reporters thought the description was apt.

The 1948 conventions were the first to be televised, but the audience was a tiny one. Even so, TV made its own contribution to this first and last convention of the Progressive party. After the Wallace acceptance speech, there was no related picture on which the TV cameras could focus. So the television pool cameras pointed straight at a full moon shining down on Philadelphia as if to emphasize the lunacy of it all.

The Communists in the Progressive party were basically stupid, but like so many stupid people, they were also arrogant. The creation of an independent and autonomous Macedonian state to be formed of the southern territories of Yugoslavia and Bulgaria had long been part of the Communist plan for Europe, but this idea had been dropped like a hot potato at the same time that Tito of Yugoslavia rebelled and got himself expelled from the Cominform. The Progressive party platform committee nevertheless urged an independent Macedonia in its report to the Philadelphia convention, though it was hard to figure out why this subject was mentioned at all in an American political party platform. Communist bosses were infuriated, so the Progressive party leaders dutifully urged and approved an amendment that deleted all references to the Macedonian issue. As I had just returned from Yugoslavia only a few weeks before, I had great fun twitting the Progressive party leaders, including playwright Lillian Hellman, asking if she had been unaware that Tito and an independent Macedonia were both non-subjects so far as the Communists were concerned. She became quite annoyed with me.

As I have remarked, the Republicans were fat and happy and sure of victory. The Dewey forces rode roughshod over local politicians in their go-it-alone, take-it-easy campaign. They made and broke promises with equal ease, including an unkept promise to make Republican House member Charles Halleck their Vice Presidential nominee if he could deliver all of the Indiana delegation to the support of Dewey at the convention. Halleck delivered, but Dewey didn't, after he saw an unhappy *Times* editorial headed "Surely Not Mr. Halleck," which chronicled Halleck's reactionary and isolationist record.

Governor Warren has never made clear to me why he ran for Vice President at all, but it was a source of puzzlement, especially since he had publicly declined the No. 2 spot on the ticket four years earlier. In any event, he was beaten along with Dewey, remained as governor of California, and after Eisenhower's election was appointed Chief Justice of the Supreme Court. On Warren's eightieth birthday in 1971, his family graciously asked me to give one of a series of toasts to the Chief Justice on that happy night.

To the surprise of many, I offered my toast to Warren's defeat for the Vice Presidency, which I described as an unimportant and tedious office that attained importance only if a President died. It was good, I went on, that Warren had lost in 1948 or we would all have forgotten him by now (1971) and the United States would have been deprived of the great "Warren Court," which had given such vital rulings on desegregation and one man, one vote—decisions that had changed the whole pattern of American life and politics.

C H A P T E R
16

Edward R. Murrow and I flew back to war in the early days of the Korean conflict. We got our first and best briefing from a bearded Bill Downs of CBS, standing at the ramp as our plane rolled to a stop in Tokyo: "Go back, go back, you silly bastards. This ain't our kind of war. This one is for the birds."

Murrow and I thought that Downs was kidding. In less than forty-eight hours, we knew that he was dead right.

The war in Korea wasn't the kind of war we had covered in Europe, or I had later covered against the Japanese in the Far Pacific. The war in Korea was a civil war. There were really no distinguishing physical characteristics between friend and foe and it was therefore hard to tell them apart. There was no fixed front line, no rear area that was really safe, and God alone was your guide when you set out to drive a jeep in the general direction of where you thought the main fighting of the moment was in progress. It was entirely too easy to pick the wrong road and wind up at the wrong end of a gun held by a North Korean. Thereafter, you might be dead, or an unwilling guest in one of his prisoner of war camps, which fell considerably below the standards of the Geneva conventions or the hospitality centers maintained by the Germans and Italians in Europe. In the first three months of the Korean battle, approximately thirty war correspondents were killed, captured, or missing in action.

The battle in Korea was one for which the United States was ill prepared. The five peacetime years of drastic cutbacks in military expenditures at home, plus some cockeyed ideas of economy-minded Secretaries of Defense, had given us an army so under-equipped and so badly organized that the troops lacked the power to fight well. Their ability to fight hadn't been enhanced by a few years of occupation duty in Japan. Soldiers of occupation simply are not the world's best combat warriors. Occupation troops are better trained for hand-to-hand combat with geisha girls.

Murrow and I found ourselves among old friends from World War II as soon as we hit the Korean peninsula. There were Homer Bigart, Don Whitehead, Hal Boyle, Frank Conniff, Harold Levine, Pat Morin, and a host of others with whom we had been to war five years earlier. Now we called ourselves "retreads" from World War II, and we practiced a stern discipline among ourselves. Nobody would ever listen to anybody else's stories about the last war, or even post-war adventures. The sharp period applied to anybody's anecdote was, "God, I get tired of the reminiscences of old men."

Among the troop commanders we found old friends too, including General Walton Walker, commanding the Tenth Army, and Major General Hobart R. (Hap) Gay, who commanded the First Cavalry Division in Korea but who in Europe had been chief of staff for the legendary General George Patton. In the Army a new star was rising on the battlefield. He bore the name of Mike Michaelis, and won his first star as a general on the Korean battle-field and his fourth star about twenty years later when he took over as commanding general for the 50,000 troops that still remained in Korea to maintain an uneasy armistice.

In those dark days in July when it looked as if we might be overrun on the Korean peninsula, Hap Gay pointed out to us the extreme vulnerability of the American position.

Boyle, Whitehead, Murrow, and I found Gay one afternoon on a narrow dusty highway beyond the Naktong River above Taegu at a tense moment in the fight. His undermanned First Cavalry Division was being flanked on both the right and left, and the North Korean enemy was driving hard for a knockout blow. We found Gay sitting in a field with others of high command and he greeted us as old friends from Europe. We sat on the ground and talked for some minutes about the fighting in Europe. Gay was interrupted from time to time for urgent discussions with officers who had come from the front. On every occasion, Gay listened until the officer had finished, then shook his head in the negative.

At one point, Hal Boyle asked Gay what had been the maximum forces under his command as Patton's chief of staff.

Gay smiled a little grimly, and then replied.

"Eighteen divisions in the line, seventeen divisions in reserve, mostly armored."

"What are your reserves now?" Boyle wanted to know.

The general's smile got a little grimmer.

"That is what all these interruptions have been about," said Gay. "My reserves amount to about half a company—maybe 120 men. And the argument is whether I now should commit all of them, half of them, or just part of them. So far my answer is to hold them back until I need them more desperately. But, gentlemen, this situation is getting more desperate every minute so I recommend you get back to Taegu if you want to file your stories today."

Gay's thin line held that day, and it was about two days later that Whitehead and I again visited the First Cav forward positions still beyond Naktong.

We were surprised to see the Tenth Army's commanding general, Walker, there, and he was laying down the law to Gay's top commanders for one final retreat to the Naktong River line, and no farther.

"On the Naktong," said General Walker, "we must stand or die. There can be no Dunkirk for us. There aren't enough ships to pick us off the beaches so we must hold or die on the Naktong line."

This was a hell of a story, and Whitehead and I were anxious to get it off at once. It was mid-morning in Korea, but in New York it was late the night before, so there still was time to make the late editions of the *Times* if we were lucky enough to get through with a quick telephone call to Tokyo. I had come forward in a small single-engined artillery observation plane and it was waiting for me on an improvised airfield to the rear. It was agreed between Whitehead and me that I would return quickly to Taegu to telephone both his office and mine with the news. At the correspondent's billet, in a little gray schoolhouse on the main street of Taegu, there was a single telephone line available to correspondents. Not infrequently we waited for hours to get a connection to Tokyo. But this day I was lucky. I got through quickly to AP, Tokyo, and the man who took my message passed it along to the *Times* office just a few doors away.

It was a dramatic story, the first time that an American field commander had told his troops that in such a desperate situation they must stand or die because there would be no hope of rescue. It shocked the American people, who had assumed that a handful of Americans could quickly overcome the North Korean Army. It showed up the grave weakness of the American military situation, made worse by false economies at home. It helped bring about the ouster of Louis Johnson as Secretary of Defense. One of the Defense Department's major errors was a new organizational structure for the Army divisions, with two regiments instead of three in each division and two battalions instead of three in each regiment. This economy in manpower assignment made it look like we had a lot of divisions, but no division was really prepared for battle because with only two regiments there was *no* provision for reserves.

I have always wondered why the North Koreans chose to fight us head on in Korea instead of making a rush for the last southern port, Pusan, and simply ignoring the thin line of American troops in position on a few of the main roads. If they had simply bypassed Walker's little army, they could have achieved victory quickly, and we probably would not have been able to bring sufficient force to reinvade Korea. But the enemy commanders erred, and they paid for their mistake when we held Pusan, when we held on at the Naktong, until, finally, we could mount an offensive behind the enemy lines, putting fresh troops ashore at Inchon just a few miles from Seoul, the South Korean capital that the enemy had held for many weeks.

During those few weeks that Murrow was in Korea, he and I were inseparable. Once I saved his life, and once he saved mine.

During our first week, we were asked by China Morrison and some other British correspondents to go forward with them one morning, and we agreed tentatively. But I learned of some trouble at Pohang, an air base on the eastern coast of Korea, and Murrow chose to accompany me and not the British reporters. Their jeep hit a land mine a few miles from Taegu and they were killed instantly. Murrow and I were pallbearers at a simple English religious service on the grounds of a small mission near Taegu, an event that came back to haunt me when I read the delightful love story told in *A Many-Splendored Thing* and realized that I had carried the romantic hero of that book to his grave on a Korean hillside.

When we fell back to the Naktong, Murrow, Boyle, and I decided to take a quick look at the new defense line on the first morning our troops were in their new position. We gambled the enemy had not yet brought up full strength to the other side of the river, and we set out by jeep alone on the American side of the Naktong. It was a fully exposed road, and we had a few scares before we traveled many miles, but found protection when the road turned inland a few hundred yards between some hills. We had a quick lunch with officers of the Twenty-fifth Division. It had been so badly battered that nearly all of its officers were thoroughly defeatist by the time we visited them in early August. One said that "if we retreat again, our next line of resistance will be on Hawaii." The leaders of the Twenty-fifth Division were dismayed we had risked our lives on the river road that morning, and recommended another road back to Taegu for our return trip. They said the other road hadn't been tested, but they hoped it was free of the enemy since it was to the east of the Naktong.

Murrow, Boyle, and I were in a merry, mellow mood as our jeep moved through the high hills to the east of the river and headed for Taegu in the late afternoon. At one point, we became entranced with the scenery. Murrow and I, who had played a lot of golf together, thought the terrain was ideal for a golf course, and as we moved along we decided where we might place a water hole, or build a par five, or place a short par three. Suddenly we looked up, and on all the trees lining the road there were red flags flying.

Our first thought was that we had stumbled into an area held by the enemy, perhaps as the result of a local uprising unknown to American troops. The flag-bedecked road continued for miles ahead, and our apprehensions mounted.

Suddenly two trucks bearing armed men who were not in uniform came whipping around a curve heading in our direction. From my front seat position in the jeep, I said to Murrow and Boyle that we might as well stop "and get it over with." I had no doubt these were enemy troops when their trucks pulled to a stop opposite our jeep.

When we dismounted, we asked them if anyone spoke English. A man from the second truck came forward, and asked us if we had encountered any North Koreans in the hills through which we had just passed. There were rumors the enemy had infiltrated beyond the Naktong, he said, and these two trucks of South Koreans had been sent to rout them out. We breathed huge sighs of relief when we found the armed men we were now talking to were friendly.

I demanded to know what the red flag on every tree meant. Our new friend explained it was the flag of the South Korean Young Men's Association.

The South Korean trucks headed westward, and Murrow, Boyle, and I returned to our jeep. Murrow and Boyle got in the back seat but I stood beside the road for another minute or two.

"Come on," said Murrow, "get in the jeep. It's getting late and we want to get to Taegu before dark."

"Just a minute more," I responded. "I'm letting all the butterflies out of my stomach."

A few days later, Murrow and I found ourselves in much greater danger—and this time the men who threatened to kill us were United States Marines who thought because we did not know the password that we might be North Korean infiltrators.

That day had begun happily. General Earl Partridge had loaned me a C-45, twin-engined Beechcraft for a trip to the southern front in Korea, and I had collected Murrow, Bill Dunn of NBC, and James Hicks of the Afro-American Press to travel along.

When we found out that the pilot, Major Woody Ingram, had no specific orders except to give us transportation, Murrow and I proposed a quick flight to Japan to stock up on Scotch whiskey, which was in short supply in Korea, and to leave behind some money to finance further orders. We flew into Itazuke, Japan, quickly purchased three cases of Scotch for about $25 a case, and left behind $500 to finance the shipment of one case a week in wooden boxes that were to be marked "Photographic Supplies, Do Not Expose." The fraudulent labeling was our only hope that the Scotch would not be stolen from the pipeline before it reached the correspondents' billet in Taegu. The order for future Scotch deliveries was faithfully carried out, and we never lost a bottle due to pilferage.

Once the whiskey had been purchased, Major Ingram flew us to a small airfield on the southernmost tip of Korea and made a controlled ground loop so as to avoid disaster when the C-45 ate up all the grass runway. It was twilight by then, but we were anxious to push forward to join the Marines who only days before had been landed in Pusan. A South Korean general with the common name of Kim provided us with a small truck and an escort of South Korean troops, and we headed north toward the Marine positions. They had dug in that night in the area between Pusan and Masan, miles from any enemy troops.

Under the dateline "Somewhere in Korea, Aug. 5," I reported how our small convoy moved through many South Korean positions, challenged everywhere, and that, "we proceeded with a feeling of safety into the area where the Marines had established themselves."

On the first challenge by Marines, we managed to get through, but a nervous youngster wouldn't tell us the password even though I asked for it. We kept driving north, until in the darkness we heard the curt command "Halt." It was followed a few seconds later by the order "Advance and be recognized."

I was riding in the lead vehicle, so it was my responsibility to answer the challenge.

"Okay," I responded. "I'll get out to be recognized, but I'll be damned if I know the password."

Murrow, Dunn, and Hicks piled out behind me into the road. We could hear rifle bolts click menacingly a few feet away as we told these U.S. Marine sentries that we were American correspondents who had not been told the password for that night because we had just arrived from a brief visit to Japan.

A Marine, whose voice betrayed his nervousness, told us to stand in line one yard apart, to turn out the lights of our vehicles, to drop all weapons, and to keep our hands in front of our bodies so they could be observed.

First we were told we could smoke, but somebody countermanded that order. These Marines were scared, their guns were ready for action, and I thought they intended to shoot us. They would not buy the idea that we were Americans.

I have no idea how long we stood there, but it seemed like hours. Finally, Murrow suggested that he be allowed to see their commanding officer, and the Marines agreed. But they assigned a young Marine to guard Murrow. In a nervous voice, the young man, whom Murrow guessed to be about seventeen years old, told Murrow he was his prisoner and he was to walk in a certain way, keeping his hands at his side.

At the artillery position command post, Murrow found Captain

James Ordan of Orinda, California, who quickly recognized Murrow. The captain apologized for his men, explained that the Marine artillery position was in a condition of "flash red," meaning that they thought the enemy forces were very close. The captain sent a corporal to tell the Marines who were holding us prisoner to turn us loose. But, as the courier approached us, our captors refused to accept his story that he was a messenger from Captain Ordan and ordered him to stand in line with us. Now we were sure they would kill us. The situation grew more tense.

Suddenly, out of the darkness, Murrow returned, told the Marines guarding us that we were okay, and they should bring us to the commanding officer. Reluctantly they agreed, and in a few minutes we were drinking coffee with Captain Ordan. We bedded down for the night in the open air near him. That was the first time I learned that Murrow, when tired and tense, ground his teeth in his sleep like a small child.

The night was filled with the sound of rifle and automatic-weapon fire as the nervous Marines we were with, and those in nearby areas, shot at everything that moved. My first dispatch records that two Marines were killed and several others were wounded, all from "friendly" fire. In truth, there were no enemy troops for many miles, but these Marines had been frightened. They had been scared to death by the shipboard lectures they had received on the dangers of infiltration in Korea and the dire results for troops that didn't learn their lessons about infiltration. During the night, the Marine officer commanding the first division, Major General Edward A. Craig, emerged cursing from his tent to direct that the firing stop.

Murrow returned home shortly afterward to continue his CBS nightly radio broadcasts, and I stayed on to cover a war where the American position improved daily.

With other correspondents, I was ready for the big invasion at Inchon, but we had a weekend in and near Tokyo just before we sailed for that engagement. On our final day ashore, there was a severe earthquake as we were eating lunch in Tokyo, and that night we passed through a typhoon with 100-mile-an-hour winds aboard the troop transport *Simon B. Buckner*, named for the commanding general on Okinawa who had been killed on the very last day before that island was declared secure.

The Navy had snafued our orders for Inchon, so though Whitehead, Bigart, and I were among the correspondents supposed to get first priority, we were among the very last to land. This was a daring and in many ways unprecedented amphibious assault. Never before had Americans made a major landing at twilight, on a beach with twenty-six-foot tidal changes that made impossible any hope of rescue or reinforcement before the next tide at dawn. Most other military landings had been made at dawn, with a full day ahead to survey and provide what the military situation might demand.

I will always remember the experience of Joe Alsop, the columnist, who got ashore on an early wave of assault troops but who was landed on the wrong beach at dark far from other Americans. It was too risky to try to join our other forces, so Alsop and a few Marines spent the night in splendid isolation, taking cover beside a seawall. I asked Alsop what the hell he did during that long and terrifying night.

"Well, old boy," the elegant Alsop replied, "I simply took two sleeping pills and slept it out."

Alsop was a walking pharmacy, a hypochondriac of immense physical courage.

Once ashore, the Marines and Army troops quickly smashed through the slim defense line of North Koreans, heading for Kimpo airport and Seoul.

One day on the way to Kimpo, I hitched a ride with Keyes Beech of the *Chicago Daily News* and his friend Marguerite Higgins of the *Herald Tribune*. With me was an Associated Press correspondent, Bill Ross, and as we reached the very "point" of the Marine advance forces, Beech asked Ross to get out of the jeep which Beech and others had "liberated" in Seoul before the Communists could grab it.

I've been to a lot of wars and I've never before or since seen anything like this happen. War correspondents usually stick together, especially in the most dangerous areas, but Beech explained to Ross he wanted him out of the jeep because he regarded Ross as a competitor. The AP, Beech said, had faster facilities for moving stories into Chicago and thus Ross might beat Beech with his own story. At this point, I too left the jeep. Beech protested he had not asked me to leave, but I responded coldly that "I came forward with Ross, and I'll go back with him."

It was a hell of a dangerous place to leave the jeep, because the snipers had not been cleaned out behind us. But we made it back on foot to a main road where we hitchhiked back to the command ship. Just as we boarded the ship, we got word that Kimpo had been captured, and we beat Beech and Miss Higgins with the story. They didn't get back for a long time.

I think the Inchon operation was the high point in General Mac-Arthur's military career. It was a superb master stroke and executed brilliantly. MacArthur watched the landing himself from the command ship, and entrusted the ground command to a separate corps headed by his own chief of staff, Major General Edmond Almond.

Carl Mydans of *Life*, Tom Lambert of AP, and I were with General Almond on the day our troops made a flanking move and river crossing southeast of Seoul to insure its recapture. We stood on a hill that was technically in no-man's-land and watched the Seventh Division troops take the enemy by surprise with this new crossing of the Han. As we stood on the hilltop, clearly visible to the enemy across the river, there was one burst of mortar fire that landed perhaps 100 yards to our right. We hit the dirt, and stayed down so as not to invite additional fire, but I never felt we were in any serious trouble that day.

You can imagine my surprise a few weeks later to read in the Army newspaper *Stars and Stripes* that General Almond had received the Distinguished Service Cross for exposing himself to heavy enemy fire while in no-man's-land on this operation.

"Hell," I muttered to myself, "I didn't get a medal, but I was not five yards from the general."

Even after Inchon had been a brilliant success, MacArthur insisted upon keeping Almond's corps separate from the Tenth Army command of General Walker. MacArthur wanted Almond to shine even though it looked like we might be running out of war. Correspondents said this was "Operation Third Star, Last Chance," meaning that if Almond didn't get his promotion to lieutenant general quickly, he would never get another chance.

We never had adequate or satisfactory communications facilities for the correspondents stationed in Korea, and not a few of us suspected this was no accident. This left the main reporting of the war to the "communiqué commandos" stationed in Tokyo, and they took their editorial guidance from the briefers in MacArthur's headquarters. The correspondents in the field who might have witnessed the action could not get their stories back to New York as fast as the men on duty in Tokyo. Though Press Wireless, an independent company organized by several newspapers, offered to ship out a mobile transmitter, MacArthur's headquarters always found excuses why it could not be placed in operation. We in

Korea were forced to rely on the military facilities, already over-burdened with priority military traffic, or on the few existing tele-phone lines into Tokyo.

After the recapture of Kimpo, we organized our own airlift system, which proved physically exhausting in my case and nearly brought death to one of my *Times* colleagues, Harold Faber, whose Flying Boxcar crashed and burned on landing at an American base in Japan. After a full day at the front, we would walk or hitchhike back to Kimpo to board at twilight the last military air transport heading for an American air base in Japan. On the flight from Kimpo to Japan, I usually would write my dispatch so as to have it ready for instant filing by telephone or teletype when the airplane touched down in Japan. Then I would have dinner in the American mess, catch a few hours of sleep, and be awakened for the trip back to Korea on the first transport out, which was scheduled to land at Kimpo just after daylight. Then it would be back to the front until dusk, another flight to Japan, and back to the front again the next morning.

It was on one of these later flights that Faber, a fine correspond-ent with a brilliant future, was wounded so critically in an air crash that we feared he might die. His recovery was not assured until many weeks later, when at Walter Reed Hospital in Wash-ington his leg had been amputated. This ended his career as a cor-respondent, and he became an editor on the national desk in New York.

After Inchon's brilliant success, and the recapture of Seoul, the North Korean armies that had been opposing us to the south simply evaporated and made their way back helter-skelter to North Ko-rean territory behind the thirty-eighth parallel.

We had come into this war simply to halt aggression, and I wondered as I flew south whether General Walker's armies would stop at the thirty-eighth parallel or whether he would seek to destroy the enemy armies.

I saw Walker in his old headquarters at Taegu, and he said his troops were moving north. He carefully had refrained from asking for any clarifying instructions, he said. The next day, Major Ingram flew a group of correspondents up to the thirty-eighth parallel on the east coast, and we looked down as South Korean troops moved across this unmarked boundary against little or no opposition.

I left Korea in November, 1950, before MacArthur launched his ill-fated "Win the War by Christmas" offensive toward the Yalu, and took a terrible beating from the Chinese. One reason for this American defeat was the divided command and lack of communication between the forces commanded by Generals Walker and Almond.

I was back in Washington, once again assigned to the White House, on that night when President Truman decided at long last to remove General MacArthur from all his commands and to replace him with General Matthew Ridgway. Simply stated, MacArthur had been guilty of insubordination to his Commander-in-Chief, and Harry Truman never hesitated for a moment when he decided to fire him.

It was one of the great stories of my career, that night when Truman fired MacArthur, and the *Times* scored a tremendous beat over the *Herald Tribune* even though we started dead even. Never have I dictated a story so fast, so cleanly, as I did that night working directly with the New York office, where the copy was pulled from the typewriter paragraph by paragraph and rushed to the composing room, then to the waiting presses.

On his homecoming, MacArthur made an emotional appeal to a Congress that wasn't quite sure whether Harry Truman was right. But Truman stood his ground, and MacArthur, in his own words, simply faded away, though he entertained until the last minute the hope that he and not General Eisenhower would be the Republican Presidential nominee of 1952.

CHAPTER
17

As the Presidential election year of 1952 dawned, both major parties faced major questions:

Would President Truman seek reelection to a third term?

Would General of the Army Dwight Eisenhower reenter the Presidential arena he had renounced for military men as recently as 1948, and if he did, could he capture the Republican Presidential nomination from Senator Robert A. Taft of Ohio, who was known as "Mr. Republican"?

Mr. Truman had already made up his mind in December, 1951, not to run and had informed his closest White House aides. For public consumption, however, he was playing coy about it, hinting one day that he might run and another that he might not. At one stage, answering my question, he strongly reiterated what he had told General Eisenhower in 1945, that there was no public position, including the Presidency, that the Supreme Allied Commander might want for which Mr. Truman would not back him. Seconds later, Mr. Truman, smiling, qualified his statement to say he would back General Eisenhower only if he ran as a Democrat, but he now had concluded that Ike ·was a Republican.

I cannot even pretend at this late date that I did a good job in covering the Truman story; indeed, I must admit that I lost at least one golden opportunity to forecast his refusal to seek another four years inside the White House that he referred to as his "jail." My chance had come during a pre-Christmas holiday at Key West, Florida, when Merriman Smith of United Press and I were sharing a cottage together. Smitty and I both liked to cook—I specialized in steaks and Smith in Chinese foods—and one of our favorite people around the White House was the venerable white-haired correspondence secretary, William D. Hassett, who had served FDR as well as Truman.

One night after I had cooked a steak for Hassett, the three of us resumed our discussion of Subject A: Would Truman Run Again. Hassett told us both he now knew that the President would not run again.

Smith and I spurned Hassett's information. We doubted that he knew any such thing, we told him, and we were well aware that what he had said about Truman not running again was the product of his wishful thinking because he loved the President and didn't want to see him killed off by the terrible responsibilities of the Presidency. We were, I'm sure, quite rude to Hassett, who simply smiled and asked for another drink and changed the subject.

In any event, neither Smith nor I wrote anything about Hassett's forecast, for Smith and I had been at the White House too long to fall for a story like Hassett's. You can imagine our chagrin when Truman did announce that he wouldn't run again.

Truman had told Hassett and other staff members of his decision not to run on the same day that Hassett tried to convince Smith and me that he knew the President wouldn't run; but we, in our arrogance, had simply refused to report what we had been told on excellent authority.

I had one more chance to print the news first that Truman wouldn't run—an exclusive interview with the President on February 12, 1952. But after granting me the interview, the President withheld permission for me to publish it because he had been made angry by a visit that morning from the aging Illinois Democratic Representative, Adolph J. Sabath. Sabath told reporters outside the White House that the President didn't really want to run, but might be a candidate at the risk of his health and personal happiness if he felt the nation needed him.

The interview Truman gave me has never been published, because the White House would not release it while it was still news, even after the President dramatically made his announcement on March 29 before a stunned audience at the $100 a plate Jefferson-Jackson Day dinner in the National Guard Armory in Washington.

Truman interpolated into his prepared speech that night this declaration:

"I shall not be a candidate for reelection. I have served my country long and I think efficiently and honestly. I shall not accept renomination. I do not feel that it is my duty to spend another four years in the White House."

There were cries of "no, no" from the audience, but the President told reporters as he left the Armory that there was no chance whatsoever that he would change his mind.

I had left the primary campaign trail in Wisconsin to come back to Washington for the sole purpose of covering that speech because the President had given me a hint during that unpublished interview of February 12 that the March 29 dinner might be the time and place for his third-term announcement.

The copy paper is yellow with age now, but the fact that I've kept it all this time reflects my pride in that accomplishment that might have won me a Pulitzer Prize if Truman hadn't withdrawn his permission for publication.

The President and I had talked alone in his oval office for perhaps thirty minutes before I wrote this account, which by prior agreement he had the right to edit:

Washington, Feb. 12—President Truman has given friends in recent days the first comprehensive account of the various factors bearing upon the decision he must announce reasonably soon as to whether he will run for reelection, or retire, voluntarily, from the Presidency on Jan. 20, 1953.

Mr. Truman didn't tell these friends his final decision— if indeed he has made it—but he did outline in detail the pros and cons concerning seeking another term as he sees them.

One of these friends [journalese for Mr. Truman himself] gave *The New York Times* today a summary of Mr. Truman's views remarking that "if the President should be asked whether this is a true account of his current state of mind, I feel certain he would reply in the affirmative."

This was the summary:

If the President felt free to do exactly what he wanted to

do, he would not be a candidate for reelection under any circumstances.

But events—in the world, in the country, inside the Democratic party and inside the Republican party—may lead him to seek another term.

Friends who have discussed the situation with Mr. Truman recently believe he would be a candidate for reelection if he felt that his failure to run and a resultant division in the Democratic party might lead to the election of Senator Robert A. Taft of Ohio, General of the Army Douglas MacArthur, or some other Republican who shares their views on foreign and domestic policy. He describes their views as backward-looking and the prospect of either's election to the Presidency as the most terrible thing that could happen to the country.

While the President feels that his own 1948 victory established the Democratic party as a national party, able to win elections without the electoral votes of New York or the "solid south," he would fear a Republican victory if the Democratic party were divided by a dog fight within its own ranks, concerning the Presidential candidate of 1952, by reason of his retirement.

Mr. Truman has told friends many times that he does not believe in the doctrine of the indispensable man. Acceptance of that theory by any people, he believes, would lead inevitably to rule by "Caesars" and to dictatorship. He does not regard himself as an indispensable man.

Another factor pointing the way toward a "do-not-choose-to-run" statement is the effect of the Presidency upon the Truman family. The President is irritated by all the precautions the Secret Service feels it must take not only for his own safety, but for that of his family ever since the unsuccessful assassination attempt by two Puerto Rican nationalists in November, 1950.

Mrs. Truman has never been enthusiastic about political office for her husband and finds burdensome all the things a First Lady must do to carry her share of the White House entertaining.

Margaret Truman is the idol of her father's eye, and he resents the restrictions that are placed upon her freedom as the daughter of a President. He also feels strongly his presence in the White House places handicaps upon the activities of the rest of his family.

There also is the personal fact that the burdens of the Presidency are so great in modern times that prolonged tenure inevitably shortens the longevity of any incumbent. Mr. Truman has been speculating of late that his predecessor, Franklin D. Roosevelt, would be alive today if he had not run for a third term in 1940, and remarking that he (Truman) had no intention of dying at his desk. By next inauguration day, Mr. Truman will have been in elective office for thirty years, and three decades of public service have left their mark.

On the other side of the ledger, among the factors pushing the President toward another campaign for the Presidency is the well-known fact that Mr. Truman regards the continuity of American foreign policy as the most important issue facing the country today.

He feels that foreign policy is inescapably linked with the proper domestic policy, and that unless the country is prosperous and united, it cannot support the kind of foreign policy necessary to deal with the Soviet threat.

Mr. Truman's views on party loyalty and the importance of preserving the two-party system also are well known. Having been given by the Democratic party the chance to win the highest elective office in this country, Mr. Truman would be swayed by arguments that his failure to run would amount to sabotaging the party's chances to win the next election. Certainly he is under great pressure from leaders within the party to seek another term.

But those who have seen the President recently are convinced that he hasn't made up his mind finally about what he will do in the 1952 campaign. His personal decision would be to retire on Jan. 20, 1953, but that decision may be changed by events in the weeks and months ahead.

If the President wants to run again, he undoubtedly can command renomination from his party convention. He probably can force the nomination of the man he would want to succeed him, but there is a chance that in this process the Democratic party might split over succession.

If that prospect seems likely, Mr. Truman might decide to run again to keep the party from destroying itself.

The prospect is that the President will make his announcement within the next sixty days, the basis of this forecast being that by that time it should be clear whether Senator Taft will head the Republican ticket and whether the Democrats will be sufficiently united to nominate an international-ist-minded candidate whom the President believes can defeat the Ohioan in the November elections.

The national Jefferson-Jackson Day dinner here on March 29 would offer a good forum for Mr. Truman to make his announcement. Another likely date might be April 12, the seventh anniversary of his succession to the Presidency, following the death of President Roosevelt.

I was, of course, crushed by the White House decision to deny permission for the interview to be published after Mr. Truman had agreed to my interviewing him and to my publishing what he told me in indirect fashion. My bosses in Washington and New York were ready to break the big story that next morning, and the dispatch I have quoted above bears the marks of editing in the handwriting of Arthur Krock.

But once the President declared our talk off-the-record, that was the way it stayed until the publication of this book. Reporters now often break off-the-record commitments and find some excuse for themselves for doing so, but it never occurred to me or to my editors at the *Times* to in any way violate the commitment we had given to Mr. Truman even though he had in his own way chosen to violate the commitment he had given to me. His only excuse was that he was just "damned mad" at Congressman Sabath, whom he described in typical Truman language as a "shithead."

By the time the President announced his unwillingness to run, he had already chosen his successor, Adlai E. Stevenson, then governor of Illinois. Stevenson, typically, was unable to make a quick yes-or-no decision, and finally was "drafted" by the Democratic national convention that met that year in Chicago. Stevenson was a brilliant orator, and the darling of most liberals and intellectuals, but he was hampered by indecisiveness throughout his long career, including his last chore as Ambassador at the United Nations during the Kennedy and Johnson administrations. Stevenson had two campaigns for the Presidency against Eisenhower, and was beaten more decisively in the second than the first.

Over on the Republican side, in early 1952, General Eisenhower had allowed friends to put him into the Republican Presidential race. At first Ike had the idea that he might be nominated by both parties if he did not work hard to win either nomination. Republican leaders beat a path to the Eisenhower headquarters in Paris, but for many months they could not get him to launch a meaningful campaign against Senator Taft, who had the almost solid backing of the Republican establishment, except for the Eastern "internationalist" sector, including such men as Governor Dewey and former National Chairman Herbert Brownell. The Eastern newspapers, led by the New York *Herald Tribune*, gave potent editorial support to the Eisenhower campaign, and the general was an easy victor in his first test of popular strength with Senator Taft in the New Hampshire primary.

The history books will say that Eisenhower beat Taft for the Presidency in Chicago, but I say that the battle was fought and won in a little Texas town called Mineral Wells, where the Taft "organization Republicans" steamrollered Republicans newly recruited to back Ike. The Taft group grabbed a Texas delegation with thirty-eight votes in such high-handed fashion that it became known as the "Texas steal," and it was, in the final analysis, the issue on which Taft went down to defeat at the Chicago convention.

Before 1952, the Republican parties in the Southern states had been small, almost private clubs, closely held by "Old guard" leaders who preferred to keep the party small in each state so they could control it more easily. These Southern Republicans were important chiefly for the delegate votes they could provide at national conventions at four-year intervals, and when a Republican President was in power, to dispense a little federal patronage. Usually they did not run statewide candidates in the one-party states in the South where the Democrats were dominant.

But the rise of Eisenhower changed all that, and especially in Texas. Republican caucuses to elect convention delegates were filled with standing-room-only crowds—the new Republicans determined to elect Ike to the Presidency. These former Democrats easily outnumbered and outvoted the regular Republican leaders who had committed themselves to Taft, but the Taft people would not accept defeat. They argued the new Republicans were not "card-carrying" Republicans and weren't properly representative of the Texas Republican party.

Henry Zweiffel, the Texas Republican national committeeman,

told me quite frankly in advance that his group planned to unseat the Eisenhower delegates and to elect Taft delegates instead through their control of the machinery at the Republican state convention to be held in Mineral Wells. Zweiffel said he would rather lose with Taft than win with Ike, and he was not disposed to let Texas Democrats recently turned Republican take over his party.

On hand to represent Taft's national interests in Texas were the Ohio Senator's cousin, David S. Ingalls, and a long-time Tennessee Taft leader, Representative B. Carroll Reece. Ingalls and Reece approved the Zweiffel tactics. I asked Mr. Ingalls in advance if he did not see in these maneuvers the prospect that Taft might be hurt nationally because of what went on in Texas.

"Why should he?" Ingalls responded.

I tried to point out that Republicans, since they were the minority party, probably couldn't elect a President unless they got help from unhappy Democrats, but he would not concede that the Eisenhower Republicans had made the switch in good faith.

Herb Brownell was in Texas for the Ike forces, and he summarized the issue: "The Taft people have found out now they can't win the nomination so they are out to steal it."

Until then, Eisenhower had been unwilling to campaign against Taft on any substantive issue, even that of foreign policy. Now the stolen Southern delegates provided a battle cry, and the Eisenhower backers paraded in Texas and later in Chicago with "Rob with Bob" signs.

After Mineral Wells, I had no doubts myself that Ike would win the nomination and I told the Taft leaders my opinion. There was one big primary still to be fought in South Dakota, and I moved on to Sioux Falls from Texas. But before I left Mineral Wells, I telephoned a Taft lieutenant, Earl T. Barnes of Cincinnati, then working for Taft in South Dakota, and told him bluntly, "You've just lost the nomination by what your people have done in Texas." Barnes bet me I was wrong, but paid off after the first ballot in Chicago.

When Taft entered the South Dakota primary, he thought it would be an easy victory for him, and a meaningful triumph over Eisenhower since it would come just before the convention in Chicago. But South Dakota turned out to be surprisingly close, and Taft's final margin of victory over Eisenhower was less than 1,000 votes.

The Taft people had great mobility in South Dakota, thanks to the generous contribution of an amphibious aircraft, a Grumman Marlin, with crew and gasoline provided by the wealthy Florida oil man Charles Wrightsman, who in later years was to be a confidant and occasional host at Palm Beach to Democratic President John F. Kennedy.

The slugging in South Dakota was pretty rough. One night Barnes and the other Taft leaders showed me a newspaper advertisement that had been prepared for publication in weekly newspapers throughout the state. It was a direct appeal to the voters of German descent, quoting the conservative Washington newsletter *Human Events*. The letter had described Eisenhower as having authorized taking German workers into the Soviet Union as "slave laborers" to repair the damage from the Nazi military machine.

The advertisement was already in the hands of South Dakota weeklies for publication when Barnes showed it to me.

"Well, I think it might help you in South Dakota, but ruin you across the country," was my bluntly stated reaction.

Early the next morning, Barnes and his aides chartered several airplanes to fly around South Dakota recalling the "slave labor" ad, making certain it would not be published.

The controversy over "the Texas steal" mounted in the weeks before the convention delegates assembled in Chicago. And the Eisenhower forces had a piece of rare luck in that the National Governors' Conference convened in Houston just before the convention. Angry pro-Eisenhower delegates, robbed of their convention seats, went to work on the Republican governors. The Eisenhower strategy called for a new convention rule, one that would bar contested delegates from voting in the convention until the controversy over their seating had been settled. Every Republican governor, including some who were for Taft, signed the proposal for the "fair play" amendment, much to the dismay of the Ohio Senator and his campaign managers.

The first vote taken at Chicago was on the "fair play" amendment, and Taft lost by approximately 100 votes, thanks in large part to the seventy votes provided by the California delegation which was pledged to the Presidential candidacy of Governor Earl Warren, later to be named Chief Justice by a grateful Eisenhower and his Attorney General, Brownell.

The field marshal for the losing Taft forces was Tom Coleman, a white-haired, blue-eyed party leader from Wisconsin who fought the good fight for Taft and never really acknowledged the Eisenhower victory. Coleman was one of my closest personal friends, before and after the Chicago convention, until his death. He never tried to conceal from me the troubles Taft had after the Mineral Wells convention and the charges of delegate-stealing became a national issue.

Taft had control of the Republican National Committee and its chairman, Guy Gabrielson of New Jersey. On every convention arrangement the National Committee sided with Taft, only to be upset by the delegates themselves.

Taft himself had picked General MacArthur to be the Republican keynoter that year. MacArthur, I think, had an idea that he might be nominated if Taft couldn't make it. Certainly MacArthur thought himself a preferable nominee to General Eisenhower, who earlier had been his subordinate both in Washington and in the pre-war Philippine Islands.

But MacArthur's keynote address, though well received, did not start any MacArthur stampede. MacArthur came into Chicago hoping that a single speech would bring him the nomination just as the famous "Cross of Gold" speech had won an earlier Democratic nomination for William Jennings Bryan back in 1896. But when the speech was over, MacArthur knew the prize was not to be his.

He left the convention platform in company with Chairman Gabrielson and with a key Taft lieutenant, Representative Clarence Brown. It was the general's plan to return almost immediately to his Waldorf-Astoria apartment in New York City, but Senator Taft telephoned from his Hilton Hotel headquarters in downtown Chicago to urge that MacArthur remain on the scene in Chicago. The general refused.

"This stage is not set for Macbeth," MacArthur said to Gabrielson and Brown.

With every hour, the tide rose for Eisenhower and slipped away from Taft. By the time the first ballot was taken, General Eisenhower had 595 votes and Senator Taft had 500, with a scattering of other votes for Governor Warren, for General MacArthur, and for Harold Stassen. Ike was just nine votes short of the majority when Warren Burger, chairman of the Minnesota delegation, stepped to the platform to switch nineteen votes from Stassen to Eisenhower, and with those votes the Republican Presidential nomination was settled. Years later, Burger was rewarded for that

Minnesota vote change when President Nixon made him Chief Justice of the U.S. Supreme Court to replace Earl Warren.

Eisenhower, watching on a television set downtown, told me later he had been "bored" by the first-ballot delegate tabulations and didn't fully realize that the recognition of Burger meant that his nomination was now assured. His first instinct was to visit Senator Taft, and this he did, helping to close Republican ranks for the battle ahead.

Then, on the recommendation of New York's Governor Thomas E. Dewey, Eisenhower chose young Senator Richard Nixon from California to be his running mate.

The Democratic team of Adlai Stevenson for President and Senator John Sparkman of Alabama for Vice President never had a chance to beat the Eisenhower-Nixon combination. The Democrats were caught up in the "mess" in Washington, plus the unpopularity of the limited war being fought in Korea at heavy cost in men and money.

Eisenhower promised a campaign crowd in Detroit that he would go to Korea himself, and this one stroke alone brought millions of votes to the Republicans.

Stevenson was magnificent in defeat. "I'm too old to cry, and it hurts too much to laugh," he said on television.

CHAPTER
18

There were many days during 1953 and 1954 when the most powerful man in the United States was not the President of the United States, but the junior Senator from Wisconsin, Joseph R. McCarthy.

McCarthy achieved power as a hunter of alleged Communists, although it is doubtful if he ever turned up a genuine Communist someone else had not uncovered first.

I spent months covering McCarthy's activities and I got to know him extremely well from the closest personal observation.

From the time he first claimed in 1950 that he held in his hand a list of 205 card-carrying Communists—a number that he would reduce progressively to eighty-nine, and finally to just one— McCarthy was always reckless with the truth, and careless with the constitutional rights of those whom he might choose to charge with wrongdoing.

McCarthy was a bully boy, and made members of the Eisenhower cabinet and other federal officials cringe with fear when he threatened to use the full power of publicity against them.

If he was caught in a lie, or about to be caught in one, he quickly changed gears and came up with an even more sensational charge that would capture the headlines, and bury forever the evidence that he had lied in the first case. It made no difference to him that the second charge was perhaps more untrue than the original accusation just disproved.

He had all the nerve of a Mississippi riverboat gambler, and he soon concluded he had nothing to fear from President Eisenhower. Ultimately this turned out to be wrong, because Ike helped to destroy him. But for a long time, lesser officials of the Eisenhower administration knew they could expect no help from the White House if they tangled with McCarthy.

The Wisconsin Senator had good reason for questioning whether President Eisenhower would stand up to him. General Eisenhower, as a Presidential candidate, surrendered to McCarthy in their first direct confrontation during the 1952 campaign.

The Eisenhower staff had sought to demonstrate to me the courage they believed their boss would show in choosing to defend General George C. Marshall before a Wisconsin audience. This audience had heard McCarthy denounce Marshall as a willful conspirator with the Communists.

That first McCarthy-Eisenhower showdown came in October, 1952, when Eisenhower was campaigning in the Middle West. As he traveled through Illinois on one day, and headed toward Wisconsin on the next, a big question among reporters was whether General Eisenhower would give an unqualified blessing to McCarthy, who was up for reelection as a Senator.

Among those of whom I inquired was a top Eisenhower aide, an old friend from Nebraska, Fred Seaton, who later was to be Eisenhower's Secretary of the Interior.

Seaton told me that Eisenhower would endorse McCarthy at the first stop in Wisconsin that next day, but he urged me to form no judgments until I had read the general's speech for the final rally in Milwaukee that evening. In that speech, Seaton predicted, Eisenhower would defend vigorously his old chief General Marshall against the unfounded attacks made by McCarthy.

"And your publisher [Arthur Sulzberger] is very much interested in this," added Seaton.

Our final stop before Wisconsin was Peoria, Illinois. McCarthy was there, accompanied by his old backer, Republican National Chairman Arthur Summerfield. In a hotel room that night, Eisenhower read to McCarthy what he proposed to say in defense of General Marshall when he got to Milwaukee.

McCarthy told me later he had listened politely to the Presidential candidate. McCarthy told Eisenhower that he was free to say whatever he liked, of course, but it was McCarthy's opinion that a Wisconsin audience might boo the Republican Presidential. nominee's defense of Marshall.

"I told him," Joe McCarthy went on, "that he would be better off choosing another state, another city, and another day for his defense of General Marshall."

Early the next morning at Green Bay, Senator McCarthy was the first to speak to a rear-platform crowd from the Eisenhower train, but went back inside before General Eisenhower himself appeared to urge the reelection of Senator McCarthy and the election of all other Republicans.

There was real concern at this point among some of General Eisenhower's backers about the probable reaction of important Eisenhower supporters who disliked McCarthy. But Seaton continued to insist to me that the pro-Marshall paragraph would be in the Milwaukee speech, and that this would satisfy the anti-McCarthy forces among the Eisenhower backers.

As the train rolled across Wisconsin, I made repeated efforts to see Senator McCarthy, and finally in the late morning I succeeded. He was sitting with Tom Coleman from Madison, who had been Taft's floor leader at Chicago. They both told me that the pro-Marshall paragraph had been deleted. I told Senator McCarthy I didn't believe him. He laughed and said, "Wait and see."

In late afternoon, in a Milwaukee hotel, Eisenhower's prepared speech for Milwaukee rolled off the mimeograph machine page by page. On each page I looked in vain for the paragraph defending General Marshall and denouncing those who had defamed him. I couldn't find it as I read the speech again and again.

Then I sought out Eisenhower's press secretary, James C. Hagerty, and finally Seaton. Both acknowledged the paragraph had been in the speech, but now it was gone.

I wrote a tough story that night, telling how Eisenhower had failed to defend his old Army friend while calling for the reelection of Senator McCarthy. The story was something of a splash on page one of the *Times*.

The next day in answer to inquiries, the Associated Press quoted a high source in the Eisenhower camp as saying that the

Times story was in error, that there never had been a pro-Marshall paragraph in the Eisenhower speech. I got an inquiry from my New York office asking my reaction to the AP's story. I replied that my account had come from highly trustworthy sources and was accurate.

I never heard any more from the *Times* about the Marshall paragraph until the election was nearly over, and I was back in New York. Then Managing Editor Catledge said he supposed I might have wondered about the reaction in New York to my story from Milwaukee.

"Yes, Turner, I was wondering but I wasn't going to be fool enough to ask," I told him.

"Boy, you were never in any trouble," Catledge said. "That paragraph about General Marshall had been written by Mr. Sulzberger himself and he had a telegram from General Eisenhower saying it would be used in Milwaukee. Then it wasn't used, and your story told us why."

I heaved a sigh of relief because I had never been sure whether I could prove the existence of a paragraph that I had not in fact ever seen myself.

After Eisenhower's landslide victory, which I again reported for the *Times'* radio station WQXR, I got the following letter, on November 6, 1952, from Arthur Sulzberger:

> Dear Bill,
> I thought you did a very good job again on election night. You certainly should be grateful that Eisenhower won with a landslide though I understand there is a possibility that you did not wish to see him elected President. At least it let you finish at a fairly reasonable hour instead of having to go through that marathon you endured four years ago when you also acquitted yourself so well.
> Congratulations and all my best to you.
> Faithfully yours,
AHS

To Mr. Sulzberger, I replied as follows:

> Thank you for your very generous and thoughtful note about the radio broadcasting job of election night, as well as

for the comments Mr. Catledge has relayed concerning the campaign coverage in general.

It was fun, as it always is, to work on a fast-developing story, whatever the outcome. And even though Orv [Dryfoos] insists that I will be credited with only half a working day since, by comparison with 1948, my radio stint added up to only about 7 hours as compared with 17½ hours.

As for the "possibility" I did not wish to see Ike elected, let's put it this way. I would be very content if I could be sure, as some of the General's supporters are sure, that the "real" Ike is the ghost-written Ike who called himself a Vandenberg Republican in Michigan and delivered the Al Smith dinner speech in New York; and that it wasn't the real McCoy when he stood on his real platform in Illinois and extemporized like the Chicago *Tribune*. I still don't know which is which, but finding out will make reporting interesting during the next four years.

One reason the Eisenhower administration had trouble dealing with Joe McCarthy and his red hunts was that the administration had a split personality. Ike, who was no politician, simply abhorred McCarthy and all that he stood for. But other campaigners, including Vice President Nixon, saw a rich harvest of votes in red-hunting and blaming the Democrats for "treasonous" acts.

For a long time, McCarthy was appeased when he started making trouble, and like others who had been appeased in other places, McCarthy fed on his powers and had nothing but contempt for those who dared not face him head on.

For a long time, the Wisconsin Senator had been talking about "twenty years of treason," meaning all the five terms that Presidents Roosevelt and Truman had served, but now, in his contempt for the Eisenhower crowd, McCarthy stretched his oratory a little and began to talk about "twenty or twenty-one years of treason."

I had a grandstand seat for all of this because reluctantly I had bowed to Scotty Reston's urgings and agreed to become the McCarthy expert—not just five days a week in Washington, but also on weekends when the Wisconsin Senator went home or out on his lucrative speech-making circuit. It was a hard, distasteful task and those of us assigned to McCarthy privately referred to it as "the sewer beat."

At one point, during the French struggle to hold Indochina, it was announced that there would be one final drop of paratroopers into the doomed fort of Dien Bien Phu. I sent a note to Reston volunteering to jump with the French paratroopers into Dien Bien Phu. On Monday morning, in my typewriter, there was a note from Reston which read: "Look, you coward, go on back up to Capitol Hill and cover McCarthy."

Reston had put me on the McCarthy story because he thought I had both the physical endurance and the courage to report the news as it happened. That had not always been true of *Times* men on the story; one of them, we found out later, had been a former member of the Communist party and it was necessary to move him out of the Washington bureau in a hurry. But he wasn't fired, even though he passed the word around New York for a while that his transfer had something to do with rivalry with me. He quit talking that way after Reston told him face to face that if the rivalry nonsense persisted, he (Reston) would find it necessary to tell the real reason for his sudden departure from Washington.

It was perhaps curious that even though I pulled no punches on McCarthy, the Senator and I enjoyed friendly personal relations. We ate and drank together, both to excess. McCarthy had a habit of huddling on late afternoons with his close journalistic supporters including the reporter from the Chicago *Tribune*. I got into those meetings too.

When the big fight with the Army developed, it was Secretary of the Army Robert T. Stevens who first defied McCarthy. But then, at the urging of other Republican Senators, Stevens surrendered to McCarthy and agreed to provide him with witnesses that the Army had said would not be allowed to testify.

That was at the famous fried chicken luncheon arranged by that old compromiser, Senator Everett McKinley Dirksen, where Stevens was so confused he thought he was the victor, not the loser.

Late that afternoon, I called Senator McCarthy and the following conversation took place:

"Well, Senator, it looks to me like you not only got your pound of flesh [from Stevens], but you weighed your hand as well," I said.

"Bill, have you ever thought you'd like to be a general?" McCarthy asked.

"Good God, no, Joe. Why?" I replied.

"Well, if you want to be a general, I can fix it. I'm running the Army now," McCarthy asserted.

It was a short-lived triumph for McCarthy, what might be called a Pyrrhic victory, because now the Wisconsin Senator had gone too far even for a President who did not want to fight a Senator of his own party. Ike could not allow the Army to be so humiliated, and the charges and countercharges that led to the Army-McCarthy hearings soon developed.

Those hearings, lasting thirty-six days, were the instrument that destroyed Joe McCarthy. Much of the credit should go to Robert Kintner, then president of the American Broadcasting Company, who decided to provide complete coverage even though it cost about $500,000 for a network that was already losing money. The bigger, richer networks didn't stay with the story full time. Earlier, the first important television program that helped bring McCarthy down to size was the famous CBS "See It Now" documentary by Ed Murrow, who used film clips of McCarthy in action to show the public the Senator's real character.

But it was ABC's minute-by-minute scrutiny which was the most effective. Now the public didn't have to believe me, or Phil Potter of the *Baltimore Sun,* or Homer Bigart of the *Herald Tribune* and the conclusions we might draw about McCarthy's conduct. Now people at home could see McCarthy on their own television screens, snarling and smirking, constantly interrupting with his "points of order."

On the home screens too, the American audience watched that dramatic confrontation between McCarthy and the old-fashioned Yankee lawyer from Boston, Joseph Welch. Welch cried out after McCarthy struck out at one of Welch's law firm associates who was not associated with the hearing. McCarthy said the young associate, Frederick G. Fisher, originally had been slated for a job in the Army-McCarthy hearings until identified as a member of the National Lawyers Guild "long after it had been exposed as the legal arm of the Communist party," as McCarthy put it.

"Until this moment," Welch cried out, "I think I never really gauged your cruelty or recklessness. If there is a God in heaven, it will do neither you nor your cause any good."

And Welch flatly refused to question McCarthy further.

From that time on, Joe was doomed, and Joe knew it. There followed the Senate censure resolution, and the hearings before a special committee headed by Utah's Republican Senator Arthur Watkins.

Finally, on the Sunday before the censure debate began in the

Senate, I was one of a panel that questioned Senator McCarthy on the premiere of the CBS television program *Face the Nation.* I remarked something about the censure debate beginning on the morrow, and McCarthy snapped back that "the lynch bee begins tomorrow."

"Senator," I said, "did you refer to the Senate of the United States as a lynch bee?"

McCarthy was astounded by this direct question, and began to evade, and duck, saying that I could call it what I liked.

"No, Senator," I responded, "let's call it what you called it . . . a lynch bee. . . . Are you referring to a constitutional organ of the United States government as a lynch bee . . .?"

When the program ended, McCarthy told me, "You are a worse ham than I am, Bill. You know that you do not have any more respect for the Senate than I do."

"That may be true," I responded, "but I'm not a member of the Senate, and I'm not on trial starting tomorrow."

In the debate that followed, the charges against McCarthy were amended, and the final count on which he was convicted was that he had spoken contemptuously of the Senate itself when he called it a "lynch bee."

What Joe had done in his moment of recklessness was to insult the Senate as a whole, and this was too much for its Republican and Democratic leaders. The Senate likes to think of itself as the most exclusive club in the world, and its own deliberations are controlled largely by a kind of inner club, the establishment, and that establishment had been gravely offended by McCarthy's reference to the Senate as a "lynch bee."

In the censure hearings, McCarthy was represented by Edward Bennett Williams, a celebrated criminal lawyer, but Williams often found it impossible to restrain his client. At one stage, Williams, working with Senator Barry Goldwater, the Arizona Republican who later was to be the 1964 Presidential nominee, believed they had worked out a face-saving compromise under which McCarthy would apologize and the Senate would drop the censure charges. McCarthy refused to go along with the proposal of Williams and Goldwater unless the deal was also acceptable to another McCarthy cheerleader, Senator Herman Welker, Idaho Republican. Welker said no, and so did Joe, and the Senate moved to its final vote.

Senator Lyndon Johnson, then minority leader but later to be President of the United States, played a major role, bringing his flock of conservative and liberal Democrats into close alliance against McCarthy. When the final vote was taken, every Democrat in the Senate voted against the Wisconsin Senator. The final vote was 67 to 22. McCarthy and McCarthyism were dead politically.

By now, Joe was drinking far too much, and none of his friends, not even his pretty wife, Jeanne, could persuade him to take it easy.

Before McCarthy died, he gave me tremendous help on the exposé that led in 1955 to the enforced resignation of Harold Talbott as Secretary of the Air Force. Joe provided the documents with which I demonstrated that Talbott had used his office and the stationery of the Air Force to seek business for a private management engineering firm, Mulligan and Company, in whose profits Talbott continued to share after he took government office.

I was not the first newsman to disclose Talbott's conflict of interest in office. The story was broken originally by Charles L. Bartlett in *The Chattanooga Times* and he got a Pulitzer Prize for it. But Bartlett's story in the Tennessee paper attracted little or no outside interest. A Democratic party official, Clayton Fritchey, told me about it with a suggestion that I might have more impact than Bartlett had had.

I made my way to Capitol Hill where Robert F. Kennedy, then counsel to the Senate Permanent Subcommittee on Investigations, confirmed the Bartlett story with the added information that he (Kennedy) now planned to question Talbott soon.

The Air Force Secretary was attending a high-level Defense Department meeting at the Marine Corps base in Quantico, Virginia, but I was able to get him on the telephone. Talbott told me he was leaving the conference early the next morning to make himself available for questioning by young Kennedy. Talbott assured me he had done nothing wrong, and would cooperate fully with the Senatorial investigation to demonstrate there had been no wrongdoing.

We gave the story a big ride the next day. Now people began to pay attention to the inquiry into Talbott's business affairs. When he had been up for confirmation by the Senate, Talbott had agreed to sell his stock in major defense contractors, but he had told the committee that his private management partnership couldn't be sold. However, he had promised to take no active part in its management while in office.

President Eisenhower was in Geneva attending a summit meeting with Soviet leaders, and in his absence, most Republican leaders in

Washington derided the idea that Talbott had done anything wrong.

Newsweek magazine, for example, published a story attacking Bartlett and me under the caption "Back page story with a front page name." *Newsweek* suggested that I didn't know what I was writing about.

A few days later there were signs within the investigating committee, headed by Senator John McClellan, Arkansas Democrat, that the whole Talbott affair could be forgotten if Talbott would now resign from Mulligan and Company and stop taking money from the firm.

But Bob Kennedy didn't want the matter to end there. He had copies of correspondence that Talbott had turned over to the committee and this file of documents now was ready for circulation to the members of the subcommittee. Bob tipped me off these letters would reach the Senators about 4 P.M., and suggested that I use my contacts to get hold of the letters from one of the Senators. If I failed, Bob added, I should call him back.

Promptly at 4 P.M. I called Senator Stuart Symington, a Missouri Democrat and a long-time friend of Talbott's. Symington admitted he had the documents but said he wouldn't give them to me. As I called Symington, he was on his way to Burning Tree Club to play golf and he decided to make certain that no member of his staff would slip the documents to me or any other reporter. Symington took his file with him to Burning Tree and placed it in his locker, which was next to that of President Eisenhower. For the first and only time, as Symington later told me, he locked the door of his locker before he went out on the golf course.

After failing with Symington, I decided my next effort must be made in person. I went directly to Senator McCarthy's office and found him there. I wasn't at all certain of the reception I would get because McCarthy had been defending Talbott in the private meetings of the subcommittee.

"Did you just get some documents from the committee about Talbott?" I asked McCarthy.

"Sure," said he, "there they are."

The documents were in a large manila envelope that bore the stamp "Confidential." It had not been opened.

"Could I maybe borrow those documents for a couple of hours if I return them tonight?" I asked McCarthy.

"Sure," he said, and handed me the unopened envelope.

I started for his office door, then said, "Joe, I can't get out of the

Senate Office Building with this envelope marked 'Confidential' all over it."

Joe called in his secretary, Mary Driscoll, and told her to get me a new, larger, and unmarked manila envelope. I put the Talbott documents inside and headed out of the Senate Office Building for my office downtown.

Inside the taxicab, I tore open the envelope and the first thing I saw was a letter from Talbott, on the stationery of the Secretary of the Air Force, soliciting business for Mulligan and Company from defense contractors.

This was a rich find for a reporter, and I was so anxious to get it into print that I thought for a moment that I probably could run the couple of miles downtown faster than the taxicab could carry me. But I stayed in the cab, and at the office I made three copies of all the Talbott letters, one batch to be sent to New York for photographic reproduction, a second set to be kept by me to write the story, and a third set to be given by me to Sherman Adams, the President's principal deputy in the White House. I felt the White House deserved this courtesy from the *Times*.

Once the story had been written, the New York office insisted that I call Talbott and give him a chance to comment on the letters. I was not anxious to do this because I feared he might make the whole file public and my story would lose its exclusivity. Finally, I was ordered to call Talbott on his unlisted telephone at home.

I told Talbott that I had his letters, and he said, "I don't want to talk to you. I don't care what you print. I have nothing to say."

At this point, the telephone was taken from his hand by his wife Peggy, who said, "It's a pretty snide, low, sneaking group that has done this. My husband is tired. Don't you call him anymore."

Once the letters had been front-paged in the *Times*, Talbott demanded and got a public hearing before the McClellan subcommittee.

There was no hope now that a quiet resignation could save him.

Senator McClellan called me to his office to ask where I got the committee documents. I refused to tell him.

Senator McClellan indicated to me he might subpoena me before his committee to force disclosure. I told him it would do him no good because I would plead constitutional privilege under the First, Fifth, and all the other Amendments, and if necessary go to jail rather than tell my source. McClellan reminded me we had always been friends, and said I should cooperate with him.

"Well, Senator," I responded, "I guess this is the end of a beautiful friendship."

McClellan got up and came around his desk, and put an arm on my shoulder.

"I don't think so," he said with a smile. McClellan never again asked where I got the documents.

During the Talbott hearing that afternoon, McCarthy called me to a place beside him at the committee table. With a grin, he asked if I had told anyone where I got the documents which had safely been returned to him the night before. I assured Senator McCarthy I had told no one of my source.

"Well," said McCarthy, with a straight face, "I think you should tell this committee."

"Well, Senator McCarthy, if you think so, I will tell them I got the documents from a young Army officer who put his duty to country above any phony stamp of secrecy."

Deliberately I had parroted the answer McCarthy himself had given when pressed for the source of a secret FBI report he had in his possession during the Army-McCarthy hearings.

McClellan's committee heard Talbott's explanation and then sat back to let the Eisenhower administration handle its own problem.

I found out one morning there was a secret meeting in progress at the White House, and that Vice President Nixon was there. The President was still in Geneva. Through a White House aide, I sent a note to Mr. Nixon asking if he would give me a ride to Capitol Hill in his limousine when the meeting was over. Word came back that I was to disappear from the White House lobby and to wait on West Executive Avenue for the Vice President.

When Nixon emerged, we got into his chauffeur-driven limousine and headed for Capitol Hill.

"Talbott will have to resign," Nixon said. "We could explain away everything except using the Air Force stationery. . . . We can't duck that one."

The next day I published another front-page story saying that Talbott's fate had been decided at the high-level administration meeting, but, of course, I did not reveal at that time that Mr. Nixon was my source. My story was promptly denied by Senator Karl Mundt, South Dakota Republican, who even asserted that no such meeting had been held at the White House.

When President Eisenhower got back, he was asked about the Talbott affair at a news conference. The President said his action would hinge more on ethics than on whether Talbott had obeyed the letter of the law.

A few days later, I sailed for a long-planned holiday in the Netherlands. That night I was flooded with radiograms. Talbott had been forced to resign, but first the Air Force had given him a medal.

CHAPTER
19

Grave and complex problems faced the Republican party as it looked ahead to the 1956 Presidential campaign in the aftermath of President Eisenhower's serious heart attack in Denver in September of the year before.

I flew to Denver within a few hours after the first (and false) announcement from the White House that the President had not come to his Lowry Field office because of an upset stomach. James C. Hagerty, the regular White House press secretary, was not in Denver when the false announcement was made, but he flew in from Washington as soon as he was informed of the seriousness of the attack. Under Hagerty's direction, the American people then were told the truth about a Presidential illness for the first time in history.

For the reporters it was a kind of death watch as Eisenhower fought for his life those first few days. Army cots were brought into corridors near the main press room at Lowry Air Force Base, and the reporters worked round the clock until a team of doctors headed by Dr. Paul Dudley White of Boston could give assurance that the President was mending, slowly but surely.

Because Eisenhower regularly and daily saw his own doctor, Major General Howard Snyder, who had detected nothing amiss, the heart attack came with dramatic suddenness and shock to the President, his family, and the staff that had accompanied him to Colorado for a long summer holiday. On the day he was stricken he had returned from a fishing trip at Fraser, Colorado, high in the Rocky Mountains, worked at his desk for a short time, and then gone out to Cherry Hills Country Club to play twenty-seven holes of golf. After eighteen holes, they paused for lunch, and Ike had a hamburger with a piece of raw onion on it. In fact, he ate the raw onions of the other players at his table. One of them remarked that he was afraid to eat raw onions because they brought on indigestion, and the President responded that in earlier years raw onions had bothered him too, but not now.

Soon after the afternoon round began, the President complained to his playing partner, Ralph (Rip) Arnold, that he was suffering "a little heartburn."

"Oh, oh," the President told Arnold, "those onions are backing up."

He shot a 40—four over par—on his third nine, and went in the late afternoon to the home of his mother-in-law, Mrs. John S. Doud, for dinner. Someone suggested a drink, but the President declined. About 2 A.M., he awoke with intense pains and Dr. Synder was summoned. The doctor first prescribed a dose of milk of magnesia because the abdominal pain from the heart attack was not dissimilar to the many stomach upsets Eisenhower had suffered before. But it was determined soon afterwards that this was in fact a heart attack, requiring hospitalization at the Fitzsimmons Army Hospital in Denver. The President's heart attack already had been diagnosed when the first announcement was made by Deputy Press Secretary Murray Snyder that the President had an upset stomach.

One of my first stories from Denver on September 26 began:

President Eisenhower raced into his vacation like a man with no time to lose.

Some of his companions, younger in years, reported that the Presidential pace on the golf course, at the bridge table and in fishing streams exhausted them after a few days.

All of his friends agree that the President outwardly never seemed more relaxed, determined to have good time.

He was here to have a good time and and he was having it.

When the first shock of the President's heart attack wore off, public speculation began, naturally, on whether he could run again in 1956. Most of the experts, including myself, concluded he could not and would not in view of both the illness and his already advanced age of sixty-five.

I didn't cover all of the long death watch nor the convalescent period that followed in Denver, because two weeks after the President became ill, I doubled over in the press room at Lowry. A few hours later my misplaced appendix was removed in a long operation, which sidelined me for several weeks. When I was fit for travel, President Eisenhower's staff authorized transportation for me on the White House plane *The Columbine,* so I could have a bed all the way to Washington. Dr. White accompanied me because he was heading back to Washintgon.

In retrospect, one of the most interesting facts about the Eisenhower illness was that no one at the White House would permit Vice President Richard M. Nixon to assume any important Presidential duties. This occurred before there were regular and formal understandings between a President and a Vice President about what might be done by a Vice President in the event of Presidential disability. Nixon, for the most part, stayed in Washington and the government of the United States for a long period took its orders first from Hagerty and later from Sherman Adams, the No. 1 Presidential assistant. Adams had hurried back from a European trip when the President was stricken. Much later Nixon was allowed to preside over meaningless meetings of the President's cabinet in Washington, but these lacked substance because no one wanted Nixon or the cabinet to replace the President. The White House palace guard was in charge and in no mood to admit any outsider, even the Vice President.

When Eisenhower was well enough to leave Denver, he flew back to Washington on November 11, and proceeded almost immediately to his own home on a farm near the great Civil War battlefield at Gettysburg, Pennsylvania.

The pressures already were building on the President to run again. There was no visible effort among Republicans to develop a strong second team headed by Nixon or anyone else. Republican National Chairman Leonard W. Hall had insisted all along that Eisenhower would run again for President with Nixon again as his running mate.

In retrospect, I have decided that the White House staff members who wanted Ike to run again deliberately chose Gettysburg for his convalescent period so he would see how dull and grim life in retirement might be. Except for a Civil War buff, Gettysburg is one of the least attractive places in the country, bitterly cold in winter, damp and gloomy for much of the spring, and blazing hot in summer. After Eisenhower was well, whenever he left the White House for holidays, he sought out the Augusta National Golf Course or Thomasville, Georgia, in the spring, Denver for its cool weather in the summer, and Palm Springs, California, for the heat of the desert in winter. Certainly there was nothing about Gettysburg that made it attractive for convalescence or retirement, a point that was not lost on Eisenhower, who became increasingly eager for physical exercise as his heart mended.

In late December, the President's doctors persuaded him to go to Key West, Florida, for a brief holiday in the sun, but Key West simply was not Eisenhower's cup of tea. President Truman and his cronies had found Key West delightful for their long walks in the sun, their dips in the ocean, and their long low-stake poker games at night. But Ike was quickly bored. He hit a few golf shots, and resumed painting.

One of my stories pained the Key West and Florida chambers of commerce greatly. I asked Hagerty one day what the President had been painting in this tourist atmosphere of sun, sand, and palm trees and reported on page one that Ike now was painting from a colored picture postcard a scene of his beloved Rocky Mountains in Colorado. Perhaps the President got what Dr. White wanted, "exercise for his health and as a test of his function," but he didn't like it much and soon was back in Washington.

On January 13, the President had a dinner at the White House for his closest political associates from the 1952 campaign. It did not include Vice President Nixon. I had a clean beat on the story because Hagerty's office had given out in advance all the names of those attending, and someone at the White House suggested to me that I measure these names against the functions they had performed in the 1952 campaign and that I not be misled by their current titles in government. The dinner guests included party leaders such as

Leonard Hall, Arthur Summerfield, Sherman Adams, Henry Cabot Lodge, and the President's brother, Milton, all of whom argued that the President had to run again. There was not, one of them suggested, "time to build up a worthy successor." Nixon not only wasn't there, but he also went largely unmentioned.

By February 14, 1956, a team of six doctors, headed by Dr. White, gave a medical go-ahead for a second-term candidacy. The doctors concluded "medically the chances are that the President should be able to carry on an active life satisfactorily for another five to ten years."

"But the choice is his, not ours," the doctors concluded at a huge news conference.

Promptly, the President took off for Thomasville, Georgia, and the plantation home of his Secretary of the Treasury, George M. Humphrey. There he could hunt birds in the thousands of acres that Humphrey owned or held under lease, and, too, there was a delightful golf course set in the piney woods. The President lost no time. Early on the second morning he played his first full eighteen-hole round since his heart attack. Those reporters who were awake at such an early hour or who could be routed out of their beds by Carroll S. Linkins, the Western Union agent, were allowed to watch the President hit his tee shot. He hit it cleanly, and was well satisfied with that test of strength.

On February 29, the President held a news conference and announced that he would run again, but made no mention in his formal statement about whether he wanted Vice President Nixon as his running mate. Nixon was the subject of the first question, and the President replied that he could not dictate the choice of his running mate until he himself had been renominated. This was elaborate hocus-pocus because no one, least of all the President, doubted he would be renominated unanimously and by acclamation, dispensing with any roll call of delegates.

What I didn't know on February 29, and neither did most reporters, was that Eisenhower already had talked to Nixon privately about running again, and had suggested that the Vice President might be better off politically taking a cabinet post or some other big job in the next Eisenhower administration instead of serving another term as Vice President. This advice was preceded by a Presidential declaration that of course he would be happy to have Nixon run with him for Vice President again, but really for his own political good Nixon should look in other directions.

One day after Ike's own announcement, Jim Hagerty told me about the Eisenhower-Nixon talk in response to a question. Hagerty said that the President had told Nixon to chart his own course, but that he would support Mr. Nixon if he chose to run again.

It was a big exclusive for me and the *Times*. In retrospect, I think I missed the important point. I placed heavy emphasis on Ike's willingness to back Nixon again for Vice President, and gave secondary attention to his suggestion that Nixon might better himself politically if he came into the cabinet instead.

If I had reversed the story and hit it hard enough, the big front-page headline would have reflected Ike's proposal that Nixon run for something else, and not for Vice President.

Perhaps I over-inflate my paper's influence, but I think now that if I had written that story correctly in the first place, then Nixon might have been forced away from the Vice Presidency, and his political career might have had an entirely different ending.

It is interesting now to look at this history as told by the two participants in this conversation, General Eisenhower and Mr. Nixon.

In his *Waging Peace*, published in 1965, Mr. Eisenhower describes in great detail his meeting with his Vice President before he announced to the public that he would be a candidate for reelection.

Mr. Nixon, on the other hand, in his book *Six Crises*, first published in 1962 and brought up to date in 1968, makes no reference at all to any private talk with the President about running again in 1956, but refers only to his own tense and sometimes angry reactions to General Eisenhower's press conferences during the period when Nixon was "charting his own course." In my opinion, the Nixon book deliberately omits vital facts to bolster and explain Nixon's own course of action.

Eisenhower put it this way:

> . . . In this conversation in the early days of 1956, I emphasized to him [Nixon] that the decision to seek the Vice Presidency again would be exclusively his own.
>
> "You should," I suggested, "make a searching survey of the probable advantages and disadvantages to yourself and to the party before you give me an answer." Mr. Nixon well knew that for the entire four years of my first administration I had been searching everywhere for men of promise

and had done my best to give them political visibility. There was no difficulty in finding able administrators and leaders, but the problem of making them better known and appreciated by the public."

At this point, General Eisenhower in a footnote listed as "among the best—men whom I considered, along with others, to have the necessary qualities for successful administration and leadership— were Robert Anderson, Herbert Brownell, Cabot Lodge, Alfred Gruenther, Gabriel Hauge, Lucius Clay and my brother, Milton S. Eisenhower."

This is an interesting footnote, to say the least, revealing as it does Eisenhower's own thinking about potential Vice Presidential candidates other than Nixon.

The Eisenhower book went on:

> Indeed, except for Dick Nixon, there was no young Republican who as the 1956 convention approached was both experienced in the responsibilities of government at the White House level and so well known nationally that the public would consider him a reasonable candidate for the Presidency in 1960. That fact worked to Dick's advantage. But he had a disadvantage, I pointed out. Since the election of Martin Van Buren as the successor to Andrew Jackson in 1836, no incumbent Vice President had been elected President. Would he, I wondered, increase his acceptability to the party and the American public as a Presidential candidate in 1960 if he should decline to run again for the Vice Presidency and instead accept another post in which he would have, in his own right, obviously important responsibilities?
>
> During my first administration, Mr. Nixon had become well acquainted with the duties of the Departments. In the event he decided to withdraw from the Vice Presidential race, I was quite ready to appoint him to one for which his talents would be well suited. Already I knew two or three Cabinet officers desired to return to private life and were remaining in Washington only at my request; Defense Secretary Charles Wilson was among them. The Vice President's participation in National Security Council meetings, his legal background, and his interest in national defense would have made reasonable his appointment as Wilson's successor. I advised him to talk over this and other possibilities with his

wife, Pat, and with any other person he trusted implicitly
and to give me an answer at his convenience. He agreed. . . .
. . . One strong consideration that I had mentioned to
Dick would point toward his remaining in his present post.
This was the undeniable truth that, in view of my recent illness, the chances of my demise or complete disability within
a span of four years were, if not much greater according to
the doctors, certainly more so than they would be for one
who had no such notations on his medical record. As of that
moment, because of his unique service in the Vice Presidency, I believed Nixon to be the best prepared man in government to take over my duties in any emergency.

In *Six Crises*, Nixon's account is about as different as is possible
from that given by General Eisenhower. Nixon makes no reference
at all to this talk Ike has described above in such great detail, and
he limits his own reactions to the reports he gets secondhand about
the news conferences that Eisenhower has held. Surely, in the Nixon
case, this is a serious omission from the historical record, and, in my
opinion, is intended to distort the record. In any event, the Nixon
book tells us that when Eisenhower announced he would agree to
run, he evaded a direct reply to a question about whether he wanted
Nixon as his running mate, saying that he could not properly speak
out on the choice of a running mate until after the Republican national convention itself had picked its Presidential candidate.
The Nixon book continues:

In politics, however, not speaking can be another way of
speaking out, and the President's words set off a wave of
speculation by the public and a furor among my own friends
and supporters. This, in turn, caused embarrassment to me
because I still could say nothing before the President spoke.
At the next weekly press conference, on March 7 [1956],
the President delivered his famous answer: "I told him
[Nixon] he woud have to chart his own course and tell me
what he would like to do." His statement was telephoned
to me soon after the press conference in a somewhat garbled
version. The impression I got was that he was really trying to
tell me that he wanted me off the ticket. I told Vic Johnston,
Chief of Staff of the Senatorial Campaign Committee, who
was in my office at the time, that the only course I could
properly take under the circumstances was to call a press

conference the next day and announce that I would not be a candidate for Vice President so that Eisenhower would have a free hand to select his running mate.

It seemed to me that it was like the fund controversy all over again. But *then* [1952] Eisenhower had not known me well and had every justification for not taking a decision with regard to keeping me on the ticket until all the facts were in.

This is an interesting and self-serving declaration by Nixon concerning his anger with General Eisenhower during the 1952 controversy over the Nixon fund raised by wealthy Californians. This fund almost led to Nixon's dismissal as a Vice Presidential candidate before the Vice Presidential nominee turned public sympathy in his favor with the famous "Checkers Speech." At that time, in 1952, Nixon became so angry with General Eisenhower's indecision that he told the Presidential nominee there were times when "you must shit or get off the pot." Ike didn't like it then, nor did he really warm to Nixon perhaps until about 1968.

Picking up Nixon's discussion of how he felt about the Eisenhower "chart your own course" statement in 1956, Nixon went on to say that unlike the period of the fund controversy, Eisenhower now knew him well and had "had an opportunity to evaluate my work over the past three years, and particularly during the period after the heart attack."

If he [Eisenhower] still felt, under these circumstances, that he wanted me on the ticket only if I insisted on seeking the post, I concluded that he should have someone else in whom he had more confidence as his running mate.

Later that day, Len Hall [Republican National Chairman] and Jerry Persons [a White House assistant], who had learned from Johnston of my intentions, cornered me at the Capitol and argued that if I issued such a statement it would split the Republican Party in two.

I told them that everyone in politics knows that a Vice President cannot chart his own course. "It's up to him if he wants me," I said. "I can only assume that if he puts it this way, this must be his way of saying he would prefer someone else."

"That's not what he meant at all," said Hall. He declared

I was judging Eisenhower's statement by standards which should be applied to a political sophisticate. Both he and Persons argued that the President was sincerely interested in my future and that I ought to consider the whole thing again and at least delay my decision.

It was about this time that I finally got the Nixon-Eisenhower story published on page one and in its correct background—that Nixon had listened calmly, so far without positive reply, to suggestions that his political career would be advanced better if he did not seek renomination as Vice President.

Nixon reports that as he delayed his decision "the uncertainty, the tension dragged on" and that "perhaps the most difficult thing for me was placating my own close friends and associates," who in letters that flooded the Nixon office charged that the President was being "ungrateful, particularly in view of my conduct during the period since his heart attack."

As a White House reporter, it is difficult for me to imagine what it was Nixon had done, or had not done, in the post-heart-attack period that should cause the President to be grateful to him. But this is one of those statements for which Mr. Nixon has become much better known since he assumed the White House in his own right in January, 1969.

While Nixon sweated out his decision to run again, the New Hampshire primary, always first in the nation, was held, and there were a surprisingly large (22,000) write-in vote for Nixon for Vice President. Nixon recounts that this had a "great impact on my decision as well as the President's," and that it also persuaded the Republican politicians. Still there was no clarion call from Ike to Dick.

On April 27, Nixon went on, Republican National Chairman Hall urged

me to unbend and put an end to the wrangling, which was only hurting the party.

After Len Hall left my office, I did some intense soul-searching. Would I hurt or help the party and the course of the Eisenhower administration by being on the ticket? I telephoned the White House for an appointment and went to see the President that afternoon. I told him that I would be honored to continue as his Vice President and that the only reason I had waited so long in saying so was that I did not want to force my way onto the ticket against his wishes. The President said he was delighted with my decision. He called in Jim Hagerty and arranged for an announcement of the decision to be made from the White House, that afternoon.

The Nixon account continues with some highly interesting observations that are revealing about Nixon the man and the politician in a time of crisis:

And so ended the personal crisis involved in my decision to be a candidate for Vice President in 1956. In retrospect, it was a minor crisis, for the outcome really never was in doubt. [Here, in my opinion, Nixon seems to forget those angry panicky moments when he was ready to announce publicly his own withdrawal as Vice President and had to be argued from this action by Vic Johnston, Len Hall, and Jerry Persons.]

Yet, it [the discussion of his second term for Vice President] was part of the much more serious heart attack crisis for me—the aftermath when my guard was down. I would otherwise not have been so sensitive about Eisenhower's attitude toward my candidacy and would have resolved the situation much sooner.

The significance, at least for me, once again was that the most dangerous period of a crisis is not the preparation of the battle itself, but the aftermath when one's normal reaction, after having mobilized all one's emotions and physical resources to fight the battle, is to relax. If you cannot take off the time to let your system relax and recharge normally, then you must be alert to the fact that your temper will be short and your judgement less acute than normally. During the trying months when the President had lain ill, I had expended my energies not only in a heavier work schedule, but in treading a tightrope of political diplomacy. Then, before I could recover my equilibrium, I found myself on political tenterhooks and I reacted with less than my best judgement.

So ends the Nixon apologia.

After Nixon's White House visit, and Eisenhower acceptance of this situation, Harold E. Stassen and others who wanted to "dump Nixon" were doomed to fail, even though Presidential disability again became a fact of life as the President underwent major surgery for ileitis in early June. That second illness raised anew the whole question of whether the President would run for reelection and whether his age and health could withstand for another four years the rigorous duties of the Presidency. Naturally, this also brought up the Nixon question again. But Chairman Hall had a single answer to all inquiries. It would be the same ticket again, Hall insisted, Eisenhower and Nixon. And that, of course, is the ticket that came out of the San Francisco convention in late August.

Eisenhower again defeated Adlai E. Stevenson that year, despite a series of foreign policy crises in October involving first the Budapest uprising, and then the Israeli, French, and British invasion of Egypt. The strike against Suez by our allies came as a complete surprise to Eisenhower's government. Under any normal circumstances, this display of weak intelligence and inept diplomacy ought to have cost the President heavily, but on the contrary, the crisis atmosphere increased the heavy Eisenhower majority to almost 10,000,000 over the hapless Stevenson.

What did Eisenhower really want in 1956? I don't know for certain, but I am convinced he didn't want Nixon on the ticket again. General Eisenhower certainly was not a "political sophisticate," as Len Hall so accurately told Mr. Nixon. In fact, Eisenhower had little use for politicians, and less understanding of them.

Some highly placed Republicans, still unwilling to be quoted by name, have told me they thought Eisenhower's hope in 1956 was that the convention eventually would nominate his most trusted aide, Sherman Adams, for Vice President. None of us can ever know for certain, but that would have been an interesting chapter in history. Two years later, the public and an unbelieving Eisenhower found that Adams, a seeming paragon of New England virtue, had been compromised heavily in his personal transactions with a Boston textile manufacturer, Bernard Goldfine. Goldfine, among other things, simply quit filing federal income tax returns when his old friend Adams moved into the White House. After great pain and indecision, Eisenhower finally in 1958 had to ask Adams to resign.

CHAPTER
20

In 1958, I went off to cover two more civil wars—in Algeria and Lebanon. In Lebanon, American troops were involved, but it turned out they did not have to fight and perhaps they should not have been sent there at all.

By the time I got there in early 1958, the war in Algeria already was an old one, steadily draining away the strength of the French who could not hope to win against a hostile majority Moslem population.

But to the French, it seemed necessary to stand and fight it out in Algeria because they had just lost in Indochina.

As I look back on the war in Algeria now, I see so many parallels with the mistakes we later were to make in Vietnam when the Americans took over the burdens of fighting for the survival of the South Vietnamese government.

In Algeria, the French Army could control the big cities and most of the major roads by day, but they were vulnerable to guerrilla attack by night. In Algeria, as in Vietnam, pacification was a key program, and the government-supplied statistics showing success in this area were always misleading, if not totally false.

I liked the tough French officer, General Jacques Massu, commanding the French armies in Algeria, but he and the Army that had moved to Algeria from Indochina again were facing an impossible task, fighting a war they could not hope to win.

One bright sunny Sunday, Massu took me guerrilla-hunting and the whole venture demonstrated in the simplest fashion the terribly difficult job the French Army faced in trying to smash the rebel bands that carried out hit-and-run raids from heavily wooded mountains.

General Massu and I flew together in the same helicopter over a section of the Atlas Mountains just south of Algiers. Below us, intelligence sources reported operations by half a dozen bands of guerrillas numbering in size from seventy-five to two hundred men.

Flying in a U.S.-built Sikorsky 58, Massu and I came in low over the mountaintops hoping to draw fire from the rebels below. Just behind us, and hidden on the other side of the mountain, were other helicopters with French paratroops ready to make an instant assault on the rebels below if they fired a single shot or disclosed their location in any way.

We spent many hours flying over many mountains but the rebels refused to fire; they were far too battle-wise.

"It is as uncertain as hunting foxes from horseback," General Massu explained.

The mountainous terrain below was simply more suitable for the rebels than for their pursuers.

Even in early 1958, Massu realized this was a war that could not be won unless the French were prepared to take some drastic and revolutionary political and social measures along with their military action. Massu knew, and admitted, that the reactionary political stand of the French colonials, the so-called *pied noire*, or black feet, would have to be reversed before peace could come to Algeria. He did not doubt that the Army would have to fight the French settlers at a final stage in effecting the political reforms that might be required to make any deal with the Moslems who were banded together into a National Liberation Front, called the FLN by the French.

The French colonials lived in comfort and ease even at the peak of the fighting, but they saw no need for the social reforms that would make a better life for the Moslems.

It was always the French Army that carried the burden of social reform, whether in the form of better schools or better housing for the natives, and these efforts were limited by budgetary restrictions. The overburdened French government in Paris couldn't afford to fight a war and carry out extensive social reforms at the same time. Yet without both France was doomed in Algeria and no one knew this better than Massu.

Most correspondents, I think, looked upon Massu as a reactionary military martinet. I have never known why he chose to take me into his confidence, but he did, long before another military uprising brought General Charles de Gaulle back to the helm of France. De Gaulle didn't like Massu and soon moved him out of Algiers and into Germany. De Gaulle also decided to end the struggle for Algiers and turn it over to the FLN, an action that would have been impossible if De Gaulle had not possessed and exercised dictatorial powers over the French government and a war-weary people at the time.

But before De Gaulle surrendered, the French tried about all the devices of modern warfare that we were to try later and equally unsuccessfully in Vietnam. The French had an electrified barrier on their eastern frontier with Tunisia, just as we tried an electrified McNamara Line on the edge of the Demilitarized Zone between North and Southern Vietnam.

In mid-February, 1958, I visited the no-man's-land on the western approaches to Algeria and got a close look at the so-called Morice Line, which leaked like a sieve. It stopped barely 20 percent of the arms flow from Tunisia into Algeria.

South of the electrified barrier, I visited a French artillery position controlled by radar from a mountaintop twenty-five miles south of Tebessa and four miles west of the Tunisian frontier.

The radar equipment was highly sophisticated, and came from the supplies the United States had sent to France as a member of the North Atlantic Treaty Organization. Its use to fight rebels in North Africa was in direct violation of the agreement with the United States, but the French government blithely and continually denied it was using NATO supplies in the civil war. The French officers in charge of the artillery fire base offered no pretext or excuses in telling me where and how they had acquired a radar system so sensitive that it could tell the difference between a man and a camel crossing a mountain leading from Tunis to Algeria. Any man who moved at night in this no-man's-land was assumed to be part of the enemy force, and was brought under fire at once. But it was not really effective. Victory for the rebels was inevitable because the French were being bled white by this heavy and constant expenditure of men and money.

After several months in Algeria, I was back in Washington when President Eisenhower suddenly ordered Marines and Army troops to make a landing in Lebanon in July, 1958. The President acted after a revolutionary government in Iraq had taken power. It was assumed by the government in Washington that the revolution in Iraq had been brought about by the Russians or by their Egyptian Allies in the Middle East.

The Marines and the Army came sweeping into Lebanon for an amphibious landing. Landing boats made their way through groups of gay water skiers on the beaches near Beirut. Though they came ashore in full battle array, ready to fight on a moment's notice, they met no fire on the beaches. During the long period our troops were in Lebanon they encountered nothing more serious than sniper fire.

I was not in Lebanon for the initial assault backed up by the Sixth Fleet, but I flew there as quickly as possible on a naval air transport plane that made the long trip from Washington via the Azores, Casablanca, and Crete.

It was a crazy kind of military situation. If you wanted to visit the rebels deep in the mountains, you simply called a taxi in front of the St. George Hotel and gave the driver instructions to take you to a rebel headquarters. There were military checkpoints along the way, both governmental and rebel, but in either case your government-issued press credentials were sufficient identification to get you through the lines.

I found on arrival that the *Times* task force was having much difficulty with its communications. All the correspondents in Beirut were sending their press copy at the urgent rate of about $1 a word, and it was taking twenty-four or more hours for the copy to reach New York. From my friends in the radio networks, I learned they had clear radio transmission channels via Paris directly to the United States. So I presented myself to the Lebanese authorities as representing the *Times*-owned WQXR radio station and not as a representative of the newspaper itself. With some help from NBC, it was arranged that I could broadcast nightly directly from Beirut into the third-floor news room of the *Times* in New York. We gave up using the commercial cable system entirely and every night I broadcast by voice all the dispatches of my *Times* colleagues. Now there were no more $1-a-word, twenty-four-hour-old messages reaching New York; instead my transmission was instantaneous, and the radio broadcast cost only about $7 a minute, during which time I could dictate approximately 150 words into a recording machine. Every night I signed off as Lawrence of Lebanon, a source of great amusement to the employees of Radio Lebanon. Our rivals on the *Herald Tribune* never learned about our radio dispatches and why we beat them so consistently with the news from Lebanon.

But the American mission to Lebanon was as fruitless as it was unwise. When our troops finally left, the rebels fighting the government moved in to share power in Beirut. And the revolutionaries in Iraq proved to be native radicals unfriendly simply to their own government, but in no way directed either from Moscow or Cairo. But this was a time when America believed it must serve as policeman for the whole world, a mood that later was to get us involved so deeply and so expensively in a war we could not win in Vietnam.

In 1959, the *Times* granted me a sabbatical so that I could serve one year as president of the National Press Club. In the course of that year, speakers at the club included two major leaders of the Soviet Union, Premier Nikita Khrushchev and that old-line Soviet Bolshevik, Anastas Mikoyan. We saw and heard from Richard Nixon, then Vice President, and two of the most ardent seekers of the Presidency from the Democratic side, Senators Hubert Humphrey and John F. Kennedy.

The biggest event of the year was Khrushchev's appearance for his first speech in the United States as Eisenhower's guest. It was carried live for two hours on all three television networks. I introduced Khrushchev and, as is the custom, I fielded and asked all the written questions sent up by the members from the floor.

It was the first time that we allowed women to sit at luncheon tables with the rest of the members and guests on the ballroom floor. I bowed to that demand only because the Russian Embassy insisted upon it. But I resisted all efforts to move the luncheon to some other and larger auditorium because I knew that in the Press Club at least I was the boss and could enforce regular Press Club rules. The regular rules meant there would be no censorship of questions by the Russians, or there would be no speech. On an earlier occasion in 1959 when another Soviet official, Frol R. Kozlov, had been in Washington, the luncheon for him was sponsored by the Press Club and the Overseas Writers and held in a downtown hotel. At the last minute, the Russians demanded and won from the president of the Overseas Writers the right to screen and censor all questions addressed to Mr. Kozlov and I had no choice but to go along. But the questions the Russians allowed us to put to Mr. Kozlov were so namby-pamby that I made up my mind, then and there, that if I could get Khrushchev's acceptance there would be no censoring of questions.

In fairness to the Russians, it should be noted they never asked for the right to censor the Khrushchev luncheon questions. Perhaps it was because they had heard through the grapevine that I would be hard-nosed on that one. But they did screen and censor the questions at a subsequent news conference held by the Soviet Premier and also televised, just before he went back to Moscow. I presided at that one, too, but it was their news conference and I made it clear to my colleagues at the outset that it was being held under the rules of the Kremlin, not the National Press Club.

My old boss, Lyle C. Wilson, a UP vice president, commented about my style and my no-censorship-nonsense attitude at the Press Club luncheon in a column he wrote on September 16, 1959, for the Washington *Daily News*:

"Bill simply insists that the questions shall be asked with the bark on. Nothing insulting or offensive, you understand, but nothing subject to censorship either. Seems like a good idea."

For Khrushchev, this opportunity to address the American nation on all three networks—saturation coverage, as we call it in the trade—was a propaganda godsend, and he took all the advantages possible from it. He was on his best behavior, smiling and animated, and pouring out one propaganda line after another. His big pitch, the one that got him big headlines, was for cooperation between the United States and the Soviet Union to insure world peace lest the earth "be covered with ashes and graves."

As Khrushchev spoke in Russian, his words were translated paragraph by paragraph into English by an attractive young man, Oleg Troyanovsky, whose father formerly had been the Russian Ambassador to the United States.

After the prepared speech it was my turn to take over with a huge pile of written questions that had been collected from the more than 500 American and foreign journalists seated in the audience. But I had decided I would ask the first question myself, and with that first question let Mr. Khrushchev know that he was in a free country populated by journalists who were free and un-afraid.

"Now we come to the question period," I said after Mr. Khrush-chev had spoken his last words and young Troyanovksy had translated them.

"Written questions are not new to Mr. Khrushchev. There is a story, perhaps apocryphal—and if apocryphal, perhaps it should now be denied since it has been published in the West—that at the meeting of the Communist party congress during which he delivered his long speech about Mr. Stalin and about the crimes that Mr. Stalin had committed in the cult of personality, that someone in the audience sent up an unsigned but written question. Mr. Khrush-chev paused in he middle of his speech and read the question to the audience: 'What were you doing when Stalin was committing these crimes?' the question asked.

"Mr. Khrushchev noted the question was unsigned and suggested that perhaps the author would like to arise and identify himself.

"After a brief pause, or a lengthy pause, if you like, no one stood up.

" 'Well, comrades,' Mr. Khrushchev said, 'now you know what I was doing while Stalin was committing these crimes.'

"Perhaps the Chairman would like to comment on that story. If it isn't true, we might just as well forget it for all time."

One needs to recall now that there had not been at this time any official verification from the Soviet Union or its leaders that Khrushchev ever had made such a speech, or had denounced Stalin. My question therefore was on really dangerous ground. Out of one corner of my eye, I could see Troyanovsky whispering rapidly in the Premier's ear as I asked this anecdotal-type question. I could see Khrushchev's face blush red with anger, especially at the laughter from my colleagues when I suggested he had taken the coward's path of silence rather than face Stalin head-on about the crimes he was committing.

When Khrushchev arose to speak, he was madder than a hornet, or even a whole nest of them.

"Probably the authors of fables, including the authors of this question, wanted to place me in a difficult position, and to place me in difficulties," the Soviet leader began. "And there are laughs, there have been laughs even before I have replied to the question. But I would say that they laugh best who laugh last. I shall not reply to this question, which I look upon as being provocative, and I would like to take this occasion to deny any such malicious rumors and lies which do not correspond to the truth."

We did not know it then, but Khrushchev tells us in his memoirs, *Khrushchev Remembers,* how even the members of the Politburo carefully avoided raising any criticism of Stalin to his face because they never knew from one meeting to the next whether Stalin's secret police would deport or kill them on a second's notice.

But before the national television audience and the Press Club forum, Khrushchev did not stay angry for long. The forum and the propaganda opportunity it offered were too good to waste in a fit of bad temper.

For example, he explained at great length and in good humor what he claimed to have meant when he once threatened to "bury us." Khrushchev admitted he had used the phrase, loosely, as he explained it, but said it had been distorted. What he meant then, and now, was "not the physical burial of any people but the question of the historical force of developments," that is, communism would replace capitalism as the dominant economic force in the world. But having answered the question about "burying us" once before a Press Club audience, Khrushchev was not in a mood to entertain the same question again on his American tour. When precisely the same question was put to him later in his visit by Los Angeles' Mayor Norris Poulsen, Khrushchev cut him up for ignorance of the previous question and answer. I, too, felt that Mayor Poulsen might have done his homework better.

Some of the Press Club questions got funny answers, and some of these curious replies were due to faulty translations of the questions.

For example, I asked Mr. Khrushchev the Soviet timetable for sending a man to the moon, but Troyanovsky translated the question so it appeared I had asked the timetable for "throwing a man to the moon."

"We have no intention of throwing a man over to the moon because we value human life," the Soviet Premier said. "Therefore we would only consider sending a man to the moon when the technical possibilities are achieved. But they have not been achieved, I believe, so far."

Khrushchev also said that day that sending a Soviet rocket to the moon to plant a Soviet emblem was not a Russian desire to claim sovereignty over the moon, but was instead a triumph in science for all mankind to share. This was, of course, ten years before we landed our first man on the moon—a feat the Russians have not duplicated as this is being written in May, 1971.

Probably the second most interesting guest at the Press Club that year was Cuban Premier Fidel Castro, bearded and in his guerrilla uniform that he had worn before he achieved power in Cuba. Castro's appearance in Washington was a source of great unhappiness to President Eisenhower who declined to meet with him, although Vice President Nixon had a long talk with Castro.

It was not the Press Club that had departed from protocol to invite Castro to Washington when he was not welcome officially. The first invitation had come from the American Society of Newspaper Editors, and the Press Club simply hitchhiked on their invitation. But Castro made a big hit at the Press Club that day, keeping in the background the Communist plans he had for development of his country just ninety miles off the coast of Florida.

I always tried to get a wisecrack into the brief introduction of any club luncheon speaker. I said of Castro, for example, that with his capacity for two- and three-hour speeches he would make "Silent Cal" Coolidge seem like a deaf-mute.

I first introduced Senator Hubert Humphrey, the Minnesota Democrat, as "the only man in public life with more solutions than there are problems," a line that I borrowed from Fletcher Knebel, then a correspondent for the Cowles newspapers.

Senator John F. Kennedy chose the Press Club for one of his most important and eloquent speeches on the meaning of the Presidency and how he would employ the vast powers of the White House to get into the thick of battle, not lying back and waiting for decisions to reach him. It was about this time that Kennedy had changed his hair style so it was not so long, and I referred to him as "a young man in a hurry, determined to get to the White House, new hair-do and all."

My last big function as Press Club president was the traditional black-tie dinner honoring the President. That night Richard Nixon played the piano accompaniment for Jack Benny, the comedian and violinist. Nixon chose "The Missouri Waltz," which had been the favorite of his old enemy, former President Truman, also a piano player.

The Press Club was a men's club with a member's only bar in those days, but we were always under pressure to admit women either as guests or as full-fledged members at our lunches. I was against their admission, but I saw no problem with their covering the news from the balcony just as all of us cover the news of Congress from the press galleries and not from the floor.

Even on the one occasion when I weakened and let a handful of women reporters cover the Khrushchev luncheon, some of the women demonstrated they did not know how to behave properly in a men's club. One of them, Molly Thayer, a free-lance associated with the *Washington Post*, crashed her way into the men's bar and was escorted out by the former president, Jack Horner.

She was screeching loudly in the lobby when I heard her and heard about her invasion of the bar.

"Molly," I said, "try to act like a lady if you can while we must have you in here."

She shouted about discrimination, but I was too busy to listen.

President Kennedy was one of those who thought women should have full rights and privileges in our club, and he never let up the pressure on me to see to it they were admitted.

But I was as direct and blunt in saying no to Kennedy, who was my friend, as I would have been to any other member of the Press Club, President of the United States or not.

One day we were flying with Kennedy aboard Air Force One from Washington to Nassau for a meeting with British Prime Minister Harold Wilson. Kennedy came out where the pool reporters were sitting, spotted me, and promptly began the old argument about admitting women to the Press Club.

Merriman Smith of UP, then the best White House reporter in town, advised Mr. Kennedy to stick to "things you understand, like the Congo," which, of course, nobody understood. Smitty went on to say that feelings ran high in the Press Club over the issue of admitting women.

Kennedy again called on me to exert my leadership as a past president to get them admitted.

"Look, Mr. President," I responded, "I might sleep with them, but I'll be damned if I'll eat lunch with them."

Still Kennedy persisted, and Smitty delivered the punch line.

"If you had another brother," Smitty said to the President, "how would you like him to marry one [a newswoman]?"

The President turned on his heel and walked away.

About a year later, after the President had been killed, I was having a long talk with Mrs. Jacqueline Kennedy on the broad veranda of her parent's home, Hammersmith Farm, at Newport, Rhode Island, overlooking Narragansett Bay. I was urging her to join me on a projected ABC early morning program. But she would have none of the idea.

"Look, Bill," said Jackie, "I have the same feelings about career women that you do."

I was genuinely confused, and said I didn't know what she meant.

"Oh, you know, what you told Jack," she responded.

I said I didn't remember what I might have told her husband on the subject.

"Yes, you do," Mrs. Kennedy insisted. "You told Jack you might sleep with those Washington newspaperwomen, but you'd be damned if you'd have lunch with them."

I knew enough to quit when I was behind.

CHAPTER
2 1

I had known John F. Kennedy for a number of years but our relationship was never really close until the 1960 Presidential campaign, which brought us together on a twenty-four-hour-a-day basis, first in the hard-fought Democratic primaries and later in the close battle with Vice President Richard Nixon for the Presidency itself.

Kennedy was forced by his religion to contest all the important primaries. He had to literally force his nomination upon the leaders of his party who were uncertain a Catholic could win after their bitter experience with Alfred E. Smith in 1928.

Consequently, I traveled throughout the nation with Kennedy, most of the time in his own two-engine Convair, the *Caroline*, a gift from his family. In those days before he was nominated, Kennedy did not attract a large press corps so those of us in the early primaries had a marvelous opportunity to get to know him well. Whether in Wisconsin, or West Virginia, or Oregon, Kennedy was a delightful traveling companion. The talk aboard the *Caroline* was not always confined strictly to national politics. Kennedy was interested in a reporter's personal life as well as politics.

The Democratic race that year was marked by several active campaigns. Senator Hubert Humphrey of Minnesota quit, but only after he lost in West Virginia. The Senate majority leader, Lyndon Johnson, always insisted publicly that he wasn't running, but he still waged a very bitter campaign. Senator Stuart Symington of Missouri was everybody's second choice and the first choice of hardly anyone. And Adlai Stevenson, the Democratic loser of 1952 and 1956, was hoping against hope he'd get a third try for the White House.

On the Republican side, there was really no battle for the nomination. It was all locked up for Vice President Nixon. Nixon, with President Eisenhower, had decided that the Republican Vice Presidential candidate would be Henry Cabot Lodge, a former Senator who was the U.S. Ambassador to the United Nations.

At an early stage of the 1960 campaign (actually in 1959) New York's Governor Nelson Rockefeller made the first of his public-opinion samplings to see if he should run. He soon decided the party faithful had already settled on Nixon so there was no use in spending a lot of Rockefeller money and energy.

I toured Texas with Nelson Rockefeller and it was coldly made clear that not even the Rockefeller millions could convert the Texas Republican leadership. I remember writing that in Texas, "where oil and politics do mix," Rockefeller had just drilled "a dry hole."

The Republican national convention in Chicago would have been without any major news to report if at the last minute the Vice President and Rockefeller had not tried to rewrite the party platform to accommodate Rockefeller's views and dilute those of the conservative wing, who dominated the platform committee. Some of the changes criticized Eisenhower's policies, and these made the retiring President mad. Finally, compromises were worked out and Nixon was nominated without a struggle.

Nixon had arrived in Chicago with the choice of Lodge for Vice President already made. Arthur Krock and I got this story early from Leonard W. Hall, the Nixon campaign manager.

At the last minute (perhaps to add a little drama to the convention), Nixon assembled the top Republican leaders and pretended he was asking them for guidance on the selection of a running mate. Since I already had reported days before that it would be Lodge, I telephoned Len Hall to express some concern about the current probabilities.

"Don't worry, don't worry," Hall said. "One of the girls in the other office is typing the text of Lodge's acceptance speech as it is being read to her over the telephone."

Meanwhile, the Democrats were having a real brawl. Kennedy's first opponent was Minnesota's Senator Humphrey, a personally attractive man with little national constituency who up to that time could never convert his solid liberal credentials into any sizable delegate bloc even for Vice President. In 1964, Lyndon Johnson was to make him Vice President, and in 1968, it was Johnson's bloc of Southern delegates who made Humphrey the Presidential nominee at the divided Chicago convention.

In 1960, Humphrey's big primary campaigns were made in Wisconsin, just next door to his home state of Minnesota, and in West Virginia, where Humphrey appeared to be the favorite. West Virginia was a predominately Protestant state in which all of Kennedy's rivals ganged up behind Humphrey to stop Kennedy. Humphrey ultimately lost Wisconsin and West Virginia, but both battles tested the Kennedy political organization.

I traveled into the West Virginia coal fields with Senator Robert Byrd of West Virginia, a former Ku Klux Klan kleagle, who was the leader in West Virginia of the Johnson forces. Only Kennedy and Humphrey were on the ballot. So I asked Byrd what advice he gave to voters who might favor another Presidential nominee like Johnson.

"Everybody knows who I am for," Byrd said. "When a voter asks my advice, I say that if you are for Senator Kennedy, that's fine. But if you are for Adlai E. Stevenson, Senator Stuart Symington, Senator Johnson, or Joe Doe, you better remember that this primary, with all the national attention on it, may be your last chance."

To an audience of Democratic leaders in the coal fields of southern West Virginia, Byrd introduced Humphrey as "one who knows what it is like to wear tennis shoes to school in the snow."

Byrd's remarks provided the first solid public evidence that all the anti-Kennedy forces had joined a "stop Kennedy" drive.

Until primary day itself, it looked like a combination of anti-Catholicism and the coalition of anti-Kennedy forces might win West Virginia for Humphrey. This result would have eliminated Kennedy, but it would not have nominated Humphrey, who after his Wisconsin defeat had become only a stalking horse for the anti-Kennedy forces.

There is no doubt the Kennedy campaigners, led by his brother

Bobby and aides such as Lawrence F. O'Brien and Kenneth P. O'Donnell, spent heavily in the pre-convention campaigns, especially in West Virginia. But I never could find anyone who could document claims that the primaries were bought with Kennedy millions.

Until the very end, Kennedy felt he would lose in West Virginia and he was ready for it, praying a comeback still would be feasible in Maryland or Oregon.

On the Sunday before the West Virginia primary, Kennedy told me, "Maybe we are moving up but I doubt if I can get beyond 46 or 47 percent of the vote. . . . If I get that close, maybe I can still survive."

All of the pollsters and all of the political experts—myself included—forecast victory for Humphrey. A *Times* team that surveyed West Virginia reported all the "surface political signs" pointed to Humphrey, although there was a strong last-minute surge for Kennedy. Also, there were enough undecided voters to alter the Humphrey trend in the opinion of the *Times* team.

When the votes finally were counted, Kennedy had about 60 percent and Humphrey 40 percent. Everyone had been wrong about how the coal miners south of the Kanawha River would vote, and it was in this area that young Franklin D. Roosevelt, Jr., played a decisive role for Kennedy.

After West Virginia, the outlook for Kennedy became brighter, much to the displeasure of Senate Majority Leader Johnson who believed with House Speaker Rayburn that he still could command a majority at the Los Angeles convention.

Johnson made only a few road trips in search of delegates, relying heavily on his Congressional associates. That turned out to be his biggest mistake because members of the House and Senate had little political impact on the convention.

Just before the Los Angeles convention, Johnson went to New York to convince the publishers of the biggest, most influential newspapers and magazines that he, not Kennedy, would win the Democratic Presidential nomination. He made some converts. *Time* magazine put Johnson on the cover of an issue that would appear after the nomination had been made, and the magazine was saved from a genuinely embarrassing situation only when Kennedy, to the surprise of most, selected Johnson as his running mate.

During this same New York trip, Johnson told the editors of the *Times* that he was unhappy with my political coverage; he insisted that they run a statement by him attacking me by name. In it, he said Lawrence's "sloppy work was the product of reportorial fatigue." What made him maddest was my constant forecast that a Kennedy victory seemed certain, most likely on an early ballot; and he wasn't happy with my analysis of the political mistakes of the Johnson campaigners in depending on Congressional influence to win him the nomination.

This personal attack by Johnson infuriated me, and I did not wait long to reply. On the Sunday before the convention, I wrote that Kennedy's first-ballot nomination now seemed assured as the big-state delegations began to break away from their uncommitted stance to open support of Kennedy. I added that the "stop Kennedy" forces, including those backing Johnson, "are showing signs of early, but pronounced, political fatigue."

Johnson's denunciation of my "reportorial fatigue" had been on one of the back pages, but my description of his "political fatigue" appeared on page one. On the following morning, I ran into Jack Kennedy as he was running from one caucus to another, and the Massachusetts Senator, with a big grin, shouted to me, "I see where you returned the arrow."

Now LBJ was more furious with me. We did not speak again until after the election was all over and he had come to visit the President-elect at Palm Beach. He found me sitting on a bench in the Kennedy backyard waiting to play golf with the President-elect. Both of us decided the time had come to end our feud. Johnson made the first move, inviting me to come to his Texas ranch for "a rest," and I replied by saying how much I would like it "but right now, I'm stuck with this fellow [Kennedy]."

I was as surprised by Kennedy's selection of Johnson as most reporters, including Johnson's closest friends. One of them, columnist William S. White, began to weep openly when he learned that Johnson had accepted. White immediately left Los Angeles, thinking Johnson had double-crossed him.

After the convention, there was a lull while the Kennedy forces in Massachusetts and the Nixon forces in California got ready for the big campaign. I went to Hyannis Port and it was during this period that Kennedy and I began to play golf together, usually in mid-afternoon, generally starting too late to play more than nine or ten holes. He was an excellent golfer with a smooth, compact swing. If he had practiced or played more frequently, he might have shot in the seventies.

One afternoon in August, 1960, after golf at the Hyannis Port Club, the Senator and I went back to his home in the Kennedy compound for a drink. We were interrupted by a telephone call from Connecticut's Governor Abraham Ribicoff, who had been the first and most prominent Kennedy backer dating all the way back to Kennedy's defeat for the Vice Presidential nomination on the ticket with Adlai Stevenson in 1956.

Ribicoff was calling Kennedy to tell him that Chester Bowles, recently renominated for Congress from Connecticut, had now decided not to run again but instead to devote his full time to supporting Kennedy for President.

Kennedy was furious. He knew that Bowles was a candidate for Secretary of State if he won the Presidency, and he also knew that many might consider Bowles' withdrawal from the Congressional race as a sign that Kennedy already had promised the job to Bowles. If so, the backers of Adlai Stevenson for Secretary of State would be annoyed, and perhaps withhold their support from Kennedy.

"I hope that you will tell Bowles that I want him to run," Kennedy told Ribicoff. "Be very tough about it. Tell him I want him to hold that seat in Congress."

There was some more discussion at Ribicoff's end, which naturally I couldn't hear.

"Well, I don't want people thinking that I'm going to make Bowles Secretary of State," Kennedy said. "My own disposition right now is that I would not appoint Stevenson or Bowles as Secretary of State, but there's no need to decide that really until after election."

Ribicoff talked some more, and then Kennedy hung up the phone.

I grinned at the candidate and said I had to hurry off to my typewriter because now I had the best story of the campaign so far. He smiled and said he supposed he had put me under a heavy responsibility to keep a secret like that. I told him I thought I could bear up under the burden.

I think that was the first time that Kennedy knew for sure I was not only an aggressive reporter, but in delicate situations I also could keep a secret. And from then on, he shared many more confidences with me, both during and after the campaign, and after he entered the White House.

The post-convention interlude of rest had to be broken for another brief session of Congress—a move that had been arranged by

Speaker Rayburn and Senate Majority Leader Johnson as a tactic
they hoped would help Johnson win the Presidential nomination.
Now LBJ was Kennedy's running mate and they both were stuck
with a Congressional session that neither now wanted. It did not
benefit the Democratic party or the country as a whole. As Vice
President Nixon had minimal duties connected with government,
and seldom exercised his one constitutional responsibility to preside
over the Senate, the extra session was not as confining to him as it
was to Kennedy and Johnson. But about that time, Nixon injured
his knee, and that injury interfered far more seriously with his
campaigning than any session of Congress would have.

The 1960 Presidential campaign was notable chiefly for the televised debates between the Presidential candidates—the first in
history—and Kennedy was clearly the winner in the first encounter
with the Vice President. Nixon's makeup was poorly applied by
his own expert (he declined the services of a competent woman
makeup technician offered by CBS) and the makeup ran all down
his face as he perspired heavily. Nixon seemed nervous and in-
secure, while Kennedy was calm and confident.

Not long before the first debate, President Eisenhower, wittingly
or unwittingly, struck a heavy blow at the Nixon candidacy by
denigrating the Vice President's influence in the two Eisenhower
administrations. Eisenhower was asked at a news conference to
name some policy decision greatly influenced by the Vice President's private counseling inside the administration. With a candor
that struck terror into the hearts of Nixon's friends, Ike replied
that he couldn't think of any at the moment, but maybe if he were
given a week he might recall a policy on which Nixon's mark had
been set. That question gave the Vice President a lot of trouble
when it was raised in the first debate by Sander Vanocur, representing NBC.

After the spectacular fiasco of the first debate, and the bad impression Nixon had left visually, the Nixon campaign aides quite
naturally were deeply concerned about the "image" their candidate
might project in the second TV debate, scheduled from the NBC
studios in Washington.

Kennedy came out early to look over the NBC arrangements for
the second round, and found the Washington studio had been
chilled to a frigid 64° F. in the hope that Nixon wouldn't perspire.
The bright lights were in Kennedy's eyes, but the light on Nixon
had been softened. Kennedy at once demanded that the tempera-

ture of the studio be brought up to a normal living-room standard, about 70° F., or he threatened that he would wear a topcoat during the debate and explain why it was necessary. The network executives were quick to turn up the heat and adjust the lights.

In addition to the debates, Nixon had one other heavy burden to carry in his 1960 campaign—Henry Cabot Lodge, his Vice Presidential running mate. Lodge rather fancied himself as a policy-maker even when he held subordinate positions like Ambassador to the United Nations. Lodge always was in hot water with his State Department superiors because there can only be one Secretary of State at any one time. Policy perforce must be made in Washington, not in New York. The dissatisfaction with Lodge was not just among the career diplomats, who might have been expected to dislike the Boston Brahmin. It was just as strong among Ike's old friends like General Walter Bedell Smith, who had come in as Under Secretary of State to administer the department during the many absences of Secretary John Foster Dulles.

Now Nixon found Lodge trying to make policy in the middle of the political campaign, even though Vice Presidents have no policy-making functions, before or after election. Speaking in New York's Spanish Harlem one evening, Lodge promised his audience that Nixon would appoint a Negro—the first ever—to his cabinet. Lodge didn't even realize that Spanish Harlem was anti-Negro.

Lodge's pledge was relayed to me at once on the West Coast, and I was instructed to ask Nixon, who at the moment was speaking at the celebrated Knott's Berry Farm in Orange County, perhaps the most reactionary political center in the country. I sent a written question to Nixon, and, surprisingly, got a very prompt answer to the effect that the Lodge promise was not authorized by the Presidential candidate. Nixon emphasized that his intention was to appoint a representative cabinet of fine and well qualified persons without regard to race or religion, but he would not promise to discriminate in favor of Negroes by saying one of them would necessarily be appointed. This was a rebuke to Lodge and was meant as such, but Nixon perhaps was more worried about any adverse reaction such a pro-Negro promise by Lodge might have in the South, a part of which the Republicans hoped to, and eventually did, carry.

Lodge somehow would not take the hint, and kept making his pledge of a Negro in the cabinet even after Nixon had disowned the promise. A few days later Nixon called a campaign strategy meeting with Lodge and his aides on a Sunday in Hartford, Connecticut. It was held behind closed doors, and when the meeting was over, Lodge was the first to leave. He stopped for only a few questions but he insisted to me that the issue of a Negro in the cabinet had not even been discussed. When Nixon came out later, we held an informal news conference as we walked from the meeting place back to his hotel. Nixon was quite explicit. Not only had the Negro in the cabinet issue been discussed, but he had made his own viewpoint very clear to Mr. Lodge, who would, in the future, confine himself to agreed strategy. My story in the *Times* the next day pointed up the differences between what Lodge had told us and what Nixon had said, but I suggested strongly that Mr. Nixon's views now would prevail.

Lodge used this story to attack me personally as an enemy of the Republican ticket who was trying to stir up trouble between himself and Nixon. But from then on, he soft-pedaled his Negro in the cabinet pledge. Southern Republican leaders especially were relieved that he did.

One of Nixon's biggest blunders was a promise he had made to the Republican convention that he would carry his Presidential campaign to all fifty states for the first time in history. So, in the closing days of October, I found myself riding on Nixon's chartered campaign airplane into tiny Rocky Mountain states with few electoral votes when the outcome of the election was being determined in the bigger, more populous states like Illinois and New York. Nixon couldn't spend more time in the big states where he desperately needed a lift because he now was keeping his convention pledge to go to all the little states.

On one such trip, our chartered jet made a very dangerous landing in a snowstorm at Laramie, Wyoming—a landing so dangerous that the pilot of the jet made three approaches to the field before he could set his plane down safely. It was the first fully loaded jet ever to land on the Laramie runway. More than a few of us aboard were genuinely frightened.

Once on the bus headed for a small-town political meeting, I spoke loud and longly about "damn fool high school campaign promises" that threatened the lives of more than 100 people just so Nixon could say he had campaigned in Wyoming. The Nixon people never forgave me, and in the bitterness of defeat, Nixon often would mention Bill Lawrence as one of the reporters responsible for his defeat.

Nixon, of course, never thought to blame himself for the election he lost so narrowly. It was easier to blame me, or to put the blame on President Eisenhower whose help in the campaign was not asked until the battle was nearly over. Ike had offered to do more, and Len Hall had urged it, but Nixon wanted to win it all by himself.

Nixon, though, did have some legitimate reasons for disliking me. During the campaign, Soviet Premier Khrushchev had invited himself to the United Nations General Assembly meetings in New York, and had carried on a bitter campaign against the United States, grabbing attention by hammering on the table with his shoe. Nixon several times reprimanded Senator Kennedy for criticizing foreign policy blunders by the Eisenhower administration while Khrushchev was in the country. Nixon argued Kennedy should withhold such criticism as long as Khrushchev was here.

At a news conference in Springfield, Missouri—it was, I believe, the last open news conference Nixon held during the campaign —I asked the Republican candidate if his demand that Kennedy refrain from criticizing foreign policy as long as Khrushchev was here did not give the Soviet leader a considerable veto power. By staying indefinitely, I suggested, Khrushchev could keep foreign policy out of the American campaign entirely. Nixon denied that such was his intent, but he never mentioned again his idea that Kennedy ought to silence himself on foreign policy for the duration of the Khrushchev visit.

While Vice President Nixon was distant and reserved with most reporters covering his campaign, there was a lively, animated intimacy between Kennedy and most reporters assigned to him. He was interested in their personal and professional fortunes, their romances, the day-to-day happenings. The reporters in turn joshed him a lot about undelivered speeches which he released for publication but never bothered to read.

In the early spring of 1960 during the Gridiron Club festivities in Washington, even before the primary season had developed in earnest, Carleton V. Kent of the Chicago *Sun-Times* had taken a one-to-twenty bet with Silliman Evans, Jr., of *The Nashville Banner* that Kennedy would win the Democratic nomination on the first ballot. It was an evening of high spirits and Kent couldn't resist the lure of $25 against $500 on Kennedy. When Kennedy and Kent both won on the first ballot at Los Angeles, there was some friendly byplay between Kent and Evans before the Tennessee publisher paid up. When he did, Kent let me know promptly so I could tell Kennedy.

One of Kennedy's favorite speech lines was an attack on those in government, usually Republicans, who were "frozen in the glacial ice of their own indifference," so Kent's wire to me said: "Please tell the candidate that Silliman Evans is no longer wrapped in the glacial ice of his own indifference and has paid up."

I showed the telegram to Kennedy as he sat in an open car in front of the O'Hare Inn near the Chicago airport, and together we framed a reply to Kent that played on the Republican argument that the vast sums of money Kennedy was planning to spend were "not Jack's, but ours."

"Please remember that the Evans money is Jack's, not yours," the reply to Kent said. "Don't spend it on the Nixon train."

Kennedy's failure to follow his prepared texts gave rise to many anecdotes but none better than the one about his carefully prepared speech before the Houston Ministerial Association to deny that his Catholic religion would be an inhibiting factor if he were to be President. As we were handed the text that morning, Kennedy said, "Tell all the reporters I will not be a textual deviate on this one."

CHAPTER
22

I was not with Senator Kennedy on election night in 1960, but rather was back at my now traditional spot in front of the microphones for the *Times'* radio station, WQXR. Though Kennedy stayed away from the reporters on duty in Hyannis Port that night, awaiting the words of concession from Vice President Nixon, I was able to reach him from time to time on a private and unlisted telephone number he had given to me. I know he was disappointed at the extremely close margin, and particularly dismayed that states like Ohio and Wisconsin that he had considered "in the bag" went for Nixon. Through the long night, though, he was ahead in the vote and he never doubted that he would win.

Nor was I present at the National Guard Armory in Hyannis on the day after election when he finally acknowledged his victory following Mr. Nixon's formal concession. I was at that time still sleeping after the broadcasting job on election night.

Two mornings after election I flew to Hyannis and made my way immediately to the Kennedy compound, getting passed without any difficulty through the newly arrived Secret Service agents, who knew me by sight from my association with other Presidents at the White House.

As I started up the steps leading to the home of Joseph P. Kennedy, father of the clan, the President-elect spotted me coming, and came out the door to greet me.

"Some mandate," were his first words to me, meaning that he was President-elect with less than a majority of the popular vote and with slim party margins in both houses of the Congress—Democartic majorities that certainly were not liberally inclined but would be likely to split. The conservative Democrats, with Republican help, were likely to line up against much of the Kennedy program as it was unfolded.

The first business after election was some rest, some soul-searching, and the selection of the team that would guide the New Frontier. The chosen place for work and play was new to me, Palm Beach, Florida, but it was love at first sight with that resort city.

During the campaign, arrangements by the Kennedy camp were quite sloppy—far less efficient and comfortable than the quarters provided by Nixon for his traveling press. At least on one occasion I had to share a double bed with another man. On another, there were separate beds or cots for six men in one room. Palm Beach, a playground for the opulent, was therefore a delightful surprise at first glance, and I remember well my first contrived complaint as we turned into the palm-tree-lined driveway of the Palm Beach Towers, our new headquarters.

"My God," I said to the press bus contingent, "we're back in the slums again." There was a roar of laughter and it became a kind of ritual, a remark I always had to repeat on every trip to Palm Beach.

In the bright sunshine of southern Florida, the President-elect could relax, swim in the ocean at the back door of his father's home, and play golf with only a minimum of public sight-seeing on the pleasant fairways of the Palm Beach Country Club, then headed by its first president and founder, Morris Brown. Mr. Brown, a gentleman of the old school, made the reporters as welcome as the President-elect and his official family.

The Kennedy administration was not only new, but also young and very informal. The Secret Service agents assigned to Kennedy who had become accustomed to the formal atmosphere of the Eisenhower White House and vacation retreats never ceased to be amazed when they would be called from their guard posts to join the President-elect, his friends, and family on the patio of the Kennedy home to watch a movie or films of an old professional football game.

Caroline Kennedy, then about three, epitomized the informality best of all. One evening while Senator J. William Fulbright of Arkansas, chairman of the Senate Foreign Relations Committee, was holding a news conference on the patio about some subject of great importance, Caroline waddled awkwardly into the limelight, wearing a pair of her mother's shoes, much too large for her tiny feet. Fulbright couldn't figure out immediately why the reporters were convulsed with laughter and why the President-elect moved swiftly to intercept his daughter and escort her back into the house.

This was, I think, one of the most pleasant interludes of my life. I could and did play golf with Kennedy several times a week, and I played also with Salinger and some of my colleagues. I could and I did outreport and outwrite my rivals on story after story based on inside information I had gathered from the President-elect or his staff.

Kennedy quit pretending that I did not have an inside track barred to most other reporters. Once, announcing in Washington an appointment I had forecast weeks earlier, the United Press reported that he spotted me in the crowd around his front porch and observed with a grin, "I'm just trying to make the *Times'* predictions look good."

Then the UP story said that the President-elect "raised his hand in mock solemnity as if to tick off the names of the other appointees suggested as probable by the *Times* and asked, 'Who else is there now?' "

The *Times* had backed Kennedy for election—though the editorial in support of him lacked any great enthusiasm for Kennedy himself—and my newspaper was now the chosen instrument for many of the "leaks" Kennedy chose to use to scoop himself on the selection of his own cabinet and the development of his own policies.

Not a few of these stories also were due to the fact that Kennedy and I had become very close friends; that he knew I could both keep a secret and break a big story in an impressive way.

I started out ahead of my fellow correspondents for this reason, and, with rare exceptions, they had no way to catch up.

One thing I knew for certain, as I have related earlier, was that despite all the pressures in his behalf, Adlai Stevenson was not going to be Secretary of State. Nor was Chester Bowles. But Kennedy had not the slightest idea whom he would pick for the State Department job. There was inside lobbying by Vice President-elect Johnson for the appointment of Senator Fulbright of Arkansas, but that seemed out of the question because Fulbright had signed the "Southern Manifesto" committing Southern Senate Democrats to fight civil-rights legislation.

On one of our first mornings in Palm Beach, I approached Kennedy with the proposal that he now clear for publication the information I had kept in confidence since mid-August that Stevenson would not be Secretary of State. Even such a negative story would have been big news because the Stevenson backers, who numbered millions, were certain he would get the appointment for the campaign help he had given Kennedy after the Los Angeles convention. Kennedy still didn't want to announce the Stevenson veto so he proposed a trade instead.

"Why not a positive story?" he suggested. "You can write flatly that my first firm cabinet selection is [former Governor] Luther Hodges of North Carolina to be Secretary of Commerce."

Of course I wrote it and of course the *Times* front-paged it. My colleagues in Palm Beach who didn't have the story set out to discredit it, and found the Kennedy press secretaries willing to cooperate to the extent that they would say they had not been informed of any definite Kennedy cabinet selections. And, of course, it was many weeks before the Hodges appointment was confirmed by the President-elect. But I never had any moments of anxiety about it.

One cabinet selection, Governor Ribicoff of Connecticut to be Attorney General, seemed certain to all the reporters, including me. But early in our visit to Florida, I called Abe to arrange a golf game over the weekend at Hollywood, Florida, and casually inquired when he might be coming to Palm Beach so the appointment as Attorney General might be announced. Because Ribicoff had been his first and most persistent supporter for President, Kennedy long ago had let it be known that Abe could have any cabinet position he wanted, or a place on the Supreme Court if one were open.

Ribicoff's answer to my casual inquiry startled me.

"Bill, I don't want to be Attorney General," he said. "I would much rather have a job in which I think I can make an important contribution, and I think that opportunity lies as Secretary of Health, Education, and Welfare."

"Why don't you want to be Attorney General—the President and all of the rest of us assume that is your choice?" I asked.

"I just don't think that the first Catholic President should have a Jewish Attorney General to try to push the blacks into schools down the throats of white Southern Protestants," Ribicoff told me.

"Does the President know this?" I asked.

"No," said Ribicoff, "would you mind telling him for me?"

I dialed the President's private number, and in seconds was connected with him. I told him that Ribicoff didn't want to be Attorney General but did want to be Secretary of Health, Education, and Welfare.

Kennedy obviously was surprised. His first reaction was that he had already promised HEW to Michigan's Governor G. Mennen Williams when the Michigan delegation, ignoring the importunings of candidate Johnson, had swung solidly behind Kennedy at a critical moment on the road to Los Angeles.

The President-elect asked me where he could find Ribicoff, and I replied that I had talked to him in the professional shop at the Diplomat Golf Course in Hollywood, Florida, just before he was to tee off. I gave Kennedy the number and he called Ribicoff off the course for a brief telephone chat, inviting him to Palm Beach for lunch and golf on the following day.

Though the news was withheld, I was part of the Kennedy-Ribicoff foursome that next afternoon along with Republican Earl E. T. Smith, a Kennedy friend who had been Eisenhower's Ambassador to Castro's Cuba. Indeed, at a news conference after the round, Ribicoff said they had played as a threesome, and when asked about scores increased his own score for nine holes from 38 to 43—a rarity among golfers who always lie about their score downwards—and remarked that the President-elect had beaten him by a single shot. Ribicoff's story was a natural Democratic reaction because it had been felt by some that Eisenhower spent too much time playing golf in and out of Washington.

On the next day, Kennedy and a number of reporters flew to Austin, Texas, and the ranch of the Vice President-elect, Senator Johnson. It was a gesture to Johnson's immense ego to have the President-elect come to him. It was also Kennedy's way of saying "thank you" to Johnson for his part in swinging the election to the Kennedy-Johnson ticket. Without Johnson in the No. 2 spot, it is doubtful that Kennedy could have beaten Nixon, especially when one remembers how very close the election was.

As we flew west that morning, and read the papers, NBC's Sander Vanocur and I decided Ribicoff ought to be needled for lying about the golf scores on the previous day.

We composed a telegram for Kennedy's approval and then sent it to Ribicoff: "President-elect deeply disturbed by your lying account of golf scores and insists members of his cabinet must be cleaner than hounds teeth. Please wire when you find work."

It was signed "Vanocur and Lawrence," but Kennedy got as much fun out of it as we did. So did Ribicoff when Western Union awakened him in the wee hours of the next morning to read it to him at his hotel.

In Texas, Johnson barred most of the press from his ranch while he went deer hunting with Kennedy. We were told later they both had shot deer with high-powered rifles from incredible distances.

On the way back to Florida, I found a chance to talk privately with Kennedy in the plane filled with reporters. I inquired bluntly what he proposed to do about filling the Justice Department post since Ribicoff didn't want it.

"What about my brother Bobby?" Kennedy responded.

I almost dropped my drink.

"Good God," I responded in genuine amazement, "do you think you could get away with that?"

"Why not?" the President-elect responded. "He's been a good counsel for Senatorial investigating committees. And I certainly do not intend to discriminate against him because he is my brother."

I soon terminated the conversation and went back to my seat adjoining that of Vanocur. I didn't share my story with the NBC man, and I nervously hoped and prayed no other reporter would get into a similar conversation with Kennedy. Of course, none of them had the opening lead that I did because I alone knew that Ribicoff wanted HEW. They still thought he would be Attorney General.

On the following morning, I anxiously telephoned the Kennedy residence and talked with Kennedy's secretary, Mrs. Evelyn Lincoln, asking her to tell the President-elect that I had no idea whether our talk of the night before had been on the record, off the record, or for background, but, if he didn't object, I'd like to do a story saying that he was strongly considering the appointment of his brother Robert as Attorney General. No President ever had made a brother or any other member of his family an official part of his administration. This was a significant story also because Bobby had made enemies on and off Capitol Hill and as the driving force behind his brother's campaign for the Presidential nomination and election. There were few Democrats more controversial than Bobby. I told Mrs. Lincoln, however, that if the President wanted to consider our entire conversation off the record, I would forget that he had ever mentioned Bobby to me as a prospective Attorney General.

Mrs. Lincoln called back in a very few minutes, but the interval seemed like hours to me. She said the President-elect would not be displeased if I wrote a speculative story about Bobby, adding that I should make crystal clear in my story that he did not propose to discriminate against him because he was his brother.

As weeks went by, there was a bitter internal struggle before the Bob Kennedy for Attorney General story was formally confirmed. Bob himself resisted the idea, and it was finally Joseph Kennedy who in effect ordered the younger son to join his brother's official family.

Meanwhile, my newspaper editorially fought the idea and suggested that its reporter at Palm Beach had been taken in by a "trial balloon." I called the New York editors and told them indignantly that I didn't appreciate their denigration of an important story by a reporter who had capitalized on the background information he possessed. In New York, my complaint was filed, and promptly forgotten.

The indifferent, and indeed sometimes hostile, attitude of the New York office toward my long series of important exclusive news stories from the Kennedy administration-in-the-making was perhaps the first visible manifestation to me of the attitude that would lead to my leaving the *Times* after twenty years of service. My chief critic was Clifton Daniel, who had married President Truman's daughter Margaret, and who was on his way to becoming managing editor, a post from which after a few years he was promoted sideways.

Inside the Kennedy family, my story about Bobby's prospective appointment as Attorney General became a kind of running joke between the Kennedys and myself. I don't know whether Bobby and Jack might have talked about this job before the election, but I doubt it. And Ribicoff told me recently that when he recommended Bobby for Attorney General to the President-elect, Jack

Kennedy had seemed as surprised at the idea as I was when Jack first mentioned it to me. In any event, Bobby and Ethel always pretended to me that the whole idea had been mine, that I had made him Attorney General. Later, when John Kennedy was shot down in Dallas in November, 1963, and we had reassembled in Florida about a week after his funeral, there was a long session one night up at the Hobe Sound home of Douglas Dillon, the Republican millionaire who served as Kennedy's Secretary of the Treasury. Bob and Ethel Kennedy were staying at the Dillons' and I had been asked to come from Palm Beach for dinner.

It was a night of sorrow still unrelieved by time, but most of us did our best to remember stories about Jack and about his life in and out of government that would be amusing. Occasionally the whole thing would get to be just too much for Bob, who was hardest hit of all the Kennedys by the slaying, and he would walk off into the balmy night air for a few minutes of mourning in solitude, and afterwards would rejoin the party. Towards midnight, when the idea of my driving back to Palm Beach from Hobe Sound had been vetoed by all present and I was preparing to spend the night in one of the Dillon beach houses, I was saying my thanks and good nights to Bob and Ethel.

"Thanks, anyway, Bill, for making me Attorney General," said Bob Kennedy in a soft voice.

I mumbled something and disappeared into the night.

I can't pretend even at this late date that I was first with all the Kennedy cabinet appointments; not at all. I ran well behind on the most important, that of Dean Rusk to be Secretary of State. I had been given an early tip on Rusk's chances for this job by Orvil Dryfoos, the publisher of the *Times*, who sat with Rusk on a board of directors of Colonial Williamsburg, a project of the Rockefeller family.

But after Rusk saw Kennedy for the first time in Washington, and nothing definite happened, Rusk doubted he would get the job. He bet Dryfoos fifty cents that he wouldn't. Other members of the Kennedy staff told me Rusk was out of consideration because he had once been a member of the Institute of Pacific Relations, a New York study group that had been branded pro-Communist in that hectic anti-Communist period when McCarthyism flourished and the House Committee on Un-American Activities ran its own reign of terror on the other side of the Capitol.

Just before the State appointment was made, there was renewed pressure for Adlai Stevenson who, of course, remained unaware of that remark Kennedy had made in front of me in August, that he was not disposed to appoint him as Secretary of State.

In retrospect, I think Adlai several times missed the bus plainly marked "Secretary of State." Ribicoff, who should know, thinks Stevenson lost his big chance back in late 1959 or early 1960 when the two-time Democratic nominee was invited to lecture at Yale. Kennedy sent word through Ribicoff that an endorsement by Stevenson was most desirable at that time.

"Tell him I would like his support for the Presidency," Kennedy instructed Ribicoff. "If he supports me for the Presidency and I can't make it in Los Angeles, the nomination isn't going to be worth a damn to anybody else unless I am on the ticket for Vice President.

"If Adlai will come out for me now and I don't make it, I will agree to throw my support to Stevenson and agree to run with him for Vice President. And with that assurance nobody else would get the nomination.

"Also, tell Adlai that if I do get the nomination, and win, I will appoint him Secretary of State."

Ribicoff carried the message to Stevenson, who, in typical fashion, evaded a direct reply, but, in effect, refused. Still later, after the Oregon primary victory, Kennedy stopped off at the Stevenson Libertyville, Illinois, farm and once again urged his old friend to endorse him, but Stevenson still held off. And finally at Los Angeles, Kennedy asked Stevenson to place him in nomination for the Presidency, but the Illinois leader, mesmerized by the phony demonstrations in his behalf mostly by non-delegates, and still dreaming of the White House, delayed his answer to Kennedy for twenty-four hours or more, and then finally said no.

After that, no power on earth could have persuaded Kennedy to appoint Stevenson as Secretary of State or to any other job that required instant decision-making.

That Rusk would be Secretary of State was forecast first in the *Washington Post* on a morning when I had written a story saying the new favorite might be David K. E. Bruce, a fine diplomat who eventually served Kennedy as Ambassador to London. I played golf with Kennedy that afternoon and he said not a word to me about the correct information in the *Post* and my own bad guess. Rusk at that moment was on a train for Palm Beach from New York.

Back at the Kennedy home, Kennedy exploded in wrath about

the "leak" to the *Post* and demanded a thorough investigation of it. Pierre Salinger, the press secretary, was instructed to interrogate and to reprimand the handful of Kennedy leaders who knew that Rusk had been chosen. Among the few were Bob Kennedy, the President-elect's brother-in-law Sargent Shriver, and Kenneth O'Donnell, a top advisor. Each of them assured Salinger he had not spoken to any reporter on the *Post* or to any other outsider about the Rusk appointment. Salinger went back to Kennedy to tell him this, and after some discussion, he asked the President-elect if he was dead certain that he himself had not perhaps given the information to another person.

"Well," Kennedy replied after some reflection, "I did mention it to Phil Graham." Graham was publisher of the *Washington Post*, an aggressive and hard-working newspaperman who liked to beat his own staff on major news stories.

Salinger told me later that was the day he concluded that the Kennedy administration was "the only ship of state that leaked from the top."

Until the very moment Kennedy announced the Rusk appointment there had been pressure from Vice President-elect Johnson and others for the appointment of Senator Fulbright of Arkansas to the job. Fulbright, a Rhodes scholar and a long-time member of the Senate Foreign Relations Committee, was intellectually equipped for the job. But he had signed the "Southern Manifesto" against pending and prospective civil-rights bills. It is the easy road for politicians to excuse Fulbright by saying that if he had not participated in the filibusters against the civil-rights bills, he could never have won reelection from Arkansas. But Kennedy felt a Fulbright appointment would be a slap in the face to the developing new nations of Africa, so he finally turned to Rusk.

When Rusk reached Palm Beach, Kennedy, as a matter of courtesy, asked him to telephone Johnson in Texas and to offer to go there for a talk about foreign affairs if LBJ wanted it. But Kennedy told me that Johnson was so mad that he would not allow Rusk to come down for a talk. Johnson said simply he'd see Rusk later in Washington.

On the afternoon of the Rusk appointment, Kennedy and I again played golf. I remarked with a smile that this was one appointment he had managed to keep from the reporters in Palm Beach, including me, even if the *Washington Post* did have it right.

"Yeah," said Kennedy, "I'd been meaning to ask you where you got that lousy information about David Bruce becoming Secretary of State."

"Look, Mr. President," I replied, "I always protect my sources of information, especially when they are wrong."

Kennedy laughed and we dropped the subject.

One of the most difficult appointments for the President-elect was that of Secretary of the Army. A strong campaign was waged on behalf of Georgia's Governor Ernest Vandiver, an outspoken segregationist and an unlikely candidate. Vandiver had backing from the two powerful chairmen of the Congressional armed services committees, Senator Russell and Representative Carl Vinson of Georgia. There had been Atlanta newspaper stories that Vandiver was assured the job, but my own investigations indicated he would not get it. One evening I wrote a story saying that the new President had made a "very gutty" decision against these two powerful Capitol Hill committee chairmen. But even before my story was in print, Kennedy had a copy of it, and sought me out in the Palm Beach Towers by telephone to suggest that my story might be too positive and needed qualification because if both Russell and Vinson insisted on the Vandiver appointment, he might have to accede.

Kennedy really was doing me an enormous favor by pointing out this possibility of error, but I'm afraid my instant reaction was not too polite.

I told the President-elect that I didn't really know how I could qualify the story unless I said, in effect, that perhaps Kennedy was not so gutty after all. He had every right to hang up on me then and there, but our friendship weathered my discourteous response.

"Well, Bill," Kennedy persisted, "I'm just telling you I may yet appoint Vandiver to that job so you can fix your story any way you wish."

I did a carpentry job on the story referring to a fierce battle over Vandiver with the final outcome still in doubt.

On the following day, Governor Vandiver announced in Georgia that Kennedy had offered him the position but he had refused it. He went on from there to criticize a trouble-making *Times* reporter named Lawrence. Kennedy issued a statement confirming Vandiver's announcement. I recognized it all as a face-saving gesture for Vandiver, and since I bore Kennedy no malice I sent him a note which said, "O.K., Mr. President, I can take my lumps with my leaks."

Kennedy answered by sending me a copy of a still-unpublished telegram from Senator Russell which was a roughly worded declaration that the Senator from Georgia never had, and never would, make any patronage suggestions to President Kennedy. Russell had been embarrassed partly because Governor Vandiver was related to him by marriage.

During the pre-inaugural period, we moved in and out of Palm Beach, but spent a lot of time in Washington after Mrs. Kennedy prematurely gave birth, on Thanksgiving Day, 1960, to their son, John Fitzgerald Kennedy, Jr.

Along with Tom Ross of the Chicago *Sun-Times*, I had been invited to Thanksgiving dinner with Bob and Teddy Kennedy and their wives in the Kennedy home in Palm Beach while brother Jack went back to Washington to be with his pregnant wife and daughter Caroline. The elder Kennedy, as was customary, was back in Hyannis Port for the Thanksgiving holiday along with other members of the tribe.

Tom Ross and I were invited to join the Kennedys in late morning for some pre-lunch athletics, which began with tennis and moved along to a brisk swim in the ocean. Then we ate a very heavy lunch, and Teddy, who had been named tour director, said the first event of the afternoon would be water skiing.

I protested I did not know how to water-ski, but Teddy assured me he could teach me in no time at all. Off we went to the "inlet" of Lake Worth where the waters of the Atlantic move into the lake, which separates Palm Beach from West Palm Beach. Ethel Kennedy, Bobby's wife, was first up on skis while Teddy labored on the beach to teach me the fundamentals. The water was choppy, and Ethel took a miserable spill, hurting herself painfully. There was a brief pause while she was rescued, and someone drove her home, and then it was announced that it was now my turn to ski. Having watched Ethel get hurt, I was scared, but I was too much of a coward ever to admit to the Kennedys that I couldn't do something. So nervously I took my place on the skis and gave the signal to the motorboat operator to get underway. To the amazement of all, but especially me, I managed to ride the skis upright on my very first attempt and had an enjoyable, if not swift, journey around the small island from which we were skiing. I got back on the skis two or three times more before that activity ended. We headed back to the house to make certain that Ethel was all right, and finding that she was, Teddy and Bobby challenged me to golf at the Palm Beach Country Club, which was down North Ocean Boulevard just a few blocks. We played nine holes, and I beat them both. After golf, we went back to the Kennedy house where the rest of the Palm Beach press corps had been invited to join us for cocktails. Ross and I acted as hosts while the Kennedys got dressed.

The President-elect was due back from Washington late that evening, so after the cocktail party, Ross and I changed from shorts into suits and went out to the airport to meet him. Just as I reached the airport, I was paged on the public address system. It was the *Times* in New York, telling me that Mrs. Kennedy had just been rushed to Georgetown Hospital while her husband was en route to Florida. The indications were that their child might be born prematurely.

When the *Caroline* landed and taxied to a halt, I rushed to the side of the airplane and shouted up to the stewardess-secretary, Janet DeRosier, that she should tell Kennedy that his wife had just gone to the hospital. Janet told him, and he came rushing down the ramp, heading straight for a telephone. After a brief conversation, he said he wanted to go back to Washington at once. The *Caroline* needed refueling, but an American Airlines press plane charter that had preceded him had been gassed again and was ready to go. He jumped aboard and so did all the reporters, including me, without even a topcoat to guard against the chill of the Washington winter. En route north, there was a lot less drinking than usual among the reporters and photographers as we worried about Mrs. Kennedy. Mrs. Kennedy had a history of miscarriages and all of us, inwardly, were praying this would not happen now to Kennedy at the peak of his power and happiness, just a few weeks away from entering the White House.

While we flew over North Carolina, the pilot on the intercom announced that Mrs. Kennedy had given birth to a son, and that both mother and child were doing well. There was a burst of applause and shouts from everybody aboard. Kennedy was grinning like any other young new father. We landed in Washington before dawn, and made our way to Georgetown Hospital so the new father could see his wife and his first son. Leaving the hospital, he made it clear the boy would be "Junior" unless Mrs. Kennedy had some serious objection. She didn't.

After the birth, Kennedy decided to move his pre-inaugural headquarters to Washington. The press left the warm sunshine of Palm Beach for frigid vantage points on "N" Street in Georgetown outside the Kennedy home. Happily, NBC had rented an empty house across the street in which to place its cameras for Inaugural Day. Although the house was unheated, Sander Vanocur shared it with his colleagues, leaving only a sentry outside the Kennedy home to tell us when to go back to gather some more news.

It was about this time that Republicans publicly were saying they wanted a vote recount in Cook County (Chicago), where they charged that Mayor Richard Daley had stolen enough votes to make Kennedy President. Snow was falling as Salinger went by me one day, headed into Kennedy's house.

"You can tell Kennedy for me," I said, "that there are a lot of us out here who may join Nixon's recount committee in Illinois if a certain President-elect doesn't get enough sense to move back to Florida."

The message was delivered, because Kennedy thereafter kidded me about my belated conversion to Nixon's cause.

The Republicans, by the way, never really pressed for the Chicago recount because they knew Republican officials in downstate Illinois had not always counted votes honestly, even in that particular election. It is a sad commentary on the state of public morals and ethics in Illinois that both Republicans and Democrats decided the best course would be to recount none of the votes. Republicans still had the issue of the Chicago vote steal, but Kennedy had the White House.

We did go back to Palm Beach as soon as Mrs. Kennedy and the baby were well enough to travel. It was during this period that Pierre Salinger and Kennedy decided the President's future news conferences would be "live" on television. This proposed change in White House operations made me very unhappy because I feared that many of my colleagues, given an opportunity to perform before cameras, would become hams, acting out a part, and that the press conference, as I had known it since FDR's days, would lose its intimacy.

When Salinger made his announcement, I yelled from the back of the room, "As you get deeper and deeper into things about which you know absolutely nothing, had you ever . . ." That was as far as I got. Salinger shouted back at me, and there followed a furious battle in public. When Salinger reported back to the President a little later, Kennedy grinned and said, "Yes, I could hear it all from several miles away."

In fairness to the Salinger style, I have to admit today that the press conference, even though televised, took on new life and vibrancy under Kennedy and became a vital Presidential weapon in the conduct of public business. Without television, for example, Kennedy could not have forced "Big Steel" to roll back price increases. Without television, the public would have lacked information about other decisions on which public support was required.

Just before inauguration, Kennedy kept a promise he had made to me right after election but on which he had held back for many weeks. This was a frank and full disclosure of what he meant to do with his private fortune to avoid any conflict of interest while in the White House.

There obviously had been a lot of family consultation before the veil was lifted on the size and nature of the fortunes possessed by the Kennedy brothers. When they finally decided to tell me, it was the father, Joseph P. Kennedy, who took over the job, just as he had provided the money to start with. The elder Kennedy asked me to join him in his study at the ocean-front house before 9 A.M. one morning.

Patiently, Joseph Kennedy explained that each of his children had approximately $100,000 a year in net income after taxes from three trust funds which they would control eventually. This meant that each Kennedy conservatively was worth about $5,000,000, and the money was invested in a wide field, much of it in oil.

As we were talking, Jack Kennedy, barefooted and wearing shorts with his bathrobe hanging open, walked into the room. For the first and only time since he had been elected President, I violated the rule that he should be addressed as "Mr. President." Instead, I said, "Hello, Jack," but I got to my feet at the same time as a gesture of respect for his office.

"I suppose you and Dad are discussing my money," he said sourly. "I won't interfere with your discussion."

He left the room and headed for the breakfast table. Never again did I call him "Jack," even on the golf course, though it had been a "Jack" and "Bill" relation for a long time. Now it had to be "Mr. President."

As his son left the room, the elder Kennedy resumed his discussion of the trusts and their strict control beyond the possibility that his children, even the President, could affect the investments. Again, the elder Kennedy brought up the oil investments, and the possibility of conflict of interest.

"Him," he said of his departing son. "He's no help anyway. He always votes against the oil-depletion allowance."

This was an exclusive story for the *Times*, at least for the first edition. Afterwards, Salinger briefed the other reporters on the Kennedy money. He did the briefing from a typewritten summary sheet I had prepared to show the elder Kennedy that I had understood correctly the financial information he had given me.

Just before Inaugural Day, we headed north to Boston and a farewell speech to the Massachusetts legislature. The Kennedy speech writers deliberately had modeled it on Lincoln's farewell to Springfield, Illinois, little dreaming that their President would be shot down as Lincoln had been.

It was an eloquent and moving address, but as I looked over the caliber of the Massachusetts legislators, I thought it was wasted on a bunch of political hacks.

When we got on the airplane to fly back to Washington, I stopped the President-elect briefly as he was passing me.

"God, but you must be rich, and not only in money." I said. "Imagine wasting a speech like that on a bunch of clods when you must give an inaugural address in less than a week."

A big grin spread over Kennedy's face and he responded, "Don't you worry, Bill, I've got a good inaugural." He did too.

On the night before his inaugural, Washington had one of the worst snowstorms in its history, and the Army had to be mobilized to clear the line of march for the inaugural parade on Pennsylvania Avenue.

It was to be a top-hat inaugural by Kennedy's dictation after two homburg inaugurals for Eisenhower. I showed up at the Kennedy home that morning in my black homburg, and Kennedy spotted me as we came back from church.

"There's always some bastard who doesn't get the word," he said, smiling.

CHAPTER
23

The telephone on the wall of that small cubicle I occupied inside the White House press room gave a loud ring, as if it might ring right off the wall. I reached out to answer it, and the voice at the other end was President Kennedy's.

"Go ahead and take it," he urged. "That will show the bastards."

It was perhaps the most critical moment of my professional career. The issue on which Kennedy was giving me advice and encouragement was whether I should quit *The New York Times* after twenty years and at age forty-five accept an offer to join the news team of the American Broadcasting Company.

It was typical of Kennedy that he should know of my problem, and also that he should intervene. He did not really mean that those who ran the *Times* were "bastards," nor did I, but he knew that I was angry at the moment, and had been for several days, over the decision of the *Times* that I would not accompany the President on his first European trip even though I was the White House correspondent. Kennedy had, in fact, been the first to know from me that I wasn't going, and that I was damned mad about it. And on this particular day, late in May, 1961, Kennedy had been kept informed by his press secretary, Pierre Salinger, about job negotiations between me and ABC.

In fact, it had been Salinger who had initiated these negotiations earlier that day at my request, telephoning his old friend, the former White House press secretary in Eisenhower's time, James C. Hagerty, to tell him that Lawrence was so mad this might be a ripe time to approach him. Hagerty was a vice president of ABC. Over the years I had talked to all three broadcasting networks about jobs, always at their request, not mine, and in all previous cases I had decided to stay with the *Times,* where I had worked so happily for twenty years in Washington and in most parts of the world.

For reasons that were not made clear to me then, or since, the *Times* had decided that I should not accompany the President on his first trip abroad—a journey that would take him to Paris to visit French President De Gaulle, to Vienna for his first meeting with Soviet Premier Nikita Khrushchev, and finally to London to confer with British Prime Minister Harold Macmillan. James Reston, my chief in Washington, had decided to make the trip himself, which was fair enough, but the *Times* management in New York, with or without Reston's approval, had decided the other man from Washington would be Russell Baker, who did not cover the White House but already was in Europe for another assignment. When I first was informed of this decision, I had urged upon Reston very strongly that it be reconsidered, and I assumed he would let me know the answer before he left for Europe himself.

But by now, Reston had not communicated with me, and had gone on to Europe. Mine was not a one-day anger, but rather a sustained and increasing one. The tentative decision to leave the *Times* had been reached over a period of several days before I ever talked to Salinger and Hagerty about it. My deep hurt was both personal and professional. I had decided that I could no longer serve the *Times* as its White House and top political correspondent if I could be bumped off a story like the one ahead with so little thought as to its undoubted effect on me.

So I was an easy mark for Hagerty when he made his call. He pointed out the greater economic advantages of becoming ABC's White House correspondent and he baited the hook even more by saying that if I could join ABC at once, I could make the European tour with Kennedy. It was while I was weighing this offer that the President telephoned.

Moments after our conversation, I called Wallace Carroll, the news editor of the Washington bureau under Reston and informed Carroll that I had decided to leave the *Times* to join ABC, that this was not a negotiable decision, and that my new employer would like it, if possible, for the resignation to be effective immediately so I could undertake the Kennedy European assignment for him. I told Carroll that surely there could not be serious objection to this since my own assignment for the *Times* was Kennedy and my services therefore would hardly be needed by the *Times* while Kennedy was away. Carroll agreed to put the matter up to New York. As it turned out, the principal executives of the *Times* were away from the office that Friday—Managing Editor Catledge was in New Orleans and the publisher, Orvil Dryfoos, had slipped away for a few days rest. This left an assistant managing editor, Clifton Daniel, at the helm. Daniel was at first annoyed because Carroll's telephone call interrupted him at a conference where the shape of the *Times* for the next day was being discussed. He told Carroll he'd call him back. In a few minutes, he called back to say that my resignation was accepted.

I called Hagerty and his associates at ABC at once to tell them of my decision, and then I talked briefly with both Salinger and the President before I left the White House.

In the *Times* Washington bureau, I notified only two people in addition to Carroll. One was my first chief there, my old and dear friend Arthur Krock, and the other was Miss Emmet Holleman, who over the years had been executive assistant first to Krock and then to Reston. Both understood my decision, and both were very unhappy with it, and I felt the need to get out of the office instantly before I too became deeply depressed. But first Carroll telephoned to Reston in London, and, over the transatlantic telephone, I said a few brief words of farewell and we agreed to talk when both of us reached Paris in the next few days.

Back in New York, the news of my abrupt departure circulated swiftly among my friends in the news room, and several telephoned to say they were sorry. Even Clifton Daniel made a formal telephone call to express his official regrets.

The news was also telephoned to the retired publisher, Arthur Sulzberger, who had supported me so kindly and generously over many years. Mr. Sulzberger at once dictated the following letter:

Dear Bill:

I have just been told that you are leaving and I write to express my very real regret.

You and *The Times* just seemed to go together and it won't be quite the same place without you.

But good luck to you and all the best in your new undertaking.

Yours,
AHS.

This reached me a few days later, and it was read over the telephone to me by Miss Holleman from Washington. It moved me to tears, and I admit, even now, that if the Sulzberger letter had been in front of me when I had to make the decision to quit, I could not have quit. But I must also say, ten years later, that I have never regretted the decision to join ABC to cover the news for them.

It was only a couple of days after I left Washington that Hagerty and I flew to Paris to begin coverage of the Kennedy trip, arriving in the French capital ahead of the President so we could broadcast the arrival ceremonies.

But there was one amusing incident before I left Washington. One of my oldest friends is John Charles Daly, and he had married Virginia Warren, daughter of the Chief Justice, whom I had dated before their marriage. On the night I quit the *Times* to become a broadcaster I had gone to Chief Justice Warren's apartment in the Sheraton Park Hotel in Washington. Daly was quite persuasive about my need for a higher-quality colored shirt in front of TV cameras, and had urged that I buy a dozen or more at about $25 a copy from a shirt-maker he had found in Paris. After the conversation, Mrs. Warren had telephoned to advise me to "pay no attention" to John Daly, and certainly not to buy the expensive shirts Daly bought "from a dressmaker in Paris."

"Tell me your size, Bill," said Mrs. Warren, "and when I go shopping for Earl [the Chief Justice] next week, I'll buy you a dozen new blue shirts." She did, too.

In Paris, the press was headquartered in the Crillon Hotel, and there I had my reunion with Reston, who greeted me with a shout and a smile as his first "defector." This was the term widely used to describe officials who left the Soviet Union to join the Western Allies.

During the Kennedy-De Gaulle talks, I had my first exclusive story for radio and television, a "leak" out of the first session that the French and American Presidents were in full agreement on how to deal with the Russians over Berlin. Since De Gaulle seldom agreed publicly with any Western leader, or even discussed his foreign policy strategy with them, this was a pleasing beat for me, and one for which the ABC networks interrupted their transmissions at home to carry my broadcast direct from Paris.

In Vienna, Kennedy found it hard going with the Soviet leader Khrushchev, whose first impetuous reaction to the American President was that here was a man he could bluff and who would not face up to realities. It was perhaps an understandable error since Kennedy in recent weeks had authorized the disastrous Bay of Pigs invasion of Cuba, and had assumed full responsibility for its failure. Later the President told me that the Bay of Pigs had been "an unrelieved disaster, for which no adequate excuses or explanations could be found."

In any event, Khrushchev took the toughest possible line with Kennedy during all their Vienna talks, and it was not a happy few days for the new American President.

I flew out of Vienna to London aboard Air Force One, the President's own plane, as one of four pool correspondents who always accompanied Kennedy whenever he flew. The pool consisted of the reporters from the AP, UPI, a daily newspaper, and one of the radio networks; and in this case the pool correspondents were AP's Whitney Shoemaker, UP's Merriman Smith, *Chicago Daily News'* Peter Lisagor, and myself.

While we were in Vienna, the daily news briefings by the Russians and the Americans had not reflected the deep disagreement between the American President and the Soviet Premier; we were unaware how very rough and threatening Khrushchev had been in his dealings with Kennedy, especially on the issue of a separate Soviet peace treaty with East Germany that would affect Berlin.

During the flight to London, we saw nothing of the President, but we gathered from the President's military aide, Major General Ted Clifton, that all was not rosy despite what the official briefers might be saying in Vienna at that moment.

Just as the plane landed, and my fellow correspondents moved quickly toward the open door, Kennedy came up to me, struck me lightly on the back to get my attention and said, "Tell them [meaning the American people] that I left Vienna in a somber mood."

This he said only to me, and not to the rest of the reporters, but when I reached the pool car that was to carry us to the London home of Princess Radziwill, sister of Mrs. Kennedy, I reported on the conversation to Lisagor, and as soon as possible I telephoned the other network offices in London. Kennedy obviously did not mean to be quoted directly, so I described to them the Presidential mood and offered them a wide variety of adjectives, including "somber." In my own report, for which ABC again interrupted the network, I said Kennedy had been somber as he flew out of Vienna after meetings with Khrushchev that obviously had not been successful.

This, then, was my debut as a network radio broadcaster. On one of the biggest stories, I had led the pack, thanks to some extremely good news sources who were willing to confide in me.

Over the years, as I occasionally entertained ideas of leaving the *Times*, I had always wondered whether my extraordinarily good supply of news sources in Washington came entirely because of the *Times* or whether some were sources I might have acquired for myself as a reporter with or without the *Times*. After a few months of broadcasting, I was satisfied that I could keep the sources I already had, and acquire others without the *Times*. I'm also sure that in this I was not hampered in the slightest by the fact that the President was known to be my friend. But I must also add that none of my important Republican news sources lost confidence in me. Nixon might be the exception, because he had become a bitter personal critic of mine from the moment of his defeat in 1960 or before. But my relations improved, if anything, with former President Eisenhower, with Senator Everett Dirksen, and with the other top leaders of the GOP. And it was about this time that I began to develop a genuinely close relationship with Senator Barry Goldwater, the conservative Republican who later was to lead his party as the Presidential nominee in 1964.

The most difficult part of my transition from a print journalist to a talking journalist was learning how to condense my reports into the comparatively tiny space that radio and TV allowed in contrast to the many columns of the *Times*.

Some of my journalistic colleagues and friends always called me "the human vacuum cleaner," because I put so much into every report in the *Times*; but now I found myself working against forty-five seconds as the total allowed for a report on ABC radio. And it was not easy.

During my first year at ABC, I shared anchor duties on the *Evening News Report* with an old friend, Bill Sheehan, later to become an ABC-TV News vice president, and it was during this period that President Kennedy once urged me strongly to accompany his wife Jacqueline to India. He said Jackie very much wanted me to go, and surely I could talk ABC into it.

"I'm sorry, but I simply can't do it, Mr. President," I told him one afternoon in the presence of NBC's Sander Vanocur and CBS' George Herman.

"Why not?" Kennedy asked.

"Because I must do that news show every evening," I responded.

"Hell," said Kennedy, "I watch that show, and they wouldn't miss you."

When he could, Kennedy tried hard to get away from Washington for weekends on Cape Cod, in Palm Beach, and, occasionally, in the hunt country of northern Virginia where Mrs. Kennedy liked to ride.

We golfed out of town with regularity but he seldom played in Washington, mindful of the criticism that had been directed at President Eisenhower because of his regular rounds at Burning Tree Club. Kennedy too was a member of Burning Tree, but he used the club infrequently both before and while he was in the White House.

Once in Hyannis Port, Steve Smith, the President's brother-in-law, and I teamed up against the President and the club professional. On No. 17, a par three 134-yard hole straight at Nantucket Sound, the choice of clubs varies widely depending on the direction and strength of the always changing wind. One day Steve hit first and knocked his ball on the green only a few feet from the cup.

"What did you use?" the President asked.

Steve put his hand over the top of his No. 6 club so its number could not be read.

"Does Macy's tell Gimbel's?" Steve asked the President.

Feigning humility and deep hurt, Kennedy replied, "No, but they might tell the little store on the corner."

During another round, I very nearly holed out my tee shot on a short par three for a hole-in-one, and the President conceded me the putt for a birdie. As we walked away from the hole, Kennedy grinned and said, "And I suppose if that ball had gone in you would have wanted me to telephone a radio report about you and your golf to ABC?"

"Well, it's a nice thought," I said.

"And I would have," he said.

This will not be a review of the Kennedy administration and all of its deeds and problems, any more than this book has tried to chronicle the ups and downs of other Presidents I've covered in Washington. It is enough to say, I think, that *no* President ever performed more magnificently than Kennedy did during the critical week or more of the Cuban missile crisis of 1962 when World War III was so very close you could almost hear, smell, and feel it. When that week ended with Khrushchev's concessions on a Sunday morning, Jack Kennedy said to his brother Bob that this was a week in which he had surely earned his salary and that night might be a good night to go to the theater, as Lincoln had gone to Ford's Theater and been killed. If so, Bob replied, he wanted to go along.

During that week, ABC News virtually gave me control of the network, allowing me to interrupt on my own motion when I felt a news briefing by Salinger or some other Kennedy administration source warranted it. As a result, I was on TV and radio all during the week, day and night, and my paycheck at the end of the period was very large indeed. Kennedy heard from Salinger about how much money I had made. The President sought me out in the White House lobby to observe, "Lawrence, you have a vested interest in catastrophe."

On another occasion the President told me of his intention to appoint a New York lawyer as head of the Central Intelligence Agency, but a few days later appointed the same man to run the Agency for International Development (foreign aid.) When he announced the appointment, I whispered something to the effect that this was certainly a surprise.

"Yes," he grinned, "you better check out your news sources."

On a happier night, the President and his wife gave a small and fun black-tie party for Steve Smith who was leaving the administration to return to New York to run the Kennedy financial empire.

As I joined the group, the President smiled and said, "Don't leave early tonight, Bill, we may make some news."

I told him I had no intention of rushing home, but little did I think the party would keep on until after 3 A.M. Then it was possible to announce by agreement with the Russians that the imprisoned U-2 pilot, Francis Gary Powers, had been brought out of a jail in Moscow and traded in Berlin for the Soviet master spy, Colonel Rudolf Abel, who had been in prison in Atlanta. It was so late I had no network left in operation, but I telephoned the news to a few stations still operating, one in Los Angeles and also WMAL in Washington. Then I fell into bed, exhausted.

During the 1962 mid-term elections, ABC had given me a half-hour political program on Sundays, and these were, I think, some of the best broadcasts I ever made. Some made news and were unprecedented, including exclusive interviews back to back with President Kennedy for the Democrats and General Eisenhower for the Republicans. And both of these were taped just days ahead of the Cuban missile crisis, which would have made both appearances impossible.

Toward the end of 1962, in December, Kennedy participated in another precedent-shattering TV interview for an hour with three network correspondents—NBC's Vanocur, CBS's Herman and myself for ABC. Fred Friendly of CBS was the producer.

We taped questions and answers for about ninety minutes, then the networks in New York edited the program back to an hour. It was a smashing success for the President and for the correspondents involved. Kennedy liked to kid me about it, calling that one hour the "Bill and Jack Show."

"No, Mr. President, you must say the 'Jack and Bill Show,' " I insisted. But he kept calling it the "Bill and Jack show."

Finally I said that I was well aware of the star's identity (me), but protocol and respect for his high office demanded that top billing go to him, not me, and it would therefore be known as the "Jack and Bill Show."

I went to Palm Beach with him for that final weekend that he was alive, but I did not go on to Texas because I had long before arranged to spend my vacation in Palm Beach. I asked him to play golf in those final days but he begged off because, he said, "my back hurts." And I was at the helicopter pad when he flew off to get back on Air Force One.

On the afternoon that he was shot in Dallas, I was playing golf at the Palm Beach Country Club with Mrs. Barbara Mandel, the club champion, when a cart came out from the clubhouse to tell me there was "an emergency."

Inside the locker room, the radio told me what the emergency was . . . that the President had been shot.

ABC in Washington telephoned instructions to go to Dallas,

then switched me back to Washington when word came that Kennedy was dead.

I was on the White House lawn in the rain and winter chill from 7:30 P.M., November 22, almost without sleep through midday November 25 and the departure of the President's body from the White House for the last time on the way to the funeral at St. Matthew's Cathedral, a few blocks away. I went inside the White House to watch the funeral on television. I had not shed a tear nor really realized my deep personal loss until young John Kennedy snapped that salute at the flag-draped coffin of his father. Then I broke up and cried like a baby.

CHAPTER
24

Lyndon Johnson never had a finer hour than his first hour in Washington as President of the United States. While a nation mourned President Kennedy as it had never mourned before, on television, on radio, in churches, and in the privacy of individual dwelling places, Johnson provided that absolutely vital link of continuity that kept a country going, a government functioning, and a saddened people aware that while they had lost one leader, all was not gone. The tall Texan had a simple dignity about him as he rallied his countrymen to survive, to push forward, or as he phrased it in his first message to Congress, "Let us continue."

From the vantage point of the White House lawn, in the cold, cold rain, I watched the leaders of this and other nations come for their first meetings with the new President, as President. Even those who had known him longest were most impressed with the quick grasp he had of difficult situations.

Yet in these first moments of glory, when for him all seemed to be going well, he was to make a decision that would profoundly affect his place in history, turn many millions of Americans against him, and, to a large degree, wipe out the good of all his domestic accomplishments.

The fateful decision, of course, concerned the war in Vietnam, to which he was to commit all the pride, power, and treasury of the United States both in men and material. Vietnam killed Lyndon Johnson's Presidency as surely as bullets struck down John F. Kennedy in Dallas.

The first step down that road from which there would be no turning back was taken on the second day of the Johnson administration, on a Saturday morning while LBJ still was using his Vice Presidential office in the old Executive Office Building across the street from the White House. Movers were clearing out the Kennedy possessions from the Presidential oval office.

As I waited on West Executive Avenue with a live television camera, I saw Henry Cabot Lodge, the 1960 Republican Vice Presidential nominee now serving as Ambassador to South Vietnam, coming out of the EOB. I approached him to request a live interview and Lodge was most cooperative.

Lodge had been called back from Saigon for consultations by President Kennedy, he said, but his appointment now had been with the new President. The President had authorized him to say he had reached his first decision of substance—that American aid to the Saigon regime would continue at present levels.

Lodge went on to observe that this demonstrated the continuity of American foreign policy even as Johnson's other moves already had proved domestic continuity. It was obvious to me that LBJ had hoped for just such an opportunity—a live television interview with Lodge as he left the new President's office so the Ambassador could tell about the first foreign policy decision of the new administration.

I will not pretend now that I recognized it then as fateful or as anything more than Lodge said it was: news about the first decision.

But in retrospect, as this is written in 1971, it is easy to trace the path that LBJ followed to his own political destruction. And this decision was the first step down that path.

Over the five years and more that Lyndon Johnson sat in the White House, he never had a better chance to get out of that war before the war left its mark on him. Indeed, it was his fate to escalate the war so it involved more than half a million Americans fighting on the soil of South Vietnam, and bombing its northern industrial and military centers, but incapable of winning the war, or even of forcing a compromise peace.

I spent much of those five-years-plus at the White House with LBJ. I reported his domestic triumphs, his passage of legislation that had been stalled for a full generation, including such bills as federal aid to education and a medical care program for the aged. I watched as the first President from the Southwest forced civil-rights advances that as a Senator from Texas he could never have supported if he wanted reelection.

And, of course, I watched LBJ in his great triumph over Barry Goldwater in 1964 when the White House incumbent pledged again and again that American infantrymen would not be sent to fight the war that Asians ought to fight for themselves.

Goldwater was a stubborn conservative, who sometimes seemed foolhardy in his refusal to trim his sails even momentarily to adapt to the political mood of the area in which he was campaigning. He never tried to conceal his view that Indochina, especially Vietnam, was in danger from the Communists and its loss would be a peril to the free world—the line that Johnson in 1964 discounted in attacking his rival as trigger-happy and bomb-foolish.

Even more striking was Goldwater's outline of his domestic views. Ideologically and practically, the Republican nominee thought the government should get out of business and even sell the Tennessee Valley Authority to private owners. So he said that in Tennessee, right in the heart of the area that the TVA had done so much to help. Goldwater constantly campaigned for major changes in Social Security, towards a voluntary not mandatory system, and this view was emphasized, rather than played down, in St. Petersburg, Florida, the capital of the senior-citizens movement.

When the campaign was over, Goldwater had lost only the election. Johnson had won the Presidency—with a record popular-vote majority—but Johnson had lost something much more important—his credibility.

There were few reporters in that campaign who did not believe that the President was shading the truth in many of his campaign statements, but none of us knew for certain the extent of this deception on the Vietnam war issue until much later, in the summer of 1971, when the *Times* published the "top secret" Pentagon papers tracing the U.S. involvement in the Vietnamese war. These established that the administration was preparing in the early part of the 1964 campaign to bomb North Vietnam beginning in 1965, at the very moment when Johnson was attacking Goldwater as "bomb-happy."

And so the President was barely launched in his new term, backed by a landslide, when his foreign policy began to look less like his campaign promises and more like what Barry Goldwater long ago had said would be necessary.

When Lyndon Johnson lost his credibility on the war, he discovered he had lost his credibility on all issues, domestic as well as foreign. When you deceive the people on one thing, it does not take long for them to realize you would deceive them on all things. Johnson had proved again that old aphorism that you can't be only slightly pregnant.

It was about this time that the incumbent President began to think more seriously about voluntary retirement, long before his enemies and critics could even dream that the man from Texas would surrender his powers gracefully and go back to his ranch in the Texas hill country.

It was less than eighteen months after the 1964 landslide that I began to wonder inwardly if LBJ would be a candidate for re-election. At first it was only a hunch, but there followed some vigorous night-and-day reporting, intensive questioning of the Presidential staff, and finally of the President himself.

My suspicions were aroused first in the fall and winter of 1965 when LBJ was confined to the Bethesda Naval Hospital with a combination gall-bladder and kidney-stone operation. At first he snapped back quickly, but then he relapsed. His staff, including Press Secretary Bill Moyers, openly admitted his pain, his fatigue, his need for a long rest and rehabilitation.

Such talk of pain, of tiredness, of a need for rest would not have been unusual or unexpected in the ordinary patient. But now we were talking about LBJ, who, up to then, had been depicted as a kind of superman, who, disregarding the massive heart attack that had almost killed him ten years earlier, now thrived on work, work, work and no sleep in the White House. LBJ and his staff had made the President at least ten feet tall, but now they seemed to be talking about an ordinary mortal.

I had now been a reporter at the White House with Presidents Roosevelt, Truman, Eisenhower, and, briefly, John F. Kennedy. Now I thought the Johnson staff was trying to give me a message and I brooded about what it might mean for several weeks.

Then, in June, 1966, right after the California gubernatorial primary election, I came back to the White House with some direct questions for Moyers.

"Has the President ever told or intimated to the staff that he might not be a candidate for reelection in 1968?" I wanted to know.

Moyers replied indirectly, saying there had been nothing that positive, but that the President in moments of tiredness or frustration had been heard to cry out, as every President has cried out, that he would be happy indeed when his term of office ended and he would be rid of frustrations, problems, and so many critics.

"Do you think the President will be a candidate for reelection?" I asked.

Moyers then was closer to LBJ than any person with the exception of Lady Bird Johnson, and his answer therefore astounded me.

"I wouldn't bet you a nickel either way," said Moyers.

We then talked about some of the reasons why Johnson would not want to run. One obviously was his health and a desire to spend as many years as might remain with his family, whom he adored. The Johnsons had grown rich buying and operating television stations and land while he was a Senator, and he could easily afford to quit.

In June, 1966, when Moyers and I had our conversation, the war in Vietnam was not nearly as unpopular with Americans as it later was to become. Therefore it was conceivable to us that LBJ might want to run again simply to make sure that the war came out all right, and to make certain that a Republican would not replace a Democrat in the White House. The President, I felt, would want to influence the Democratic convention to choose a Presidential candidate he approved of, and he certainly wouldn't approve of former Attorney General Robert Kennedy, brother of the late President.

After talking to Moyers, I did broadcasts that night for radio and TV. I didn't plunge in where angels fear to tread. I said cautiously that LBJ's bid for a second term wasn't the automatic assumption that most politicians thought it to be; that there were close associates of the President who wouldn't bet a nickel either way.

Then I listed reasons on both sides of the question.

My broadcasts created only a mild ripple, except among my colleagues in the White House press room who said bluntly that

either I had taken leave of my senses, or I had been taken in by
LBJ and his aides. Twenty-four hours later the President sent
word to ABC news that he'd like copies of the broadcast scripts
about the possibility he might not run. These were furnished to
Mr. Johnson.

On the following Saturday, the President held a news conference in his office which was not televised. But, in an unusual move,
he agreed afterwards to go on camera for taping one question
each from each of the network correspondents. I covered the news
conference, asked my question for later broadcasting, and went on
to lunch at the National Press Club.

In mid-afternoon, just as I was finishing lunch, I got a telephone
call from the White House saying that the President would like
to see me at once. I hurried to the White House.

I was ushered into the President's office almost at once, and he
said "How about lunch?" I didn't tell him that I had just finished
lunch because I am always willing to eat one, two, or three lunches
if one of them might be with the President of the United States.
The President and I were joined by Bob Fleming, the deputy
White House press secretary who had been my old boss at ABC
news, and the three of us proceeded to the family dining room on
the second floor of the White House.

The President's own records indicate that we were together
from 4:05 P.M. to about 5:25 P.M., but my own impression is that
I came about 4 P.M. and didn't leave him until about 7 P.M. First
we had lunch, and during lunch we talked about a wide variety of
subjects, but mostly Vietnam, and new ways that were being proposed to carry on the war there. I was shown a number of "Top
Secret" and "Eyes Only" cables which I couldn't reveal then or
now, and which as far as I'm concerned, are still secret.

After the luncheon table conversation lasting a couple of hours,
the President, in the center hall, turned toward his bedroom and
I bade him farewell. But he said not to leave, but to come into
the bedroom with him and Fleming, which I did. Mrs. Johnson
was away from Washington, he explained, so he planned to take a
nap, but he would talk to me for a few minutes more before his
eyes got tired. He removed all of his clothing as we kept on talking, put on his pajamas and stretched out on the bed beneath the
sheets. We kept on talking about Vietnam.

Finally he asked me if there might be a question I wanted to ask
him.

"Sure," I replied with a grin, "you sent for those broadcasts I did the other night suggesting that you might not run again in 1968. Was there a word of truth in what I had to say?"

LBJ, whom I had now known for more than fifteen years, grinned right back and once again evaded a direct reply. First he said I obviously had been thinking more about 1968 than he had. He told me how he had never really wanted to run for President, either in 1960 (when he lost the nomination to Kennedy after a bitter dogfight in Los Angeles) or in 1964 (when he had beaten Goldwater).

Then the President inquired the reasons I had for thinking he might not want to run again.

I repeated to him all the reasons I could think of, bearing down heavily on his desire to spend as much time as possible with his family. As we kept talking—he in bed and me beside the big bed— I noted that Mr. Johnson did not seem to be arguing very hard or heatedly with any of the reasons I put forth for his not running again. Indeed, he seemed to be confirming or tolerating my ideas, though never at any time did he say in so many words that he wouldn't run. Certainly he was not mad at me because of my suggestions.

As I remember it, he kept Fleming and me at his bedside for not just five minutes, but fully an hour as the conversation ranged from Vietnam to politics, then back to Vietnam again. I think I'm right about the time because the U.S. Open Golf Championship was being broadcast from California that day, and Fleming and I made it back to the press secretary's office just in time to watch it. Bob Fleming agrees with my estimate.

After this meeting, I was increasingly doubtful that LBJ would run again, began to bet against it, and never lost an opportunity to express my doubts on and off the air. Every time I interviewed a politician, Republican or Democrat, I asked him if he was dead certain in his own mind that LBJ would run again. With the possible exception of Vice President Humphrey, no politician doubted it. The politicians, like the other reporters, thought I had taken leave of my senses. Once I think I took Vice President Humphrey off-guard with the question, because he responded that "We certainly hope that he'll run." But when I pressed Humphrey for more information, he ducked.

Nearly every year, ABC assembles its top foreign and domestic correspondents and asks them to review the year just passed and the year ahead. In December, 1966, our moderator, Howard K. Smith, asked me in view of the Vietnam war pressures whether I thought Mr. Johnson would run for reelection in 1968.

"Howard, I am one of a tiny minority that doubts it," I replied.

Smith asked me for my reasons, and I said then that there was first the reason of health, and, secondly, the breakup of the White House staff, people like Moyers and Jack Valenti. I said I doubted these men would leave the power of the White House if they thought LBJ would be there for another six years.

"I don't know he is not going to run," I said. "I don't think the President has made up his mind for certain, but I have this feeling [that he won't]."

My colleague, Edward P. Morgan, dissented vigorously and immediately, saying that Johnson would run because "his ego is as big as the state of Texas."

I countered Morgan by asserting my doubts the President would run simply "because his ego is that big."

"I don't think he has any chance at all, come what may, of surpassing in 1968 the margin of victory he achieved in 1964," I continued. "Goldwaters just don't grow on trees. He'll have to run against somebody stronger, backed by probably a united Republican party."

In an ABC documentary, "Who in '68?," broadcast on August 17, 1967, I said in part:

> The story of the Democratic party is the story of one man—Lyndon Baines Johnson. He fiddles the tune and the supporting cast of Democrats dances to whatever tune he plays, although there are some protests and mumblings.
>
> But if the President should decide not to run, and I'm one of a tiny minority who thinks that he might not run, then the Democrats will be locked in one of the most bitter convention floor fights this country has seen in many a year.

Still later in that same documentary I spelled out my "feeling" that Johnson might not run again for a variety of reasons, including his health, frustrations over Vietnam, and a desire to maintain his 1964 landslide record. I concluded the Democratic section of "Who in '68?" by saying that although one had to accept publicly the assumption that the Democratic ticket would be repeated from

1964—Johnson and Humphrey—"if it isn't, it's a brand new ball game."

In a December, 1967, round-up, Howard Smith commented that "one of the worst things you can do to a reporter is to remind him of his predictions," and then went on to ask me if I thought LBJ would run again. It was a graceful opportunity to retreat.

"Well, nothing really has happened since I said last year that I had my doubts," I replied. "As Mr. [Frank] Reynolds says, he doubts whether Lady Bird even knows for sure. I'll stick with the prediction."

I do not want to pretend I did not have my doubts at times, nor that it did not get lonely out on that limb.

As 1968 dawned, there certainly had been no clear sign from the White House that Mr. Johnson intended to quit. Indeed the surface evidence was to the contrary. His closest political associates already had announced they were planning a reelection campaign, and the President himself showed up for his annual State of the Union message before a joint session of the Congress with a new hair-do and looking very much like a candidate. His speech was a standard Great Society speech with no hint of retirement, although we were told later, much later, he was carrying his abdication paragraph in his pocket and *might* have read it that night.

In any event, joining in the commentary after that State of the Union message as I traditionally did, I noted that Mr. Johnson looked very much like a candidate, even though I clung stubbornly to my belief that he would not be a candidate.

I took the usual joshing from my ABC colleagues for my stubbornness, and at one point in his remarks from Capitol Hill, my colleague Bob Clark said "everyone" knew that Mr. Johnson would run again. Clark paused for a second or two, smiled, and then amended his statement to say "Everyone except Lawrence, that is, knows the President will run again."

In the meantime, Minnesota's Democratic Senator Eugene McCarthy had announced his candidacy for President on an anti-war platform, but he didn't seem to be making much progress, especially in New Hampshire where he was campaigning in the primary against a Democratic establishment pro-LBJ delegate slate that was expected to win even though the President would *not* campaign in person.

Then suddenly, with little warning, the "Kids' Revolution"

broke into the open, and youngsters swarmed across New Hampshire seeking votes for McCarthy. One essential precaution was taken. The kids first had to get haircuts, take baths, and generally dress respectably so as not to turn off the above-twenty-one age group that alone could vote.

Only at the last minute did Democratic Governor John W. King and other ranking Democrats come to realize the serious threat from the McCarthy supporters. The King group then panicked, and resorted to character assassination, claiming in full-page ads that Hanoi would welcome a McCarthy victory, but the United States would suffer. The King group and LBJ guessed wrong, and the result was a tiny popular majority for the President in the head-to-head race with McCarthy, but McCarthy captured nearly all of the delegates because the pro-Johnson delegate candidates, more than could be elected, fragmented the pro-Johnson vote.

Before New Hampshire voted, there already were signs in Wisconsin that a McCarthy bandwagon was rolling there and that LBJ's unpopularity was coming home to haunt him and all his friends. Many LBJ cabinet members joined the campaign for the President in Wisconsin, hampered because they could not answer questions whether he would run. Bob Kennedy had stayed out of the early primaries, but on the night the New Hampshire votes were counted he told newsmen he was now reconsidering his position. The Kennedy people say he had decided to run before this anti-Johnson development occurred.

At the White House, LBJ had a television speech scheduled for March 31. The advance word was that he would deal mostly with Vietnam, but it would not be a political speech. I volunteered to work in the ABC Washington studios along with my colleagues, Frank Reynolds and John Scali, but the bureau chief, John Lynch, said he saw no need for my services that night. Lynch could not have been more wrong. But I went along to New York on other business and was sitting alone in my Essex House hotel room when LBJ suddenly bowed out as a candidate in a surprise ending to his prepared speech. Scali and Reynolds, like other broadcasters for other networks, were taken so much by surprise they could hardly bring themselves to talk about the Johnson political abdication.

In New York, ABC producers, learning that I was in town, summoned me quickly to take part in the late-evening news show.

There I was asked for reasons that were never made clear to me to interview Republican Senator Jacob M. Javits about the President's dramatic announcement. Javits, of course, knew less than I about the Johnson move, but New York's idea seemed to be to get a reaction, any reaction.

A few days later, however, ABC News capped my triumph with a full-page advertisement in *The New York Times* which said in boxcar type "Even the President of the United States couldn't keep a secret from Bill Lawrence." A few weeks later, I obtained a small copy of the advertisement and got LBJ to autograph it "To Bill Lawrence, from his friend, Lyndon B. Johnson." It is one of my finest souvenirs and hangs in my apartment.

CHAPTER
2 5

Once President Johnson decided not to run again, the Democratic spotlight was expected to shine on his conqueror in two primaries, Senator Eugene McCarthy. But this was not true, even briefly. The attention was on Robert Kennedy, now the oldest of the Kennedy clan, who had been reluctant about doing political battle with Lyndon Johnson in 1968.

By the time Bob Kennedy got into the race it was too late for him to enter the Wisconsin primary, but he was in time for the primaries in Indiana, Nebraska, Oregon, California, and South Dakota. All of these were head-to-head matches with Senator McCarthy. Kennedy and McCarthy would fight it out in the primaries while Vice President Humphrey stood by on the sidelines waiting to inherit the nomination from LBJ just as LBJ wanted him to do.

During early 1968, I was out on the primary trail, enduring the snows and cold weather of New Hampshire and Wisconsin, finding things somewhat better for the traveling reporter in Indiana and Nebraska, before the green and pleasant landscape of Oregon, and finally, California.

Kennedy blitzed McCarthy in the middle primaries of Indiana and Nebraska, and rolled into Oregon expecting another victory there. But Oregonians were not impressed with the young Kennedy, and for the first time in history a Kennedy lost an election. McCarthy walked off with all the Oregon delegates, and now the stage was set for a bitter and final showdown in the nation's most populous state, California, whose primary election date fell on the same date as that in rural South Dakota, the birthplace of Humphrey.

In Oregon, Kennedy had declined to debate McCarthy and this probably hurt him with the Oregon voters. Now, defeated in Oregon and desperately needing a California comeback, Kennedy agreed to debate McCarthy on a special ABC *Issues and Answers* to be broadcast in prime time from San Francisco. I took part in it along with Frank Reynolds and Bob Clark. It wasn't really much of a debate, and nothing very memorable was asked or answered, but it did show the two candidates side by side dealing with questions. The result of the debate was not nearly so decisive as the first debate in 1960 between John F. Kennedy and Richard Nixon, which Nixon lost both on oratory and makeup.

By the time Californians voted I was back at ABC election headquarters in New York where with Howard Smith I was to report on the primary results in both South Dakota and California, and to comment on their political meaning.

Young Kennedy won them both; his margin was bigger proportionally in rural South Dakota than in California. Alone among the networks, ABC stayed on the air into the early morning hours to broadcast the victory statement of Bob Kennedy from the Ambassador Hotel in Los Angeles. He was in a triumphant mood that night, the victory in California having wiped out much of the sting of the Oregon defeat, and he urged his supporters on to Chicago and the final battle for the Presidential nomination.

Bob Kennedy ended his speech, Howard Smith and I wrapped up our broadcast, and Smith said good night to our viewers, a cue for the theme music to be played over a network that was ready to go to bed. So were the tired reporters, especially me, who had not had a single day off for seven or eight weeks while on the primary campaign trail.

As the theme music sounded, our closed circuit to California still was open to ABC headquarters in New York, and over it we heard sounds very much like gunfire. From California, somebody said that there had been a shooting, and one of the ABC production crew, William Weisel, had been wounded. There were suggestions that others, possibly even Senator Kennedy, had been hit.

Walter Pfister, Jr., executive producer for special events, kept the theme music playing on and on, and we stayed on the air while urgent inquiries were being made from New York to California. Finally Bob Clark got through to New York directly and confirmed that Kennedy had been shot, though we could not know how seriously at that time.

The ABC broadcast from New York resumed, with Howard Smith giving the first word that Kennedy had been wounded by a revolver shot, that we did not know how serious the injury was. I broke in with some commentary and read some press association stories about the shooting and the wild scenes that ensued thereafter. Bob Clark came on camera and microphone from the Ambassador Hotel, and the broadcast continued for many more hours and days as Kennedy's life ebbed away.

I have already mentioned my utter exhaustion, and those last four days before Bob Kennedy finally was buried next to his brother in Arlington National Cemetery late on a Saturday night drained my resources to zero. Sometime in the next week or so, as best the doctors could figure from the changes in my electrocardiogram, I had a heart attack—a thrombosis of one of the main arteries leading to the heart. But I was unaware of the attack until in late June I began to experience a series of attacks of pulmonary edema. When the doctors asked whether I had felt a pain on my left side, I told them that I ached all over, and one more pain, even that of a coronary thrombosis, was not sufficiently different to make me aware that something very damaging had occurred. It was a rough year physically, but I insisted on attending the Republican convention in Miami Beach and the Democratic convention in Chicago.

The Democrats chose Chicago as their meeting place on direct orders from President Johnson after the national committee's site selection committee, headed by Democratic Chairman John M. Bailey of Connecticut, informally had agreed to recommend Miami Beach, where the Republicans were to convene first.

Chicago was an unwise choice for the convention city, and the violence that marred that convention came as no surprise to me.

Long before the Democrats met, Hal Humphrey, the television critic of the *Los Angeles Times*, published an interview with me on January 18, 1968, that said in part:

> Despite Chicago Mayor Daley's assurances, Lawrence thinks the Democrats are foolhardy to hold their convention in Chicago at the International Amphitheater.
>
> We'll need two cameras inside and nine outside the Amphitheater to cover the Negroes "demonstrating and maybe worse," Lawrence states.

The crowds that demonstrated in Chicago were mixed, white and black, and I have always felt that the Chicago police over-reacted to the disorders. Nothing has come to light since then to change my opinion.

What the American television viewer saw was the picture of a convention of a divided party, in a city marred by riots and bloodshed. Though Vice President Humphrey won an easy first-ballot victory, with the Southern delegations kept in line for Humphrey by the retiring President, it was a Pyrrhic victory for the Minnesotan who deserved kinder treatment than this city was giving him.

As a broadcaster assigned to look ahead at convention developments, I felt early that Senator Edmund Muskie of Maine was the likely Vice Presidential nominee and said so several days before he actually was chosen.

As the convention ended, my voice was getting weaker and weaker, more gravelly and more indistinct with every word. I already had missed most of the Republican convention at Miami Beach because of recurrent pulmonary edema. When the Democrats ended their meeting, I headed at once for the Mayo Clinic at Rochester, Minnesota, for treatment of my heart ailment and a look at my throat. There a malignant tumor on my right vocal chord was diagnosed. Daily X-ray treatments for my throat, more than thirty of them, consuming more than six weeks at the Washington Hospital Center after I left the Mayo Clinic, and a strict regimen to correct my heart and pulmonary edema conditions took me out of the play for most of the Presidential campaign that followed.

The pollsters, especially Gallup, had recorded a big lead for Mr. Nixon right after the unhappy riot-marked Democratic convention in Chicago. It was the kind of lead that looked so insurmountable

that Democratic leaders feel the polls discouraged potential campaign contributors as well as rank-and-file campaign workers. The
Nixon lead melted away like snow exposed to a hot summer sun in
the final weeks. Nixon won finally by about 100,000 votes in the
raw vote column, and there are some, including high officials of the
Nixon administration, who believe the Republican candidate might
have lost if the election had been a bit later.

I had fully recovered my voice by election night and I worked
for more than seventeen hours alongside Howard K. Smith and
Frank Reynolds from ABC election headquarters in New York. I
provided the commentary, and shortly after 8 A.M. on Wednesday, after we had Illinois recorded for Nixon, I declared flatly that
Mr. Nixon would be the next President. Our rivals at CBS and
NBC still were debating the Nixon-Humphrey outcome two hours
after we had left the air.

Nixon carried to victory with him a little-known Vice President,
Spiro Agnew, the governor of Maryland, whose campaign did not
distinguish itself for tolerance and moderation in his use of such
terms as "Polacks" and "fat Japs." It was a tiny preview of things
to come.

CHAPTER
26

It was a wintry day in Hampton, New Hampshire, near the Atlantic coast, but the tiny American Legion Hall was filled to overflowing in mid-morning with a crowd of Republicans who had turned out to greet and hear Richard M. Nixon, the former Vice President, the man who lost the Presidency in 1960 and the California gubernatorial race in 1962. Now Mr. Nixon was trying for the Presidency again. In Hampton, he was to make, without advance notice, perhaps the most significant of all his 1968 campaign pledges.

Even in New Hampshire, which prides itself on fierce patriotism and strong Yankee stock, the people were getting weary of the endless war in Vietnam. Although Richard M. Nixon had no real competition for the Republican Presidential nomination, he was about to cash in on the anti-war and pro-peace sentiment. His top advisors had urged him to make that move and Hampton was the place he chose to make it.

Nixon said that he had a plan that would end the war in Vietnam and win the peace in Southeast Asia. It was a carefully contrived and limited promise. He did not say he would "win" the war in

Vietnam; all he said he would do was "end" it. It was the peace he promised to win, but without a word as to how the Communists might be forced to keep peace with their neighbors in Asia, or Europe, or Africa, or even in South America.

But a promise to end the war and win the peace was an attractive one for nearly all Americans, on the left or the right. The left might think of it in terms of an early withdrawal; the right could dream that Nixon might use the military power Lyndon Johnson had been unwilling to use to bomb Hanoi or Haiphong or to blockade the ports of North Vietnam.

When reporters asked just what the Nixon plan encompassed, the future President quickly assumed the pose of a statesman. It would not be fair, he said, to reveal his plan and thereby possibly interfere with any negotiations that would still be the exclusive province of President Johnson. Nixon also said he would not be so rash to try to tell the President in office what to do. It would be better, Nixon continued, for him not to speak in any greater detail about Vietnam lest he decrease the chances for peace.

In the seven months of campaigning that followed, Mr. Nixon offered not a single clue as to his "plan" for ending the war and winning the peace. The very vagueness and generality of his promise helped to win him votes on both sides of the fence. Certainly, the voters were unhappy with Lyndon Johnson and his self-appointed heir, Vice President Hubert Humphrey.

This one sentence in Hampton may have made Richard Nixon President. He won by such a very narrow margin and became a "minority" President because of the ten million votes siphoned off by the rightist campaign of segregationist George Wallace. In fairness, it was not any more vague than Dwight Eisenhower's promise in 1952 to "go to Korea." However, Eisenhower did go to Korea and he acted quite promptly to end the war in Korea, though on terms that probably would have put a Democratic President into a lot of trouble.

What Nixon did after he became President was to start withdrawing American forces from South Vietnam in large numbers. To date, these actions have not ended the war nor have they won the peace. American disengagement and Vietnamization are not substitutes for ending the war.

This was precisely the problem when Mr. Nixon spoke to the nation in November, 1969, after he had been President for eight months. This speech was the start of what turned out to be a long and bitter battle between Vice President Agnew and the media.

That particular speech by Mr. Nixon broke no new ground so far as Vietnam was concerned. It did not announce any further cutback in American troops in Southeast Asia nor did it contain any new proposals for settlement of the dispute. Instead, it was simply a recital of the steps the Nixon administration already had taken or announced to reduce American involvement and to step up Vietnamization of the conflict. Coming as it did just a few days before elections in New Jersey and Virginia, it seemed to me more political than historical. But as a political speech it lacked the promise of anything new to persons who were unhappy with the continuing war that Mr. Nixon had promised to end.

I took part in the ABC commentary after the President spoke that night, along with my colleagues Frank Reynolds, John Scali, Tom Jarriel, Bob Clark, Bill Downs, Howard Smith, and an invited guest, former New York Governor Averell Harriman, who had been Lyndon Johnson's unsuccessful negotiator in Paris for peace in Vietnam.

We got a look at the speech well ahead of Nixon's delivery time and some of my colleagues had been briefed on it by "high administration sources," which in foreign affairs usually meant Dr. Henry Kissinger.

Frank Reynolds, acting as moderator, commented that it was Lawrence's job to "take the temperature of the country" and he inquired how I thought the country would react to the speech.

"Well, Frank, it is fair to talk about this politically because Mr. Nixon was out on the stump in New Jersey last week, inviting people to listen in," I said. "Politically I am not sure why he did it because there was nothing new in it [the speech] politically, and his impact will be on those who are moved by words if not by deeds.

"His appeal was not to the youth who've been raising trouble but rather to the silent majority, if they are a majority, who presumably have been with him all along. But there wasn't a thing new in this speech that would influence anybody to vote tomorrow or six months from now in a different way than his mood was set.

"Now, the Democrats engaged in a little one-upmanship on this speech after the White House announced it three weeks ago. They [the Democrats] started very vigorously to build up hope about what this speech might contain in the way of some new move toward substantively ending the war sooner. They talked about a ceasefire, they talked about greater reductions in troops. Nothing happened."

"You think they were mouse-trapping him?" Reynolds asked.

"I think that was their purpose perhaps," I replied, "and I think to that extent his speech certainly did not meet the expectations of those who turned on their television or radio sets and expected to learn some big new move in Vietnam, because it just wasn't there."

Later, after Bob Clark and Bill Downs had reacted, Reynolds turned to me again and gave his own opinion that Mr. Nixon was "an extremely skillful politician," that he didn't think there was any doubt about that, but Reynolds wanted to know if there possibly was "a full appreciation in the White House now of the depth of the discontent in the country, or of the disenchantment with the war."

"Well, Frank, I don't know whether understanding is the right word," I said. "I don't believe the White House believes there is deep discontent. I'm not really sure, despite Mr. Nixon's victory, that he is so big a politician as you suggest."

Reynolds observed that Nixon had come a long way, and I responded that might be true but "he hasn't followed up."

"He hasn't used the powers of the Presidency," I continued. "A good politician would have taken the momentum of the election and the inauguration and come forward with a program of some kind. He wouldn't be explaining Vietnam now [in November]. He would have done that in February. He had all this time to think."

Downs interjected his observation that the President had to speak in generalities because "there simply is no program that he would not regard as a cut-and-run program."

"Yes, but in his campaign he said he had a plan that would end the war and win the peace," I responded. "He said that again tonight. I still don't know where it is."

So far as the White House was concerned, my unforgivable sin was that I had even questioned the President's political skill, and had reminded an audience of millions that he had promised to "end the war and win the peace," not just wind down the war by disengaging American forces. The White House palace guard takes it as an article of faith that Mr. Nixon is the greatest political practitioner in history, and it doesn't want reporters to go around questioning this fact. Nor does any President like to be reminded of unkept campaign promises.

This provided a considerable part of the motivation for Vice

President Agnew's broadside against the media, delivered about a month later before a partisan Republican audience in Des Moines. The networks were shown advance copies of the Vice President's remarks on the afternoon that he spoke, and all three of them carried his speech live, even sacrificing their evening news shows in major markets. It is not customary for any Vice President to get national network exposure—certainly not from three networks at once. But Mr. Agnew got it because his main target that night was the networks, and the network executives felt they had to carry his speech or face charges of suppression.

Agnew slashed out at "a small band of network commentators and self-appointed analysts" who had inherited the big TV audience attracted to the Presidential talk. Agnew was angry because among these network commentators "the majority" expressed, in one way or another, their hostility to what the President had to say. Ignoring the fact that we had been briefed on the speech an hour ahead of time, Agnew found fault because we were ready with instant commentary when the President finished.

One line in the Agnew speech was aimed straight at me: "Another [commentator] challenged the President's abilities as a politician."

Then Agnew went on to rip into television generally and the great influence of its news broadcasters and news commentators.

The airwaves do not belong to the networks, said the Vice President, but rather belong to the people. And he gave his own description of how network news was determined.

"A small group of men, numbering perhaps no more than a dozen anchormen, commentators, and executive producers, settle upon the twenty minutes or so of film and commentary that is to reach the public. This selection is made from the 90 to 180 minutes that may be available. Their powers of choice are broad. They decide what forty to fifty million Americans will learn of the day's events in the nation and the world."

All of us, he pointed out, lived in Washington or New York, and he added:

"Both communities bask in their own provincialism, their own parochialism. We can deduce that these men thus read the same newspapers, and draw their political and social views from the same sources.

"Worse, they talk constantly to one another, thereby providing artificial reinforcement to their shared viewpoints."

Overnight, Agnew became a national hero to some, and a national bum to others. It enhanced a reputation he already had started to build by his attacks upon the anti-war youths, the hippies, and the "effete snobs." Suddenly the Vice President was making more news, and getting more attention than the President, or at least it seemed that way.

I had known Agnew since he had become governor of Maryland and had seen him switch, in 1968, from being a strong supporter of New York Governor Nelson Rockefeller into the Nixon camp, finally becoming the Nixon nominee for Vice President—cleared in advance with Senator Strom Thurmond and other planners of the "Southern strategy" which was to slow down civil-rights enforcement.

Among the governors in early 1968 no one spoke out more strongly in urging Governor Rockefeller to abandon his do-not-choose-to-run stance and to actively seek the Republican nomination. Agnew didn't think that a loser like Nixon should get the nomination again.

Agnew quit being a Rockefeller Republican and came into the Nixon orbit only because of the incredibly bad manners Nelson Rockefeller displayed in the spring of 1968, when he was still trying to make up his mind whether to run for the nomination. There had come a time, just before the deadline to get out of the Oregon primary, when Rockefeller supporters, including Agnew, reached the conclusion that Rockefeller would say yes, because of the withdrawal of Michigan's Governor George Romney. There was no liberal or progressive alternative to Nixon and no one likely to beat him in any primary.

Rockefeller decided to make his decision known on television without any advance warning, and I went to Oregon to cover it. Agnew fancied himself in a leading drum-beater's role for Rockefeller and accordingly made plans for a major volunteer effort that would be headed up in Maryland. Just minutes before Rockefeller spoke, a few key Rockefeller staff members, including those in Oregon, got the word that the governor of New York once again would say no. But no such word reached Agnew, and, in his enthusiasm, he invited the reporters in Annapolis to listen with him to the Rockefeller speech, intending afterwords, from the governor's office, to make known his plans for pushing the Rockefeller candidacy. At this stage Agnew could not conceive of any but an affirmative answer from Rockefeller in the absence of some private warning.

Rockefeller's first sentence, however, was another refusal to run
—flat, unambiguous, and direct. The Rockefeller name would have
to be removed from the Oregon ballot.

Agnew's smile was wiped from his face in this public humiliation
before a group of news reporters. Although Rockefeller apologized
repeatedly, especially after he did decide to enter the contest for
the nomination, Agnew inwardly never forgave him, and from that
moment was drawn into the Nixon orbit.

When President Nixon in mid-1971 surprised Americans with a
dramatic announcement of his intention to visit mainland Communist China before May of 1972, it was another spectacular rever-
sal in form for Mr. Nixon. In the 1960 campaign against Kennedy,
he had talked about the defense of Nationalist China on Formosa,
and even the defense of tiny offshore islands like Quemoy and
Matsu, with such belligerence that many who heard him thought
Mr. Nixon would risk even World War III for these tiny and
unimportant islands.

Some reporters traveling with him in the 1960 campaign had a
chant satirizing Mr. Nixon's professed great interest in Quemoy and
Matsu. It went like this:

> We want Quemoy
> We want Matsu
> We want Nixon
> To be *their* President.

It was chanted not infrequently in the late hours of a campaign
day, and it made Nixon's campaign aides angry. The reporters
thought it was hilarious, but actually they couldn't sing very well.

The so-called China Lobby, those who considered Chiang Kai-
shek a great world leader, were solidly behind Nixon both in 1960
and 1968. These included the right-wing, China-born Anna Chen-
nault, widow of the American general who had led the "Flying
Tigers" in World War II. In 1971, as Nixon moved to accommoda-
tion with the Chinese reds, these right-wing Republicans felt betrayed.

By 1972, President Nixon was three years into his first term and
I was three years into my eleventh administration at the White
House.

The Nixon administration had come into office as a minority
government, the product of a sharply divided election in which ap-

proximately 10,000,000 votes had been taken from the major parties by the third-party Presidential candidacy of Alabama's George Wallace.

Perhaps one reason Mr. Nixon won in the first place was the growing disillusionment of the American people with a war they could not win in Vietnam. Mr. Nixon had pledged to end that war, and win the peace in Southeast Asia. Over his first three years he could not keep that pledge, but he had wound down the war, and he was moving for disengagement of American combat troops on the ground. But the war still seemed far from over for the American Air Force and Navy. Peace still was well beyond the horizon.

Two other key Nixon campaign pledges remained unfulfilled. Inflation had not been stopped, though it had been slowed down at a heavy price in unemployed American workers, white and black, and pump-priming measures, including heavy deficit spending which Republicans publicly deplore like original sin, were being tried to get the economy moving more swiftly before the November, 1972, election date. In late summer, 1971, Nixon astounded friends and foes with a wage-price freeze he had repeatedly said he would not impose.

Crime kept on growing, just like Topsy, though the President had long ago installed the new Attorney General he had promised in the Miami Beach speech when he accepted the Presidential nomination.

Nixon had found out for himself, as President Kennedy once said to me, that the view from inside the White House is quite different than the view from the outside. There are limits to Presidential power, even limits to a President's power to persuade.

The election of 1970, on which the Republicans spent so much money and energy, had demonstrated anew that the Nixon-Agnew administration remained a minority government. The President wouldn't answer questions about whether Agnew would be on the ticket again. The Vice President's star had flashed across the sky like a brilliant comet when he launched his attack upon network newsmen in 1969 and 1970. But, like other comets, the Agnew star had fallen when the Republicans did not do as well as they had expected in electing House and Senate members in the 1970 election. Moreover, the Republicans that year lost a total of thirteen governors, while gaining only two new state executive mansions, for a net loss of eleven governors, more than one-third their pre-election strength.

It is true that the Democrats did not do as well in the mid-term elections as the party out of the White House traditionally does, but the Democrats genuinely had feared heavy losses in the face of the well-heeled Nixon-Agnew blitz.

While it was hard to read a clear-cut verdict into the 1970 election outcome—aside from the shattering of Republican hopes—several points seemed clear to me.

The "law and order" issue on which the President and Mr. Agnew relied so heavily could not swing an election in which the economy was slumping and widespread unemployment was increasing.

In the final analysis, I think the "law and order" issue backfired on the Nixon-Agnew campaign effort in 1970. Certainly law and order, as an issue, was no substitute for jobs for those who were unemployed, especially in the big industrial states like Michigan, Ohio, Illinois, and Pennsylvania, where the Republican ticket fared badly.

My own experience indicates that some of those who shout loudest about law and order quite often have some law or order they do not wish to obey or to enforce. In the case of Alabama's Governor George Wallace, it might be an unwillingness to integrate the schools racially as the Supreme Court commanded, or it might be Wallace sending over his strong-arm private guards to remove film he doesn't like from the camera of an ABC cameraman. Law-enforcement officers, sworn to obey the law, have been known to use third-degree tactics against prisoners and to make unconstitutional searches and seizures of evidence that the courts later had to throw out. During the first Nixon term, the Supreme Court more than once had to direct the administration to obey the earlier rulings for prompt school integration and the busing of pupils if necessary to avoid discrimination.

Sometimes I have thought of the shouters for law and order just as Dr. Samuel Johnson did about extreme patriots. It was Johnson who said that "patriotism is the last refuge of a scoundrel," and I am reminded of some flag-waving Congressmen who served on the House Un-American Activities Committee who later wound up in jail themselves. Not all those who quote the Scriptures are certain to go to heaven. And so it is with those who think law and order is a surefire election-winning issue.

Winding down the war in Vietnam was not an adequate substitute to those who expected the President to fulfill his 1968 campaign promise to end that war and win the peace in Southeast Asia.

The "silent majority," in whose name the President and Vice President had campaigned, were not in fact a majority, and its members did not vote the straight Republican ticket in any event. Nor were they very silent.

The "Southern strategy" on which Mr. Nixon relied to capture the 1968 Wallace vote was a flop. The Republicans lost ground in Florida, losing a governor and failing to gain what looked like an easy Senate seat, and they also lost a governor in Arkansas. They did not do nearly as well as they had hoped in South Carolina or Texas. The only bright spot for Southern Republicans was Tennessee, where the GOP gained both a governor and a Senator, but that was due to Democratic division in the state.

Never before at mid-term had a President campaigned so heavily as Mr. Nixon did, and the results therefore were a blow to his prestige. Nixon's highly partisan campaigning reinforced the old image of "Tricky Dick" and damaged his credibility.

Vice President Agnew had campaigned full time for months before election day—and his role was that of Nixon's Nixon, as Democratic Senator Eugene McCarthy wisecracked. Nixon had been President Eisenhower's hatchetman, self-appointed for the most part, during their eight years in office together.

Once in late 1967, before Rockefeller had destroyed his relationship with Agnew, I had a date for an early morning breakfast and TV-filmed interview with Governor Agnew at a Republican governors' conference held in Palm Beach, Florida.

When I reached Agnew's suite in the Palm Beach Towers that morning, I found him unable to talk above a whisper. Agnew had developed laryngitis. It seemed impossible for him to give a television interview.

Over the years, even before my throat cancer had been diagnosed, I had suffered from a good deal of throat trouble, and had found one medicine, Chloraseptic, that gave speedy relief when my voice was failing. I told the Maryland governor I might have just what he needed. I raced back to my own room, got the Chloraseptic, and returned to spray his throat.

He got his voice back instantly. We did the interview, which was a good one and which pointed out why Rockefeller was the best man the Republicans might name for President.

From then until now, the Vice President and his wife Judy have always addressed me as "Dr. Lawrence," a practice that did not cease even after the Des Moines speech and his personal criticism of me for challenging Nixon's qualifications as an able politician.

In December, 1969, several weeks after the Des Moines speech, the Vice President was at another Republican governors' conference, this one at Hot Springs, Arkansas.

Moving through a crowded ballroom during a cocktail party for the governors and their Arkansas hosts, the Vice President spotted me off in a corner, and shouted, "Well, hello, Dr. Lawrence, you haven't been over to treat my throat lately."

"No, Mr. Vice President," I responded, "ever since that Des Moines speech, the Secret Service won't let me anywhere near your throat."

The Vice President and Mrs. Agnew laughed heartily, and so did other spectators who understood the reference.

But I would not want anyone to think that this laughing exchange between the two of us in any way lessened the threat to all broadcasters posed by the continuing Agnew attack upon the news media. It is a threat—clearly backed up by the President—that has had the effect of intimidating some broadcasters into soft-pedaling sharp news commentary and hard-hitting reporting lest at some future date renewal problems would be created for valuable licenses.

But Agnew did not speak for all conservatives. While the Vice President was denouncing me, a Senator with even better conservative credentials, Barry Goldwater, said on the Mike Wallace show:

"I find Bill Lawrence is probably the most effective, consistently effective, down-the-middle reporter we have on the air today.

"I have never known Bill to be vicious. I've never known him to take off on anybody. I have no qualms at all about an interview by him because I know he's going to report what I said, not what he thinks I said."

From the General Motors strike onward, through six Presidents and too many wars, I could not have hoped for a better epitaph to cap my journalistic career.

BIBLIOGRAPHY

APPLEMAN, ROY E.; BURNS, JAMES M.; GUGELER, RUSSELL A.; and STEVENS, JOHN. *Okinawa: The Last Battle*. Washington, D.C.: Historical Division, Department of the Army, 1948.

CORMIER, FRANK, and EATON, WILLIAM J. *Reuther*. Englewood Cliffs, N.J.: Prentice-Hall, Inc., 1970.

Democratic National Convention Proceedings. Washington, D.C.: Democratic National Committee, 1948, 1952, 1960.

EISENHOWER, DWIGHT D. *The White House Years, 1956–61. Waging Peace*. New York: Doubleday & Company, 1965.

FINE, SIDNEY. *The General Motors Strike: A Reexamination*. New York: The American Historical Review, The Macmillan Company, 1965.

LEVINSON, EDWARD. *Labor on the March*. New York: University Books, Inc., 1938.

NIXON, RICHARD M. *My Six Crises*. New York: Doubleday & Company, 1962.

Republican National Convention Proceedings. Washington, D.C.: The Republican National Committee, 1948, 1952, 1960, 1964.

TOLAND, JOHN. *The Rising Sun*. New York: Random House, Inc., 1970.

WATKINS, ARTHUR. *Enough Rope*. Englewood Cliffs, N.J.: Prentice-Hall, Inc., 1969.

WHITE, THEODORE H. *The Making of the President, 1968*. New York: Atheneum Publishers, 1969.

WILLS, GARRY. *Nixon Agonistes*. Boston: Houghton Mifflin Company, 1970.

WITCOVER, JULES. *The Resurrection of Richard M. Nixon*. New York: G. P. Putnam's Sons, 1970.

INDEX